Books by Eric Hammel

76 Hours: The invasion of Tarawa

Chosin: Heroic Ordeal of the Korean War

The Root: The Marines in Beirut

Ace!: A Marine Night-Fighter Pilot in World War II (with R. Bruce Porter)

Duel for the Golan (with Jerry Asher)

Guadalcanal: Starvation Island

Guadalcanal:The Carrier Battles

Guadalcanal: Decision at Sea

Munda Trail: The New Georgia Campaign

The Jolly Rogers (with Tom Blackburn)

Khe Sanh: Siege in the Clouds

First Across the Rhine: (with David E. Pergrin)

Lima 6: A Marine Company Commander in Vietnam (with Richard D. Camp)

Ambush Valley

Fire in the Streets: The Battle for Hue

Six Days in June

Aces Against Japan

Aces Against Japan II

Aces Against Germany

Air War Europa: Chronology

Carrier Clash

Aces at War

Air War Pacific: Chronology

Aces in Combat

Bloody Tarawa

Marines at War

Carrier Strike

Pacific Warriors

PACIFIC WARRIORS

THE U.S. MARINES IN WORLD WAR II

A PICTORIAL TRIBUTE

ERIC HAMMEL

ZENITH PRESS

First published in 2005 by Zenith Press, an imprint of MBI Publishing Company, 400 First Avenue North, Suite 300, Minneapolis, MN 55401 USA

Copyright © 2005, 2010 by Eric Hammel.
Hardcover edition published 2005. Softcover edition 2010.

Zenith Press titles are also available at discounts in bulk quantity for industrial or sales-promotional use. For details write to Special Sales Manager at MBI Publishing Company, 400 First Avenue North, Suite 300, Minneapolis, MN 55401 USA.

ISBN 978-0-7603-3900-8

To find out more about our books, visit us online at www.zenithpress.com.

The Library of Congress has cataloged the hardcover edition as follows:

Hammel, Eric M.
Pacific warriors : the U.S. marines in World War II : a pictorial tribute / Eric Hammel.
        p. cm.
Includes bibliographical references and index.
ISBN 978-0-7603-2097-6 (hbk w/ jkt)
1. United States. Marine Corps--History--World War, 1939-1945--Pictorial works.
2. World War, 1939-1945--Campaigns--Pacific Area—Pictorial works. 3. World War, 1939-1945--Amphibious operations. I. Title.
D767.9 .H33 2005
940.54252294--dc22
                   2006297865

On the front cover: The 2d Marine Division landed in force on Tinian on J+1, July 25, 1944, at the reef off the White beaches. From there, the troops waded to shore with their personal weapons held high. Shown here is a company of the 3d Battalion, 8th Marine Regiment. *Official USMC Photo*

On the frontis page: On Saipan the Japanese put up a stubborn shoreline defense, often employing antiboat guns and plunging fire from heights overlooking the miles-long beachhead. Here, probably in the 2d Marine Division zone, a platoon commander or platoon sergeant rallies Marines prior to leading them inland. *Official USMC Photo*

Spine and title page photo: Eight minutes after the Marines hit the beach at Guam, Old Glory flies again—from a boathook mast—for the first time since December 10, 1941, when the Japanese seized the American base. Planting the flag on the beach under a hail of enemy fire are Captains Paul S. O'Neal and Milton F. Thompson. *Official USMC Photo*

Cover and layout by Tom Heffron
Maps by Philip Schwartzberg, Meridian Mapping

Printed in China

CONTENTS

PREFACE

THEY WERE AMERICA. THEY CAME FROM EVERY AMERICAN CITY AND LARGE TOWN, no doubt from every county and borough. Some were sons of American families going back to the first Siberian settlers of a vast and empty continent, while others had arrived only very recently from Europe, South America, and even Asia. Among them, they spoke or understood every major language on Earth and more minor tongues than probably thrive to this day. Their forebears had fought in every American war and most of the wars of historical Europe. They practiced religions that went back thousands of years, or a matter of months. Some, who were forbidden by their religious beliefs from going to war, had overcome those scruples in what, to them, was as obviously a war against the Devil incarnate as any war had ever been. Some, who would not bear arms, became Navy hospital corpsmen with the intent of succoring the wounded on far-flung battlefields.

Some of the older, senior Marines had fathers who had fought on either side in the Civil War, had themselves been blooded in the wheatfield at Belleau Wood, and had led Marines in little wars in Haiti, Nicaragua, and even China. Some had first fought as recently as 1939 or 1940, when their homelands had been overrun by Nazi legions.

Some were unrepentant thieves and liars, some had never worn hard-soled shoes, some had never eaten in a restaurant. Some were cowards who would always be cowards, but most were unformed teenagers who would do heroic things because heroism was the common standard to which they unthinkingly and unblinkingly adapted. Some had never spoken to, or even met, a Jew (much less taken orders from one), and some had never seen a black man, nor broken bread with a Catholic. Some had never seen an ocean or a ship, had never eaten fish, had never lived in a brick building. For some, a tarpaper barracks on a military base was an immense step up in life, but for many it was humbling. For most young Marines trained in San Diego, the fresh figs routinely set on the table at the right time of year looked like weird onions and turned out to have the most exotic flavor they would ever recall. For others, access to fresh produce of any description was a new and wonderful experience. For many, the discipline of regular exercise was a bitter shock and then a source of immense pride. For most, living out of a seabag—to say nothing of a light field pack—was a deprivation of immense magnitude, as was cooking, sewing, lying in the mud, or even just following orders. For the most part, the Marine Corps was an unforgettable waypoint in life, but a waypoint nonetheless. For some, the Corps became home for thirty and more years followed by decades of pining for that home.

Some were men of letters, eloquent and talented writers and speakers of all types, while others could not read or write—or even speak English—when they enlisted. Some were wealthy beyond description, men who had never wanted a thing money could buy. Others enlisted solely to eat or to sleep off the ground regularly. In the democracy of battle, the latter would teach the former how to survive in a self-dug hole in the wet ground or sand. And because the crucible of war does strange things to men, some of the lowest would rise to become the mightiest, and vice versa.

Friendships—indeed, a brotherhood of love—would bind men across all classes and talents for the rest of their days, and a grateful nation would offer the survivors, one and all, an opportunity to better themselves for the glorious decades that would follow their war. But that was in an unknown and unknowable future. The task these men and boys—some as young as twelve—faced lay ahead in 1940 and 1941, when the Marine Corps caught the first whiff of a war it might have to fight. No promises were made, except to some potential pilots, whose tuition would be paid to the tune of $500 a year if they enlisted for pilot training at the end of their second year of college. The rest—the immense majority—were entitled to three hots and a flop on the best of days, a little pocket money (if there was anyplace to spend it), a hope of glory, and an opportunity to look death in the face. To get any of those choice items, they had to volunteer for the most rigorous training program offered to raw recruits by the U.S. armed forces, and they might spend years beyond the reach of loved ones, cut off from even the worst their society had to offer, to say nothing of the best. Yet volunteer they did, in the tens and hundreds of thousands—even after a year or two of war, after death and maiming had become pretty much assured; even when bad and even infrequent food, crowded and stinking troop holds, and unreasonable discipline at the hands of sadists had become the least of a combat Marine's problems.

After they fought and bled, Marines were often shipped to places far worse than the sort of places you mean when you say "no place to go" and "nothing to do." They spent two and more years away from American women, or women at all. Yet they fought on, in part (they said later) because winning the war was the only ticket home. Yet, once they got home after combat early in the war, even the rehabilitated wounded clamored to go back in mid-1945, even when two complete Marine divisions and many thousands of replacements were expected to die within ten days of their storm landing on Japan's southernmost home island, Kyushu.

Think about this: The book before you is filled with photographs populated mainly by young men and teenagers in the prime of life. Yet those who survived the rigors shown in these pages, those who lived on to old age, are almost all gone. It all happened a lifetime ago, *their* lifetime ago. We owe them our freedom because they fought bravely to victory in a global war against fascism. And we owe them our lives because they were our fathers and grandfathers.

ACKNOWLEDGMENTS

FIRST AND FOREMOST, I WISH TO THANK KERRY STRONG AND THE PEERLESS STAFF she oversees at the Marine Corps University Archive at Quantico, Virginia. She, and they, went many extra miles to dig out useful, even stunning, caches of photos of U.S. Marines in combat in the Pacific. Nearly all the photographs that appear in this volume—and more than a thousand others—were digitally scanned by me in one hectic week at the archive.

Major Norman Hatch, who in my mind at least is the dean of Marine combat photographers, has always made himself available to offer advice. This project had its earliest genesis in Norm's living room in 1969, when he proudly showed me his copy of the bound collection of combat photos he had made as post-war presentations to high-ranking Marines of the day.

I also particularly thank fellow author John R. Bruning Jr. for sharing his photos, his hands-on scanning assistance, and his deep knowledge of digital scanning equipment and techniques.

Many thanks, also, to Colonel Walt Ford of *Leatherneck* magazine for some valuable instant research, and to Nancy Hoffman, also of *Leatherneck*, for photographing the second in a series of portraits of the aging author.

INTRODUCTION

Throughout the Pacific War, the U.S. Marine Corps' strength in the war zone was always vastly exceeded by that of the U.S. Army. During the Pacific War, U.S. Marines undertook twelve storm landings (at least one regiment assaulting a beach amphibiously), but the Army undertook at least a dozen storm landings in the Philippines alone in 1944 and 1945. The Marine Corps aviation arm fielded up to four division-level wing headquarters in the Pacific during the war, but the U.S. Army Air Forces establishment in the Pacific alone dwarfed that of the Marines on any given day, and the U.S. Navy almost always controlled more aircraft over Pacific waters than the Marines.

For all that the Marine Corps was invariably smaller than the raw-strength establishments of the Army and Navy, and for all that it took part in fewer operations than either of its sister services, Marines are the first troops two generations of Americans think of first when the words "Pacific War" are mentioned. How can this be? How did the Marine Corps effort in the Pacific War become so anchored in the American psyche as to become synonymous with it?

GLOSSARY AND GUIDE TO ABBREVIATIONS

IMAC I Marine Amphibious Corps

IIIAC III Amphibious Corps

VAC V Amphibious Corps

A-20 U.S. Army Air Forces Douglas "Havoc" Attack Bomber

AirNorSols Aircraft, Northern Solomon Islands

AirSols Aircraft, Solomon Islands

AirSoPac Aircraft, South Pacific Area

Amtrac Amphibian tractor

B-17 U.S. Army Air Forces Boeing "Flying Fortress" heavy bomber

B-24 U.S. Army Air Forces Consolidated "Liberator" heavy bomber

B-25 U.S. Army Air Forces North American "Mitchell" medium bomber; same as PBJ

B-29 U.S. Army Air Forces Boeing "Superfortress" very heavy bomber

BAR Browning Automatic Rifle

Bazooka 2.36-inch shoulder-fired antitank rocket launcher

D3A Imperial Navy Aichi "Val" dive-bomber

F2A U.S. Navy/Marine Corps Brewster "Buffalo" fighter

F4F U.S. Navy/Marine Corps Grumman "Wildcat" fighter

F4U U.S. Navy/Marine Corps Vought "Corsair" fighter

F6F U.S. Navy Grumman "Hellcat" fighter; F6F-5(N) variant employed by the U.S. Marine Corps as a night fighter

FMF Fleet Marine Force

G3M Imperial Navy Mitsubishi "Nell" medium bomber

G4M Imperial Navy Mitsubishi "Betty" medium bomber

LCI Landing craft, infantry

LCI(G) Landing craft, infantry, gunboat

LCM Landing craft, medium

LCT Landing craft, tank

LCVP Landing craft, vehicle, personnel

LSD Landing ship, dock

LST Landing ship, tank

LVT Landing vehicle, tracked; amphibious tractor

LVT(A) Landing vehicle, tracked, armored; amphibious tank

MAG Marine Air Group

OY U.S. Marine Corps light spotter plane

P-38 U.S. Army Air Forces Lockheed "Lightning" fighter

P-40 U.S. Army Air Forces/Royal New Zealand Air Force Curtiss "Warhawk" fighter

PBJ U.S. Marine Corps North American "Mitchell" medium bomber; same as B-25

PBY U.S. Navy Consolidated "Catalina" patrol bomber

PV U.S. Navy Vega "Ventura" patrol bomber; night fighter variant deployed experimentally by U.S. Marine Corps

SB2U U.S. Navy/Marine Corps Vought "Vindicator" scout-/dive-bomber

SBC U.S. Navy/Marine Corps Curtiss "Helldiver" scout-/dive-bomber

SBD U.S. Navy/Marine Corps Douglas "Dauntless" scout-/dive-bomber

TBF U.S. Navy/Marine Corps Grumman "Avenger" torpedo/light bomber

VJ-Day Victory over Japan Day

VMF Marine Fighting Squadron

VMF(N) Marine Night Fighting Squadron

VMO Marine Observation Squadron

VMSB Marine Scout-Bomber Squadron

VMTB Marine Torpedo Squadron

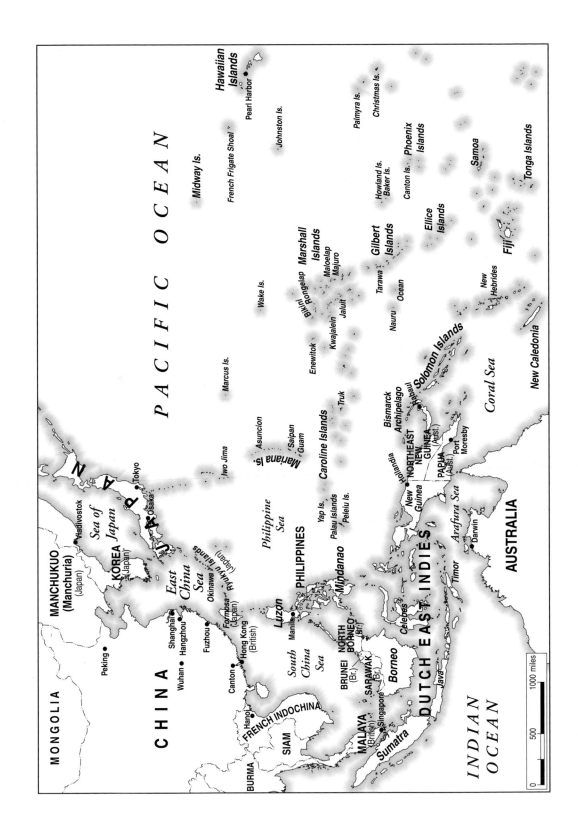

CHAPTER 1

LAND THE LANDING FORCE

1898–1941

FOR THE FIRST 123 YEARS OF ITS EXISTENCE, THE UNITED STATES MARINE CORPS was, like its British parent, the Royal Marines, a branch of the navy composed of small, ship-board detachments that usually served as seagoing police or base guards but were sometimes employed as the core of detachments that boarded enemy ships or took part in brief forays to attack enemy ports and fortresses. This changed in 1898, when at Key West, at the start of the Spanish–American War, the Marine Corps organized and trained an expeditionary battalion of infantry and artillery to seize a beachhead at Guantánamo Bay, Cuba. On May 10, 1898—just ten days ahead of a landing by the main U.S. Army invasion force—the Marine expeditionary battalion secured the objective, which it then successfully defended against a superior Spanish force.

The use of amphibiously delivered Marines to seize an advance base *and to defend it* was revolutionary. No such force was employed in the Philippines phase of the Spanish–American War and, indeed, Admiral George Dewey later lamented the oversight.

Following the Spanish–American War, and in light of its singular accomplishment at Guantánamo Bay, the Marine Corps argued that it was perfectly positioned to serve as a naval land component to assume the lead in a requirement that was emerging for the projection of American power into new areas of the globe, particularly in the Pacific.

In 1878, in the first such move of the century-old nation, the U.S. Navy established a permanent coaling station in Samoa. And in 1887 a treaty with Hawaii led to the establishment of a second coaling station, at Pearl Harbor. In 1898, Guam was seized from Spain by a landing force from one of the warships convoying U.S. Army troops to the Philippines,

A U.S. Navy destroyer fires her aft 5-inch gun at a target on Guadalcanal. Early in the war, the Navy preferred to fire against shore targets while under way at the fastest possible speed. *Official USN Photo*

The battleship USS *Idaho* fires her starboard 5-inch guns at shore targets on Guam's Orote Peninsula in August 1944. The battleship is standing in quite close to the shore and is proceeding at a deliberate pace. Fires can be seen ashore in the distance. *Official USN Photo*

and thus a third link was added to the American chain across the Pacific. The Philippines themselves became the western anchor of the chain.

For most of its history before 1898, the U.S. Navy saw itself as the guarantor of the Monroe Doctrine in the Caribbean and South Atlantic. But in 1880 a group of naval officers began to think about how their service might project force via the seizure and establishment of "advanced bases" there and elsewhere if the need arose. The U.S. Army, which was small and quite scattered at the time, would not be drawn into this line of inquiry, and no one thought of the Marine Corps in such a role, so distant was its traditional role and so small was its aggregate strength. Even with Marines at their core, expeditionary landings of all types were traditionally composed in the main by bluejackets drawn from ships' companies. No one really debated the transformation of Marines into self-supporting landing or advance-base forces until the opportunity of the war with Spain provided, first, sufficient manpower and, second, an actual mission. Only after Guantánamo Bay had been seized and defended by an all-Marine force did it become obvious that the solution to a theoretical problem existed in a real setting. Indeed, as soon as Marine expeditionary units could be organized and transported, Marines established several advance bases in the Philippines, and thus began four decades of campaigning and base work there. So, too, began the century-long focus of the U.S. Marine Corps on innovation and practice in the arts of expeditionary and amphibious warfare—a relationship so powerful as to make them synonymous with "U.S. Marines."

THE LINE OF THINKING THAT FOLLOWED THE ESTABLISHMENT OF ADVANCE BASES BY Marines in Cuba and the Philippines, and then in Panama, focused on the defense of such bases, and not on seizure of enemy bases by direct amphibious assault. The first classroom application of many theories and only a few practical examples was established in Newport, Rhode Island, in 1901, and a Marine battalion undertook an initial field exercise as part of a much larger fleet exercise in the winter of 1902–1903 at Culebra, an island off the eastern coast of Puerto Rico. No formal course was established until 1910, and it was 1913 before enough theory had been laid down to warrant the establishment of a permanent advance-base force of about 1,750 officers and men. This force was divided into two regiments—a fixed-defense regiment composed of coast artillerymen, mine troops, engineers, communicators, searchlight units, and the like; and a mobile-defense regiment composed of infantry and artillery. Note the use of "defense" in characterizing both regiments. A small aviation contingent was added in early 1914.

In 1914, Marines and bluejackets seized Vera Cruz in Mexico, in 1915 Marines took part in landings in Haiti, and in 1916 they helped to establish order in Santo Domingo. American forces quickly withdrew from Mexico, but the burden of expanding and maintaining garrisons in the Caribbean—and Nicaragua in due course—hung heavily over the Marine Corps for two decades and, while it produced veterans, it drew resources away from planning and innovation in the advance-base role.

When the Marine Corps burgeoned to 73,000 officers and men to take part in World War I, it sent a brigade of two reinforced infantry regiments to France but maintained the bulk of its fighting establishment in base-defense and expeditionary roles in the Western Hemisphere. Indeed, it is probable that no more than half of the Marine officers who would serve conspicuously and rise to high rank in the Pacific in World War II even set foot in France in 1917–1918.

As often happens in advancing theories, one man appears to have had more to do with pushing thinking toward a critical breakthrough than all the rest combined.

A U.S. Navy fast battleship fires her 16-inch guns at shore targets on Okinawa in mid-1945. A second fast battleship lies astern. *Official USMC Photo*

An American bomber attacks an ammunition dump on Guam that has been left burning by an earlier attack. Note the proximity of the Marine infantryman at the bottom right corner to the detonation. Army and Navy ground-support pilots gave it all they had, but they rarely released bombs or fired machine guns at danger-close distances to friendly ground troops. *Official USMC Photo*

The individual who drove the concept of amphibious *assault* toward its well-known conclusion was Marine Captain Earl "Pete" Ellis.

Pete Ellis became obsessed with the notion that the U.S. advance into the Pacific beginning in 1878 at Samoa would lead to a war with Japan. By 1913, he had written a brilliant and widely discussed paper that highlighted the problems of waging the land component of a naval war across such vast ocean reaches. He reasoned that the United States and Japan would defend their respective advance bases (of which Japan had *none* in 1913!), seize neutral ground to strengthen their strategic positions, and ultimately assault one another's bases against a backdrop of intense fleet activity. As part of his study and ongoing work, Ellis provided chillingly accurate detail as to how such a war would actually be conducted.

At the end of World War I, Japan—an American ally—was indeed granted mandates in former German possessions in the Pacific that enabled her to establish her own string of naval bases, west to east across the central Pacific, paralleling the American string of bases. In fact, the mandates outflanked the line of American bases, giving Japan an instant strategic advantage. This sudden advantage gave Pete Ellis's prognostications immense support and helped lead in 1924 to the first formal iteration of War Plan Orange, a strategic prescription for waging a war with Japan in the Pacific that would be supported by fixed bases such as those in Hawaii, Samoa, Guam, and the Philippines. Ellis'—and others'—chief focus on seizing neutral bases and assaulting Japanese bases was ultimately and quite naturally incorporated into War Plan Orange, and it gave a free hand to Marine Corps officers to develop specific plans and an organization for assaulting and defending island bases.

THE ADVANCED BASE FORCE AT QUANTICO, VIRGINIA, WAS REDESIGNATED THE Expeditionary Force in 1921 and was composed of infantry, artillery, engineer, signal,

The USS *President Jackson* was purchased with several of her sisters before the war and converted to transport troops to battle. Note the variety of ramped and nonramped landing craft she has embarked. This warhorse carried Marines from California to Guadalcanal in 1942 and served through the war. *Official USN Photo*

A Higgins LCVP (Landing Craft, Vehicle, Personnel) is gingerly maneuvered over the side of a U.S. Navy transport off the coast of Bougainville on D-day, November 1, 1943. Note the transport ahead and the proximity to the shore. Where possible, landing operations began quite close to shore to lessen the risk to vulnerable small craft and the troops they carried. *Official USMC Photo*

chemical, and aviation units. Its orientation was toward the Caribbean. A similar force, scheduled for basing in San Diego, for deployment in the Pacific, was hampered by post-war troop shortages and would not be effective for some years even in the face of the installation of Japanese bases in the Marshall, Caroline, and Palau island groups.

Also in 1921, Pete Ellis, now a major, modified his original treatise on amphibious assault, and it was adopted as Operations Plan 712: Advanced Base Operations in Micronesia. In a speech at the Naval War College in 1923, Ellis elaborated on his treatise in a reference to War Plan Orange: "On both flanks of a fleet crossing the Pacific are numerous islands suitable for submarine and air bases. All should be mopped up as progress is made." Ellis' genius is that he linked the role of the Marine Expeditionary Force to the U.S. battle fleet's progress across the Pacific. As technological progress was made, submarines and land-based aircraft increasingly became strategic weapons that would fill out the interstices not covered by a surface fleet. In fact, the progress of the actual Pacific War became inextricably linked to the ranges of land-based aircraft, and U.S. submarines played a vital role in holding advance lines of defense and undertaking maritime offensive operations.

Withal, the intellectual progress was not matched by physical progress. Cutbacks in military budgets and the ongoing "banana wars" in the Caribbean prevented the Marine Corps from doing much in the way of testing, evaluating, or practicing the emerging art of amphibious warfare. A reinforced regiment took part in Atlantic Fleet maneuvers in the winter of 1922, including a landing at Guantánamo Bay that incorporated a base-defense problem. In 1923, Marines conducted landings in Panama and Cape Cod.

The 1922 and 1923 exercises were instructive in that they demonstrated shortfalls in types and numbers of landing craft, naval bombardment techniques, command and control, logistics handling, and stowage of equipment aboard ship. Each of these areas would prove to be vital to success in the Pacific, but there was little opportunity to improve. The last landing exercise of the era was held in Hawaii in 1925, when an amphibious command unit oversaw the landing of a simulated force of forty-two thousand Marines. The commanders fared well, but all the other shortfalls that had showed up in 1922 and 1923 persisted.

Also on D-day at Bougainville, troops from the 3d Marine Division go over the side and climb down to their wave-tossed Higgins boat on stout rope cargo nets. Each Higgins LCVP typically carried thirty to forty combat-loaded troops at a time, or a light vehicle—usually a jeep—and fewer men. They also carried cargo ashore once a beachhead had been secured. *Official USMC Photo*

This photo was probably taken during an island invasion in the central Pacific. The exertion of climbing down a cargo net with a full combat load combined with a target made unsteady by the action of the sea often made for an awkward landing. *Official USMC Photo*

After 1925, the Marine Corps was unable to launch meaningful exercises. Its strength was cut and its mission load was increased to include a regiment in China, commitment to constabulary work in Nicaragua, and even to guarding the U.S. mails for a time. So few Marines could be based at Quantico and San Diego that both bases were for a time in danger of closure.

For all that it was hobbled by budget and manpower cuts in practical experimentation and the acquisition of equipment, the Marine Corps leadership was overjoyed in 1927 when the Joint Board of the Army and Navy officially directed the Marine Corps to undertake "land operations in support of the fleet for the initial seizure and defense of advanced bases and for such limited auxiliary operations as are essential to the prosecution of the naval campaign." This directive codified nearly three decades of intellectual and physical expenditure in the development of amphibious warfare since the 1898 landings at Guantánamo Bay and provided the Marine Corps with a strategically vital role in the projection of U.S. power and influence to the far reaches of the world.

MARINES WERE WITHDRAWN FROM NICARAGUA IN 1933, AND PLANS WERE AFOOT TO withdraw from Haiti as well. This made sufficient troops available to man the stunted expeditionary forces, undertake exercises required to test theories and equipment, and hammer out doctrine.

The 1st Marine Division stopped off in Fiji on its way from New Zealand to Guadalcanal in late July 1942. Three days of landing rehearsals at Koro Island went quite badly and caused consternation throughout the command. These nonramped landing craft are circling beside their mother ship while awaiting orders or the completion of a maneuver. Note the many other ships on the horizon. Koro was the largest amphibious landing exercise conducted to that time. *Official USMC Photo*

These LCVPs and LCMs (Landing Craft, Medium) and their transport, the USS *Heywood,* were photographed in Tarawa lagoon on November 20, 1943. Note that an amphibian tractor is being maneuvered over the side of the *Heywood,* which made her combat debut on D-day at Guadalcanal. *Official USMC Photo*

In August 1933, Brigadier General John Russell, the assistant commandant of the Marine Corps, assembled a staff at Quantico to resume organizational planning for a Marine force to be attached to the U.S. Fleet under the 1927 Joint Board directive. Russell proposed that the Expeditionary Force be renamed Fleet Marine Force or Fleet Base Defense Force. The former name was selected and all the necessary proposals were approved so that the new Fleet Marine Force (FMF) could be stood up as an integral part of the United States Fleet under the operational control of the fleet commander. The decision, codified on December 8, 1933, gave new life and focus to the 158-year-old Marine Corps.

The commandant of the Marine Corps was given responsibility for manning, maintaining, and training the FMF, and for commanding it while it was based on land. Once embarked, however, senior FMF officers and the FMF itself would come under the command of the fleet commander—a naval officer—and serve at his operational direction. The arrangement made sense in that the Marine Corps was traditionally an integral part of the Navy and thus subordinate within the Navy command structure.

Despite the creation of a staff and infrastructure, the FMF could not be adequately manned at the outset. In August 1934, a year after General Russell's recommendation, no combat units were available to serve in the FMF.

TROOPS OR NO TROOPS, PLANNING AND DEVELOPMENT CONTINUED. IT WAS RECOGNIZED, first of all, that a handful of papers and exercises did not in themselves constitute a doctrine

A pair of unladen LCVPs race through the anchorage off Kwajalein Atoll, where the 4th Marine Division invaded Roi, Namur, and several outlying islands. Note the fleet destroyer ahead of the attack transport. *Official USMC Photo*

for amphibious warfare. Thus, in November 1933, all classes at the Marine Corps Schools were terminated and all faculty and students were put to work to develop an amphibious warfare manual covering training and operations. This was issued in January 1934 and titled *Tentative Manual for Landing Operations*. It was renamed *Manual for Naval Overseas Operations* in August 1934, and *Tentative Landing Operations Manual* by the end of the year. As such, it was approved by the chief of naval operations and handed back to the Marine Corps for dissemination, evaluation, and testing. The modified but essentially intact manual was recompiled and reissued in 1938 as *Fleet Training Publication 167*. It was considered so authoritative that the U.S. Army accepted it in toto in 1941 under the title *Field Manual 31-5*.

Training and exercises were resumed in 1935 and conducted annually through 1941 in the Caribbean or at San Clemente, California. Each new exercise found kinks to be ironed out, but solutions to most of the problems waited on the development and acquisition of equipment from troopships to landing craft to ruggedized field radios. The total dependence of the Fleet Marine Force on the Navy to get it ashore in a modicum of order under a suitable umbrella of air and naval gunfire was driven home time and again, and it became essential that the junior service push the senior service toward better cooperation and integration.

Beneath an umbrella of naval gunfire and air support (note the white smoke plume at the top left corner of the photo), Marines of the 3d Marine Division prepare to run into the beach at Bougainville. The grim faces and eyes fixed directly on the camera were typical of Marines minutes or seconds away from being hurled into combat. *Official USMC Photo*

A wave of amtracs carrying follow-on troops completes the last lap to the beach at Tinian on J-day, July 24, 1944, as an earlier wave rushes back to the transports to pick up more troops or supplies and equipment. Note the airfield (Airfield 3) at the top of the photo. The only reason to take broad, flat Tinian was to turn the island into a base from which U.S. Army Air Forces B-29 very heavy bombers could reach targets in Japan. *Official USMC Photo*

THE FLEET–FLEET MARINE FORCE RELATIONSHIP CAME down to four broad, interwoven topic areas: lines of command, naval gunfire support, air support, and logistical operations—in that order. All of these were addressed in the earliest drafts of the amphibious warfare manual, and all were advanced during and between the annual fleet exercises from 1935 through 1941. By the eve of World War II, matters stood thusly:

Lines of command: Nowhere is the inherent complexity of amphibious operations thornier than in the relationship of the landing force to the fleet (or the landing force commander to the fleet commander) during the prelanding phase. The subordinate landing force is utterly reliant on the fleet to carry it to the landing site, and to land it under an adequate umbrella of air and naval gunfire support. Naval tradition and the subordinate position of the landing force assume ascendancy of the naval commander during the landing phase. But at some point the specialized training of the landing force commander and his staff must logically prevail in a form that places the burden of command *ashore* on the ground commander. This issue *seemed* to have been settled by 1941, but it consistently ran afoul of the personalities of dynamic commanders during the Pacific War and has even confounded commanders in very recent times—to the point at which a Marine general commanded a Navy task group briefly during the invasion of Afghanistan (an amphibious objective hundreds of miles from the sea!).

Naval gunfire support: A landing force is most vulnerable during ship-to-shore movement and while making a lodgment ashore. There's nothing new there; naval gunfire support of a landing force has been used since the earliest days of the availability of naval gunfire. The problem lay in the nature of modern naval guns (flat trajectory) and ammunition (armor-piercing). What a landing force requires is something akin to land-based artillery support—high trajectory and bursting rounds. Testing to 1941 showed that newly introduced bursting naval ammunition could interdict most land targets and, in fact, armor-piercing naval rounds were effective against concrete and masonry walls and emplacements. The Navy—which very much liked the idea of new missions—cooperated fully in finding the right combinations of guns, ships, and ammunition to provide comprehensive gunfire support before and during the landing phase and as a supplement to field artillery once it had been landed. It would take time—well into the Pacific War—before a doctrine for naval gunfire observers could be hammered out and provided with the best types of communications for controlling fires, but early efforts were well on the way by the time the war interceded. By 1941, Marine artillerymen were teamed aboard ship with naval gunnery officers, and in due course naval gunfire observers were trained and equipped to operate with Marine infantry ashore. Nevertheless, the butcher's bill would be enormous by the time it all came together in early 1944.

Air support: Here, no tradition existed; aerial support of ground forces already ashore was in its infancy throughout the prewar and early-war periods, and no amount of hype derived from a few exceptional instances in the long interwar period can be construed as doctrinal advancement. There was no doctrine, and thus no doctrinal advancement, until mid-1943 at the earliest; there was just a little trial and error, mostly on an ad hoc, field-expedient basis. Throughout the prewar period, air support was meant to describe prelanding aerial bombardment, postlanding aerial bombardment well ahead of advancing ground troops, interdiction of enemy lines of supply and communication, pre- and postlanding reconnaissance and mapping, guiding landing craft to the beach from the air, and direction of naval gunfire from the air. The U.S. Navy dedicated no specialized aircraft to the support of a landing force until late 1943, and even though Marine airmen defined "close air support" of ground forces—to include landing forces—as early as 1939, they did not actually conduct close air support missions, per se, as a matter of course until deployed to the Philippines in late 1944. The main factor in the evolution of air support for ground troops lay in communications between ground observers or aerial observers and the warplanes delivering the ordnance. Advances in speed and power of aircraft made it increasingly difficult for pilots to locate a target, differentiate enemy positions from friendly troops, and even fire machine guns or drop bombs accurately once a target was accurately identified. All that took training, nerves of steel, and a willingness of ground troops to risk death at the hands of well-meaning but literally misguided airmen. No prewar thinking or experiments

The 2d Marine Raider Battalion lands at Aola Bay, Guadalcanal, November 4, 1942. Note the mixture of ramped and nonramped landing craft. There was no opposition on this beach. Nonramped troop landing craft became extinct after Guadalcanal. *Official USMC Photo*

Marines wade ashore at Guam, August 1944. This is clearly a follow-on operation conducted without opposition. *Official USMC Photo*

by American soldiers, sailors, or Marines came close to defining, much less developing or integrating, adequate solutions—even though the German Wehrmacht seemed to have gotten it right, as all the world could plainly see from September 1939 onward.

Logistical operations: The first step to getting equipment and supplies ashore is correctly loading them aboard ship. It was understood early on that the best way to load troops on a ship was a battalion or a reinforced battalion at a time, so that everyone and everything was in one place. The trick with equipment and supplies was to load it in reverse order of when it would *probably* be unloaded—first on top and last at the bottom—but with enough flexibility to get at vital items that were required out of order (more ammunition, for example). Holds were not loaded to commercial capacity, with everything packed in solid; they were loaded to approximate combat requirements, with room to dig out what was needed. Eventually, a Marine "transport quartermaster" was assigned directly to each transport to oversee combat loading and unloading. Combat troops landed ahead of all others, but combat-support troops—engineers, for example—needed to get in relatively early along with their most-needed gear. Someone had to be in charge of prioritizing the landing of gear and supplies, unloading gear and supplies, locating and marking underwater and beach obstacles, designating supply dumps, overseeing and directing dump traffic, locating logistical exits from the beachheads that would service the advancing combat units, directing traffic within the beachhead, and overseeing a host of other tasks and unsnarling limitless ad hoc problems. Initially, the Navy supplied a beach party for this, and the Marines supplied a shore party, leaving the officers in charge to hash out a division of responsibilities based on the situation ashore. When this inevitably failed in practice, the rules were changed to give the Marine shore party

commander authority over the Navy beach party commander ("beachmaster"), who served as the deputy shore party commander. Initially, beach labor was drawn from any source available, especially reserve combat units. But that made inroads into a combat commander's ability to wage battle, so the Marine Corps in January 1942 stood up a 700-man shore party—"pioneer"— battalion in each division. Immense time and intellectual energy went into thinking through shore party operations, but the only sufficiently large prewar test was in the summer of 1941. The system that went to war was well intentioned, but it was by no means complete when Marines mounted their first amphibious assaults at Guadalcanal in August 1942.

As the doctrine for getting ashore was developed, the U.S. Navy and Marine Corps went to work to find the best means for transporting troops and equipment to the objective and then getting them ashore. Initially, it was thought that large warships—battleships and cruisers—would double as transports and naval gunfire vessels, but capacity was limited, gear and weapons were bulky, and too many other problems arose. A number of old destroyers were converted to transport troops, but these could accommodate only an infantry company apiece and very limited supplies. Ultimately, the Navy purchased commercial ships that were converted to transports and cargo vessels, and then went on to design attack transports and attack cargo ships, and numerous oceangoing large landing ships, from the keel up.

The design of landing craft of various sizes and types depended on the carrying capacity of the transports, and warships could carry and launch smaller craft than the later transports. All sorts of experimental craft were developed from the early 1920s onward, and much was learned, but serious design work did not take place until large transports joined

An LCVP has broached in the surf on the beach at Bougainville, and many shore party troops have been called down to free it by brute force. Note that the next boat forward also has broached—and filled with water in the pounding surf. Other boats still farther forward also might be in trouble. This was one of a beachmaster's worst nightmares: boats are taken out of service and possibly damaged, the beach is fouled, and all the careful attention to planning a swift, orderly intake of troops and equipment lies in at least temporary ruins. *Official USMC Photo*

Too much stuff. Beginning February 17, 1944, the separate reinforced 22d Marine Regiment landed to secure several islands in Eniwetok Atoll in the Marshall Islands. The landings went well, and a flood of equipment and supplies followed the infantry ashore. It is difficult to fathom how this mass of boxes and barrels ever got straightened out, but the task was indeed accomplished in due course. In many ways, too much stuff was as bad as or worse than not enough. *Official USMC Photo*

the fleet and carrying capacity was standardized. At minimum, a landing craft had to be portable via troop transport; it needed to be large enough to carry a tactical unit—an infantry platoon, for example; it had to have a powerful enough engine to get through surf; it had to be stable in the water; it had to be able to run up on a beach but also designed to be retractable from the beach under its own power; and it had to be low enough in the water to allow fully equipped combat troops to exit over the sides. This is a very complex set of demands. To make a very long and complicated story short and uncomplicated, the Navy finally accepted a troop-carrying landing craft designed by the Higgins Boat Company of New Orleans. After the final Higgins design was selected but before it was put in production, the firm's president, Andrew Jackson Higgins, was shown a photo of a Japanese troop barge that featured a bow ramp. This idea was too good to pass up, so Higgins rushed through a redesign, built a sample that worked, and went on to build thousands of ramped landing craft in several sizes. It is no small irony that the Higgins landing craft to which many credit victory in the Pacific was inspired at the end by a Japanese innovation.

Beyond troop-carrying craft, the Navy specified a range of tank lighters and other transportable landing craft. Then, as the war progressed, larger oceangoing landing ships were designed and built. (The famous LST was borrowed whole from the British.) By late 1943, also, the Navy had acquired the landing ship, dock (LSD), which had a floodable well deck from which smaller craft and amphibious vehicles could be launched.

A Roebling LVT-1 Alligator on Guadalcanal in August 1942. Note that this LVT is completely unarmed. Troops from the 1st Amphibian Tractor Battalion did mount machine guns on a number of their LVTs, and several did get into action on or just after D-day—the first hint that there was more to life for LVTs than being waterborne trucks. The LVT propelled itself through the water by means of the deep flanges attached to its tracks. *Official USMC Photo*

As all this was taking place, years of development toward an amphibious tank led the Marine Corps down many false paths. But in 1937 the Navy became aware of a swamp vehicle built in Clearwater, Florida. The fully tracked, fully amphibious Roebling Alligator was all but perfectly designed to transport supplies from a ship directly to inland supply dumps. Budget constraints kept the services from acting on the innovation until 1939, when the Marine Corps finally freed up enough money to request that Roebling build a military prototype. This was done, the design was accepted as the Landing Vehicle, Tracked, 1 (LVT-1), and a contract was let for two hundred machines. The first production LVT-1s came off the line in July 1941, and the Marine Corps stood up an amphibian tractor battalion in each division. For the time being, the unarmed and unarmored "amtrac" was relegated to a service-support role as an amphibious cargo truck, but it had a great future as a combat vehicle.

These LVT-1s—and an M3 light tank—sit in the rain at Aotea Quay in Wellington, New Zealand, in July 1942. The 1st Marine Division arrived in New Zealand in expectation of months of training, but it was called to battle almost immediately. Because the holds of the transports were "administratively" loaded, every piece of gear and box of supplies had to be unloaded in the rain and then painstakingly combat loaded.
Official USMC Photo

THINGS WERE FALLING INTO PLACE FOR THE MARINE CORPS. A BUMPY FORTY-THREE-year ride from Guantánamo Bay was leading the junior naval service down a road tailor-made for the Pacific War as it actually unfolded. It is difficult to conceive that so many vital pieces fortuitously came together so late in a game whose rules only a very few visionaries could see at the outset. But there it is—an organization rounded off on the eve of a war that began earlier than expected; last-minute acquisition of the finest assault-landing-boat design that has yet to emerge (the basic Higgins design is still going strong after the millennium); the last-minute acceptance of transport and cargo vessels good enough for a long, far-ranging war in the Pacific; and, of course, the great strides in doctrine taken in the immediate pre-war years. Beyond the scope of this study is the design of naval aircraft and the means to get them to war; strides in modern naval gunfire support enhanced by gunnery radars and ruggedized portable field radios; the upgrading of infantry and artillery weapons and tools (such as, once again, ruggedized and increasingly portable field radios); and a host of other advances that began before the war and would catch up as the warriors fought to the westward, island after bloody island.

As the modern war overtook the Marine Corps in late 1941, Marines stood exactly on a cusp between the old ways of waging war and the modern ways. When the real thing slammed the United States up against the wall, only three American military arms were prepared to absorb the shock and stand up fighting—the Navy's carrier and submarine arms, and the United States Marine Corps' Fleet Marine Force.

CHAPTER 2

READY OR NOT

AT THE START OF THE WAR IN EUROPE IN SEPTEMBER 1939, THE STRENGTH OF the Marine Corps stood beneath twenty thousand officers and men, of which the Fleet Marine Force—ground and air—counted fewer than five thousand. The FMF ground component consisted of two units grandiloquently designated 1st and 2d Marine brigades, each bolstered by a nascent Marine aircraft group, plus one scouting squadron based in the Virgin Islands. The 1st Marine Brigade and the 1st Marine Aircraft Group were stationed at Quantico, Virginia, and the 2d Marine Brigade and the 2d Marine Air Group were based in San Diego.

Things could only get better. In the face of possible war—strongly bolstered by the unseemly rapid fall of France in June 1940—the American military arms were given permission and money to grow and modernize as rapidly as possible. Thus, even though it received less attention and money than the senior services, the total strength of the Marine Corps on December 7, 1941, hovered above sixty-five thousand officers and men. The two brigades were expanded to two divisions modeled on the U.S. Army triangular infantry divisions, and the two fledgling air groups had been redesignated as Marine Aircraft wings—a total FMF strength on November 30, 1941, of nearly thirty thousand, of which nearly three thousand were aviators or aviation ground personnel. This was barely enough troops to fill a real infantry division and man a few air groups, but the call to the colors after December 7, and the enormous flow of funds, led to an unprecedented expansion that resulted in the deployment of two reinforced divisions and an effectively complete air wing, along with numerous independent combat battalions, to the Pacific by late 1942.

The Marine Corps prides itself on the doctrine that every Marine is a rifleman. This photo shows the new mingling with the old: The Springfield M1903 rifle would not be replaced with the modern M1 Garand until late 1942, the flat Kelly-type British helmet was not replaced with the modern scoop helmet until mid 1942; the new herringbone utilities were just coming into use; and this Marine is wearing an old-style khaki campaign blouse. *Official USMC Photo*

HARKENING BACK TO THE ADVANCE-BASE CONCEPT THAT HAD LED TO THE FORMATION of the FMF, the Marine Corps stood up four defense battalions in 1940. These units were built for coastal and antiaircraft defense of U.S. possessions in the Pacific athwart the presumed war zone—Hawaii, Wake Island, Midway Island, Johnston Island, and Palmyra Island.

Marines also shouldered their traditional role in the form of detachments aboard a growing number of capital ships—battleships, cruisers, and aircraft carriers—as well as guard and military police units and detachments at a growing number of Marine and naval bases and facilities.

The total involvement of the FMF in the Pacific was *not* foreseen before the United States was drawn into the war, hence the basing of a full division and aircraft wing on the East Coast—ultimately at Camp Lejeune and Cherry Point in North Carolina, respectively. Marine security detachments ended up in strategic U.S. and British possessions in the Caribbean as well as Bermuda and Newfoundland. There was even a plan afoot in 1940 and 1941 to send Marines and U.S. Army troops to the Azores to keep the islands out of German hands.

These Marine artillerymen, wearing old-style campaign covers and khaki uniforms, are practicing firing drills with an old-style single-trail howitzer. *Official USMC Photo*

The biggest single prewar job Marines tackled in the direction of Europe was the dispatch of a reinforced Marine brigade built around the 6th Marine Regiment (6th Marines) and the 5th Defense Battalion to Iceland in mid-1941. The politics of the move are byzantine, so suffice it to say that the United States meant to send Germany a clear message that the Monroe Doctrine remained a living instrument. British units also served in Iceland, presenting the first opportunity for troops of the two future allies to work together against Germany. (The formal alliance would not be cemented until the United States formally entered the European war on December 10, 1941.)

ON NOVEMBER 30, 1941, THE TOTAL STRENGTH OF THE MARINE CORPS STOOD AT JUST under 66,000 officers and men. Of these, just over 26,000 manned non-FMF billets in the United States—at 5 major bases, 43 posts and stations, Headquarters, and 4 recruiting districts. Nearly 13,000 Marines manned 68 shipboard detachments, 24 overseas posts and stations, and 3 non-FMF tactical units (the 4th Marines—moving from China to Luzon—801 officers and men; the 1st Separate Marine Battalion in the Philippines, 725; and the 1st Marine Brigade in Iceland, 3,972). Fleet Marine Force units and detachments in the continental United States stood as follows: 1st Marine Division, 8,918 (less than

Also clad in old-style uniforms and sporting old-style campaign covers, these Marines are drilling with a 75mm pack howitzer, which would be the mainstay of Marine artillery regiments until mid-1944. Note the old-style wagon wheels, which were still in use in late 1942. Be aware that, while the 75mm pack howitzer could be broken down and carried in small vehicles or by mules, you are looking at this pack howitzer's prime movers—the gunners themselves. *Official USMC Photo*

half authorized strength); 2d Marine Division (less 2d Marine Brigade), 7,540; 1st Marine Aircraft Wing, 1,301; 2d Marine Aircraft Wing (less detachments in the Pacific), 682; 2d Defense Battalion, 865; and miscellaneous units and detachments, 633. Overseas, the Marine Corps fielded 5,621 troops, as follows: 5 defense battalions in the Pacific, 4,399; elements of the 2d Marine Aircraft Wing in the Pacific, 733; and elements of the 2d Marine Division in Hawaii, 489.

The numbers above hardly constitute a war footing, but the foundation had certainly been built, the framework was in, and build-up was progressing with all due haste.

STATED IN RUDIMENTARY TERMS, IT WAS THE STRATEGY OF BOTH THE UNITED STATES AND Japan to advance their respective battle fleets across the Pacific, meet somewhere near the middle, and conduct a decisive *surface* battle that would, pretty much at one fell swoop, determine the outcome. To bolster their plans, both sides sought bases from which the fleet advances could be supported. And, as Pete Ellis had prophesied in 1913, each side laid in plans to deny the other the advantages of these bases, and indeed to seize whatever they could.

In the year or two before the onset of the war, as tensions rose, both future combatants sought new bases and built up older ones. In the case of the United States, the tiny atolls at Wake, Midway, Johnston, and Palmyra were built up, their anchorages were improved, and airfields were built or improved. The key feature of these tiny atolls was that they could more or less support one another from the air with the aircraft of the day. Naturally, also, older, larger holdings were beefed up—the Philippines and American Samoa, but not Guam, which was very close to the large Japanese base at Saipan and thus had to be conceded in the short term. Naval and Marine forces in the various smaller holdings were bolstered by civilian contracting firms that undertook most of the construction work. The bases were small, far from liberty ports, and generally abysmal in amenities.

The headquarters detachment of the 1st Battalion, 6th Marines (1/6), in Iceland in the summer of 1941. *Official USMC Photo*

Thus, through 1940 and 1941, military units rotated in and out to maintain the sanity and esprit of the troops.

On the eve of war, the Pacific island detachments were arrayed thusly: Pearl Harbor—1st Defense Battalion, 261 officers and men; 3d Defense Battalion, 863; 4th Defense Battalion, 818; and 6th Defense Battalion, 21. Johnston—1st Defense Battalion, 162; Palmyra—1st Defense Battalion, 158; Midway—6th Defense Battalion, 843; Wake—1st Defense Battalion, 424. In addition to infantry weapons, coastal and antiaircraft guns were 7-inch (three at Midway only), 5-inch dual-purpose antiboat/antiaircraft (six Midway, two Johnston, four Palmyra, and six Wake), 3-inch dual-purpose (twelve Midway, four Johnston, four Palmyra, and twelve Wake); .50-caliber (thirty Midway, eight Johnston, eight Palmyra, and twelve Wake); and .30-caliber (thirty Midway, eight Johnston, eight Palmyra, and thirty Wake). A perusal of all the numbers reveals something about the way resource-strapped senior commanders weighed the relative usefulness and survival probabilities of each base.

An unusual sight is this 1st Marine Brigade 37mm gun crew drilling in Iceland during the winter of 1941–1942. The 37mm antitank gun was outclassed in North Africa and Europe against German armor, but it was adequate against most Japanese tanks and also was a mainstay against log pillboxes and bunkers through the end of the Pacific War. *Official USMC Photo*

In addition, the 7th Defense Battalion was deployed to American Samoa beginning in December 1940. There it manned four 6-inch naval guns, six 3-inch antiaircraft guns, and a number of lighter antiaircraft weapons. It also oversaw the standing up and training of the 1st Samoan Battalion, Marine Corps Reserve, a unit that never reached authorized strength of five hundred because military-age men were needed to construct defenses, including a major air base at Tutuila.

Marine tactical aviation units were slow to reach the Pacific bases, and in fact Johnston, Palmyra, and Midway had no aircraft on hand until after the onset of hostilities. A detachment of twelve Grumman F4F Wildcat fighters from Marine Fighting Squadron 211 (VMF-211) arrived at Wake on the eve of war; otherwise the only Marine tactical aviation units were based at Ewa Field, Oahu—the Marine Air Group 21 (MAG-21) headquarters-and-service squadron; Marine Scout-Bomber Squadron 232 (VMSB-232); Marine Utility Squadron 252 (VMJ-252); and the VMF-211 rear echelon.

In addition to defense battalion and aviation units, the Marine garrison in Hawaii consisted of the headquarters and two companies of the 2d Engineer Battalion, which were building an amphibious training base on Oahu for their parent 2d Marine Division; 485 troops based at the Marine Barracks, Pearl Harbor Navy Yard; 102 troops based at the Marine Barracks, Ford Island Naval Air Station; 169 Marines guarding the naval ammunition depot north of Honolulu; and 877 officers and men serving aboard battleships and cruisers anchored at Pearl Harbor. The number of Marines at Pearl Harbor on the morning of December 7, 1941, totaled more than 4,500.

THE UNITED STATES MARINE CORPS WAS ABOUT TO BE PLUNGED INTO THE WORLD WAR. It was about to suffer its first casualties, record its first victories (such as they were), and experience its first defeats.

OPPOSITE: This 5-inch dual-purpose gun and its mate, *Belch*, probably were deployed to American Samoa before the onset of the Pacific War. Note the number painted on the sandbag beneath the gun barrel; it denotes the compass direction—138 degrees—in which the gun is pointing. Note, also, the overhead camouflage supported by chicken wire. The Marine is armed with a Springfield '03 rifle. *Official USMC Photo*

These Grumman F4F-3 Wildcat fighters belong to the 2d Marine Aircraft Wing's Marine Fighter Squadron 121 (VMF-121). They are seen here on the flight line at New Bern, North Carolina, near Camp Lejeune, in October 1941. The F4F-3 was the latest Navy-Marine fighter of the day; it was equipped with four .50-caliber machine guns and had a decent survival rate against the nimbler but lighter Mitsubishi A6M Zero fighter. At the start of the war in the Pacific, the Marine Corps had only twelve F4Fs deployed to meet the Japanese onslaught, all on Wake Island. The U.S. Navy had a Wildcat squadron aboard each of its carriers, but none saw action until early 1942. *Official USMC Photo*

CHAPTER 3

AT WAR

DECEMBER 1941–AUGUST 1942

They came out of the north in their disciplined formations, airplanes beautiful in flight, deadly in purpose and intent. The main body made directly for the mother lode of battleships tied up in the harbor and the rest went after the American warplanes, which were lined up neatly on the airfields around the harbor.

Hardly a man looked up until the death and destruction had commenced. Marines at Pearl Harbor were as stunned as anyone, as unprepared, as slow to react to the surreal circumstance of war that suddenly rained on them, enveloped them, dusted them with death.

The first to die were on the great battleships in the harbor. They died as they prepared to hoist their flags, they died in their bunks as they slept in that last Sunday moment of peace, they eventually died at their guns as they dueled Hirohito's airplanes face-on. In a few cases they triumphed, pitching the odd torpedo plane or dive-bomber or fighter into the land or water. In the end, those who could, fought the raging fires and tended to the dead and wounded.

At Ewa Field, the Marines of Marine Air Group 21 (MAG-21) were caught utterly flatfooted by the first wave of twenty-one Zero carrier fighters that was sent to strafe their little, out-of-the-way base. The officer of the day had a bare moment to sound the alarm after he recognized *Japanese* torpedo planes headed for the fleet anchorage. But the Zeros arrived before anyone at Ewa could respond.

A mile short of the airfield, the base commander, Lieutenant Colonel Claude Larkin, scrambled out of his 1930 Ford and into a ditch as a strafer opened fire on the car.

This frame from a propaganda film reportedly shows Imperial Navy Mitsubishi A6M Zero carrier fighters as they prepare to take off for Pearl Harbor. Twenty-one Zeros opened the Pacific War for Marines when they attacked Ewa Field, Oahu, on December 7, 1941. *National Archives & Records Administration*

Three battleships caught at their moorings by attacking Japanese carrier bombers. Nearest, and burning most heavily, is the USS *Arizona;* then the USS *Tennessee;* and finally the USS *West Virginia.* Marines manned guns aboard all the battleships and cruisers at Pearl Harbor on December 7, 1941. *National Archives & Records Administration*

The Ford was shot up heavily, so Larkin hotfooted the last mile to Ewa. Once there, he took cover beneath a truck as unchallenged Zeros strafed the neatly parked MAG-21 aircraft and the base facilities.

Not a single Marine machine gun responded initially, not a single Marine airplane could be driven into the sky. A Marine with a pistol took on one Zero strafer, stood tall beside a wrecked airplane, and dueled the pilot face to face.

The only opposition the Japanese faced over Ewa came from a pair of Army Air Corps P-40s that suddenly appeared and shot down three bomb-carrying Imperial Navy torpedo bombers. It was the most successful aerial encounter of the day.

In the midst of a second Japanese attack, several U.S. Navy SBD scout bombers from the USS *Enterprise* set down on the Ewa runways. The pilots were warned that the field was under intermittent attack, but only one left for another haven while the others certainly figured that any piece of ground they had reached was safer than any volume of air they might reach.

As the attack progressed, the MAG-21 Marines at Ewa broke out a few machine guns and salvaged others from wrecked planes. The spooked Marines, who shot at anything in the air, claimed one dive-bomber shot down.

The attacks ended by 1000 hours. Marines at Ewa counted three of their number killed, thirty-three of forty-seven aircraft destroyed, and two aircraft barely salvageable.

That first night of the Pacific War a jittery Marine sentry at Ewa nearly shot Lieutenant Colonel Larkin as the base commander lit a cigarette in defiance of his own order against such an act.

MARINES GUARDING THE FORD ISLAND NAVAL AIR STATION BROUGHT RIFLES AND MACHINE guns into action following a brief period of notable confusion. And a quick-thinking bugler

called out 1st and 3d Defense battalion troops at the Marine barracks in the Navy Yard. Eight antiaircraft machine guns were manned and firing within six minutes of the start of the attack, more were quickly broken out of the armory, and hundreds of Marines not occupied in belting ammunition were given rifles and ammunition, then left to their own instincts to fire at the swooping Japanese warplanes. Shortly, 3-inch antiaircraft guns were broken out of storage and 2d Engineer Battalion trucks were dispatched to the ammunition storage facility, which was twenty-seven miles from Pearl Harbor. The 3-inch guns never fired that day.

By 0820, Marines at the barracks had set up twenty machine guns and accounted for one Japanese plane, and while the attack was still under way, twenty-five more machine

The USS *Oklahoma* and USS *Maryland* in the wake of the attack. Outboard ships such as the *Oklahoma,* which capsized, were vulnerable to torpedoes, bombs, and strafing, while inboard ships such as the *Maryland* were vulnerable only to bombs and strafing. Scores of Marines died aboard the battleships. *National Archives & Records Administration*

This photo composite of Ewa Field was taken in February 1941. On December 7 the neat rows of aircraft were as vulnerable to strafers and bombers as they appear to be here. *National Archives & Records Administration*

guns opened fire. Altogether, the defense battalion Marines claimed three kills and one kill shared with ships' gunners. Nine Marines were wounded here, but many sailors and Marines from the ships in the harbor were treated at dressing stations set up at the barracks. Indeed, 102 sea-going Marines were killed that morning, and 55 were wounded in action, of whom 6 later died.

IN CHINA ON THE FIRST DAY OF WAR (DECEMBER 8 LOCAL TIME), ONLY A VERY FEW Marines remained. The 4th Marine Regiment, based in Shanghai for decades, had pulled out to the Philippines on the eve of war. That left embassy guard detachments at Peiping and Tientsin and a work detail preparing for an evacuation of the embassy guards from Chinwangtao. All three detachments received news of the Japanese attacks on Pearl Harbor and the Philippines, and all three prepared to resist local Japanese forces. Nevertheless, the cooler heads of senior officers prevailed, and all the Marines in northern China had surrendered to Japanese forces by the end of the first day of the war.

THE SMALL NAVY-MARINE GARRISON AT GUAM KNEW THAT THE WORST WAS COMING: American dependents had been evacuated in October, and on December 6 the garrison had been ordered to destroy all its classified documents. Then, on December 8 (local time; it was December 7 in Hawaii) word came of the Pearl Harbor attack. Three hours later, Saipan-based Imperial Navy bombers attacked a minesweeper in Apra Harbor. The ship was sunk, survivors from her crew joined the garrison, and the island's capital at Agana was evacuated by civilians.

The island was bombed on December 9 (local), and a Japanese naval landing force from Saipan numbering about six thousand troops began to come ashore at 0400. There were several clashes. Marines at Sumay Barracks held the attackers off, but the situation was utterly hopeless. The island commander surrendered at 0600. Four of the nineteen American fatalities were Marines, as were twelve of forty-two wounded. All the survivors were shipped to Japan on January 10.

THE ONLY AMERICAN WARPLANES BASED at Midway—northwest of Hawaii—on December 7, 1941, were seven U.S. Navy PBY patrol bombers. At 0630 (0900 at Pearl Harbor), the island command was

Fires that engulfed the Marine Air Group 21 aircraft at Ewa Field were fueled by highly flammable aviation gasoline. *Official USMC Photo*

informed of the attack on Pearl Harbor. Five of the PBYs were out on search missions, two Royal Netherlands Navy patrol bombers had just taken off for Wake Island on their way to the Netherlands East Indies, and the two remaining U.S. Navy PBYs were warming up for a mission to guide Marine Scout-Bombing Squadron 231 (VMSB-231) SB2U scout bombers that were scheduled to be launched from the USS *Lexington* that morning.

Immediately, the Dutch PBYs were recalled and folded into the Navy patrol effort, the 6th Marine Defense Battalion was placed on full alert, and the *Lexington* was diverted to search for the Japanese carrier task force.

Beginning at 1842 hours, Marine lookouts spotted activity to seaward, and at 2130 hours the island's crude surface-search radar picked up a target. The commander of the Marine searchlight battery wanted to illuminate the radar target, but senior officers quashed the request. At 2135, a pair of Japanese destroyers dispatched direct from Tokyo opened fire. The ships had no other objective beyond neutralizing Midway's air base, so aircraft there could not interdict the carrier fleet as it retired from the Pearl Harbor attack.

The initial salvo fell short, but the second struck several 5-inch coastal gun emplacements, and subsequent salvos bracketed the power plant and hit the concrete command post of a .50-caliber machine gun platoon. In the power plant, First Lieutenant George Cannon was severely wounded, but he oversaw the splicing of severed communications lines and refused treatment until an enlisted Marine had received care. The delay cost Cannon his life. He was awarded a posthumous Medal of Honor, the first of the war.

A real duel commenced at 2153, when Marine searchlights found one of the destroyers and a 3-inch dual-purpose gun battery opened fire. A battle royal ensued for five minutes before the destroyers retired. Many shore installations were damaged, four men were killed (including two from the 6th Defense Battalion), and nineteen were wounded (including ten Marines). Gunners felt they had hit one of the destroyers, but there is no supporting evidence.

VMSB-231 was returned to Pearl Harbor aboard the *Lexington*, but within a week of this sole attack on Midway—which failed to neutralize the island's air contingent—seventeen of the squadron's Vought SB2U Vindicator dive-bombers guided by a Navy PBY undertook a groundbreaking, record-setting overwater flight back to Midway. Later in the month, Brewster F2A Buffalo fighters from VMF-221 were flown off the USS *Saratoga* to Midway, and a large contingent of the 4th Defense Battalion was also dispatched.

Civilian construction workers were evacuated from Midway on December 28. On January 28, 1942, Midway was shelled by a Japanese submarine—and again on February 8 and February 10. On March 10, a VMF-221 F2A pilot shot down a Kawanishi H6K amphibian patrol bomber southwest of the atoll. The H6K had been dispatched from Wotje Atoll in the Marshall Islands and had refueled from a submarine while en route to Midway. After that, Midway was not molested for

A burned-out Marine Scout-Bomber Squadron 232 (VMSB-232) Vought SB2U Vindicator stands against a backdrop of oily smoke at Ewa Field. The SB2Us at Ewa and elsewhere in the Pacific were stopgap planes bought in low quantities by the Navy and Marine Corps to bridge the transition from much slower biplane models to the sleeker, faster, better-armed Douglas SBD Dauntless carrier scout-bombers that Marines ended up flying in combat until the end of the Pacific War. *Official USMC Photo*

nearly two months. During that time, Marine Air Group 22 (MAG-22) was stood up at Midway, VMSB-231 was redesignated VMSB-241, and the air base was prodigiously expanded and improved.

Tiny Johnston Atoll was not molested until the night of December 12, when an Imperial Navy submarine fired a star-shell cluster over the base. A Marine 5-inch coast-defense gun—one of just two emplaced in the atoll—fired one star shell of its own, and the submarine made off. This or another submarine—or perhaps several—shelled the island on December 15, causing a fire and considerable damage. Marines returned fire, and the bombardment from the sea ended abruptly. A brief, inconclusive duel erupted on the night of December 21, and again the next night. Thereafter, the tiny atoll was reinforced with more heavy guns, machine guns, and a provisional infantry company, but it was never attacked again.

Palmyra, which lay nine hundred miles southeast of Johnston, was shelled at dawn on December 24, 1941, but return fire from the 5-inch battery caused the Japanese submarine to depart. The atoll was reinforced by the end of the month, but it was never attacked again.

For all that they were isolated, Johnston and Palmyra became important links in the air route from Hawaii to the South Pacific and Australia. They were garrisoned by Marines throughout the war.

The Japanese onslaught against Wake Island, directly north of the Marshall Islands and the westernmost North Pacific outpost held by American troops, started with an attack at 1158 on December 8 (local time). The attack was delivered by thirty-six Imperial Navy Mitsubishi G3M land-based attack bombers out of the Roi Island airdrome in the Marshall Islands' Kwajalein Atoll. At the moment of attack, only four VMF-211 F4Fs were aloft, but they were searching in the wrong direction. The unopposed Japanese bombers destroyed all of the seven remaining F4Fs with their bombs, which also killed three Marine pilots and wounded four. Among the equipment and goods destroyed around the airfield was a large supply of aviation gasoline, the only air–ground radio on hand, and high-altitude oxygen tanks.

The Roi-based G3Ms returned at 1145 on December 9. This time they were opposed by the remaining F4Fs as well as accurate antiaircraft fire put up by the 422-man 1st Defense Battalion contingent based at Wake. One G3M was downed by antiaircraft fire, and a second fell to a cooperative effort between F4F pilots Second Lieutenant David Kliewer and Technical Sergeant William J. Hamilton. It was the first air-to-air victory awarded to Marines in World War II.

In California on December 9 (local; December 10 at Wake), the USS *Saratoga* and her accompanying task force departed San Diego for a direct run to Wake. Embarked in the carrier were eighteen VMF-221 F2A Buffalo fighters.

At Wake on December 10, twenty-six G3Ms attacked at 1045 hours. Two of the G3Ms were downed by a VMF-211 pilot, but this attack wave, like all others, was responsible for destroying or damaging irreplaceable facilities and equipment.

The hangar and most of the base facilities at Ewa were set on fire and destroyed by a follow-on wave of carrier bombers.

Beginning at 0300 on December 11, a 450-man naval landing force attached to the Imperial Navy's Truk-based Fourth Fleet began to move toward Wake's beaches aboard a pair of destroyer-transports. Sharp-eyed Marines spotted the silhouettes of the transports and accompanying warships, and all guns that could bear were ordered to train on targets but remain silent until ordered to fire. The landing was long delayed as the Imperial Navy ground troops struggled aboard landing craft in adverse surf conditions. Finally, at 0500, the flagship, the light cruiser *Yubari*, opened fire at shore targets; then all the warships opened fire. Despite solid hits and damage to shore facilities, the Marine commander, Major James Devereaux, continued to hold fire. Finally, a little after daybreak—0615—Devereaux ordered his Battery A 5-inch guns to commence firing. Targets were 3,500 yards distant. The Battery A guns, and those of Battery L, were soon brought on target, and Battery L struck *Yubari* twice. In the ensuing duel, nearly

This bullet-spattered ambulance served as advance notice that the Empire of Japan had not signed and would not honor the Geneva Accords during World War II. Throughout the Pacific War, American casualties and medical personnel were completely vulnerable to Japanese fire. *Official USMC Photo*

an hour in length, the Marine coastal gunners hit several other warships, possibly sank the destroyer *Hayate,* and drove off the entire invasion flotilla. Following up on the clear victory, the three remaining VMF-211 Wildcats repeatedly attacked the departing flotilla with guns and bombs. Two light cruisers, a destroyer, and a transport were damaged. During a second mission undertaken by fresh pilots, a destroyer-transport was damaged, and the destroyer damaged in the first attack, *Kisaragi,* blew up and sank as a Wildcat was diving on her—possibly the first warship ever sunk by a fighter. In return, one fighter had its engine destroyed by return fire. Also on December 11, pilots manning the two remaining F4Fs scrambled at 1000 hours to intercept an incoming strike. Two G3Ms were downed and a third was set afire.

On December 12 a pair of Kawanishi H6K amphibian reconnaissance bombers out of Majuro Atoll appeared over Wake at 0500. The two remaining F4Fs were scrambled, and one H6K was shot down. That evening, an F4F damaged a surfaced submarine.

Wake was attacked at 0600 on December 14 by three H6Ks based at Wotje Atoll whose bombs landed near the airstrip without effect. Then, at 1100, thirty Roi-based G3Ms bombed the airstrip and a nearby Marine encampment. Two VMF-211 ground-crewmen were killed, one Marine was wounded, and a bomb demolished one of the two serviceable F4Fs. Miraculously, two Marine pilots and a Navy aviation groundcrewman salvaged the engine from the wreck even as the fighter was engulfed in flames.

On the morning of December 15, the VMF-211 commander drove a submarine from the surface in what amounted to a simple look at it—because the pilot thought it might be a Dutch boat. There was no air attack on Wake that day or the next, but time was running out for Wake's gallant little garrison.

Even though each day that passed brought possible relief or reinforcement closer, it also gave the hamstrung Japanese in the Marshall Islands more time to array reinforcements of their own. Wake was a target of such strategic significance that the Japanese simply could not leave it in American hands.

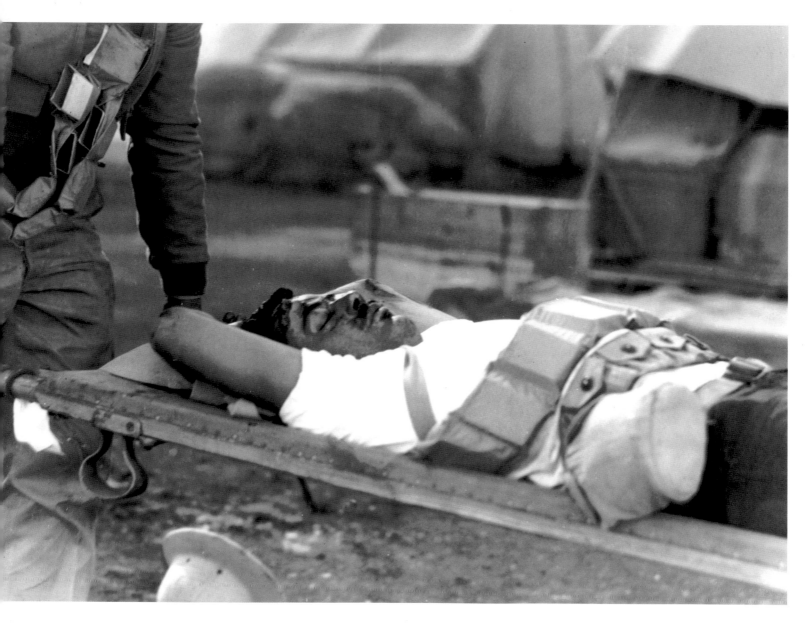

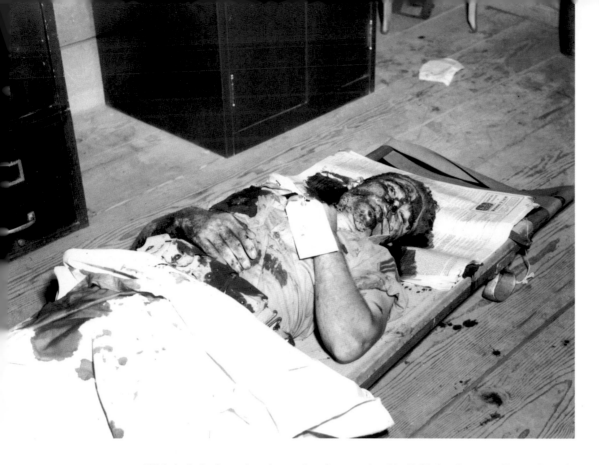

Wake's defenders pieced together four serviceable F4Fs by dawn on December 17. At 1317, twenty-seven G3Ms from Roi hit the diesel fuel main storage, wiped out the defense battalion mess hall, and damaged the salt-water evaporators upon which the garrison depended for drinking water. One G3M was shot down by a 3-inch gun, but this small victory was wiped out when one of the F4Fs fell out of the sky during a takeoff. Capping the day was a pinprick raid at 1750 by H6Ks that bombed and strafed the defenses, albeit with little effect.

The only air activity over Wake on December 18 was assumed to be a photo-reconnaissance flight by a single airplane that remained at twenty thousand feet and well out of range of Wake's formidable antiaircraft defenses.

At 1050 on December 19, twenty-seven G3Ms bombed the VMF-211 area and other previously bombed targets. Accurate antiaircraft fire was thought to hit four of the Roi-based bombers, and one of these was seen to crash shortly after its crew bailed out over the sea.

There was constrained jubilation on December 20 because bad weather over the island obviated bombing attacks. And there was yet more jubilation at 1530 when a U.S. Navy PBY patrol bomber landed in the lagoon to deliver news that the *Saratoga* task force was drawing closer in the hope of delivering VMF-221, as well as to defend the air over Wake *and* to land troops from the 4th Defense Battalion to help man the 1st Defense Battalion guns, of which there were actually too many to be fired at once by Major Devereaux's demibattalion.

The main aerial effort against the Marine bastion at Wake, from start to finish, was carried out by a group of Imperial Navy Mitsubishi G3M land-based attack bombers based at Roi Airdrome in the Marshall Islands' Kwajalein Atoll. By late 1941, the G3M, which had seen years of service in China, was being replaced by the new Mitsubishi G4M land-based bomber, known later in the war as the Betty. But the G3M Sally was not quite a thing of the past; only three days into the Pacific War, they pulled off the first-of-its-kind sinking of the Royal Navy battleships *Prince of Wales* and *Repulse* off Malaya. And, of course, they pummeled Wake until it was seized. *National Archives & Records Administration*

The sinking of the destroyer HIJMS *Kisaragi* on December 11, 1941, by a VMF-211 Wildcat pilot, was memorialized in this binder cover, whose caption reads, "Marine flyer in the defense of Wake Island sinks first Jap warship of this war. It was the first time in history a fighter plane had sunk a large warship."
Official USMC Document

With a Marine aviation staff officer and a load of reports aboard, the PBY departed at 0700 on December 21. At 0850, twenty-nine Aichi D3A attack bombers accompanied by eighteen Mitsubishi A6M Zero fighters from the fleet carriers *Hiryu* and *Soryu* struck Wake a wicked low-level blow that caused little material damage but immense morale damage. Then, within three hours, thirty-three G3Ms struck one of the antiaircraft batteries dead center on the gun-director position, where one Marine noncommissioned officer was killed and three Marines were wounded. In return for achieving a staggering blow against the accuracy of Wake's antiaircraft batteries, the Japanese lost one bomber shot down.

VMF-211 had two operational Wildcats aloft when the carrier planes returned on December 22. The pilots launched independent attacks. One shot down two Zero fighters in separate passes, but the other was shot down by a Zero as he attacked a formation of D3As. The first pilot was then wounded by a Zero, and he barely survived the crash landing of this last VMF-211 Wildcat. Wake thus had no fighter protection. Unopposed, the D3As attacked battery positions with almost no effect. After the attack, with no hope of getting any F4Fs back into the air, VMF-211 turned to for duty as infantry.

Out to sea, just 625 miles from Wake, the *Saratoga* task force, embarking VMF-221, pulled up to conduct needed refueling operations. The carrier was too far from Wake to launch the Marine F2A Buffalo fighters, but it was thought the fighters could be brought within range during December 23. Nevertheless, during the night, *Saratoga* was ordered back to Hawaii. Also ordered back to Hawaii was a task force built around the carrier USS *Lexington*. All hope for relieving Wake had been extinguished.

At 0200 hours on December 23, a total of 1,500 Imperial Navy infantrymen began the final assault on Wake. The cruel eleven-hour battle that ensued cost Japan an estimated two hundred troops killed as the Marines, sailors, and even a few civilian construction workers fought brutally in a vain effort to overcome the sheer weight of the assault. But it was for nothing. Nearly eighty Americans fell, and in the end Major Devereaux and the island commander knew they must surrender.

As details of Wake's heroic defense was brought out to the American public, many thousands of young American men and women flocked to Marine Corps recruiting stations to both honor and avenge the sacrifice. If the living spirit of the Marine Corps from that moment onward can be said to have been sparked by a single event, then that event is the defiant stand of the Marines at Wake.

THE 4TH MARINE REGIMENT ABRUPTLY ENDED ITS DECADES-LONG SERVICE IN CHINA when it sailed for Manila from Shanghai aboard two chartered liners on November 27 and November 28, 1941. Both ships had reached Luzon safely by December 1, and the regiment was put ashore at the Olangapo Naval Station to conduct field training.

The 4th Marines had been allowed to dwindle down to less than a battalion in strength—44 officers and 728 troops, plus a medical detachment—in the years before the war. Although the regiment fielded two nominal battalions, each had only two infantry companies of two platoons apiece—fewer altogether than the nine rifle platoons of a full-strength infantry battalion.

Shown in this pre-war photo is an Imperial Navy Kawanishi H6K four-engine amphibian long-range reconnaissance bomber. Although the H6K was nearing the end of its service life in 1941—it was due to be replaced very shortly by the modern H8K—it was actually retained throughout the war. The H6K looked huge in the air, but the crewmen standing on this example provide a scale that shows her to be of only moderate size. Her attraction lay in the very long range she could fly to while patrolling vast areas of the ocean. H6Ks were used only sparingly in the bomber role, as they were quite apt to flame up from bullet strikes to vulnerable fuel tanks. *National Archives & Records Administration*

News of the Pearl Harbor attack reached Olangapo at 0350 on December 8 (local), and the 4th Marines was pulled into formation in the barracks area. Its first order of business was to organize defenses for the base. Later in the morning, Imperial Navy bombers and fighters based on Formosa began the assault on the Philippines with air attacks on Army Air Corps bases on Luzon, during which they broke the back of American air defenses. By day's end, the 1st Battalion, 4th Marines (1/4), had been dispatched to Mariveles, at the tip of the Bataan Peninsula, to relieve a 1st Separate Marine Battalion guard detachment, which was returned to its parent unit at Cavite naval depot.

Marines fired their first shots in defense of the Philippines when 1st Separate Marine Battalion antiaircraft gunners downed a Formosa-based D3A dive-bomber over Cavite on December 10. The base was nonetheless soundly pummeled, dumps were set on fire, and a submarine and minesweeper were mortally damaged. Fires were so intense—and moving in the direction of the main ammunition dump—that the 1st Separate Battalion was evacuated to Olangapo and, on December 10, the U.S. Asiatic Fleet sailed south from the base to get out of the range of Japanese bombers. Also on December 10, two Imperial Army infantry regiments landed in northern Luzon.

Over the next ten days, the Marines dueled with Japanese airplanes several times, but most of their time was spent reorganizing the regiment and coordinating operations between it and the 1st Separate Battalion. On December 20, all the Marines were folded into General Douglas MacArthur's U.S. Army Forces, Far East (USAFFE), their parent Far East Fleet having left the islands by then. MacArthur immediately ordered the Marine regiment to assume responsibility for all non-headquarters naval personnel left behind and to organize them into combat units.

The VMF-211 boneyard on Wake. The unsung hero of the VMF-211 story was Second Lieutenant John Kinney, an aeronautical engineer and former Pan American World Airways employee who with very little technical assistance built and rebuilt the squadron's battered F4Fs on literally a wing and a prayer. Kinney eventually escaped from a POW train in China and made his way back to the United States before the end of the war. *Imperial Navy Photo via the Marine Corps University Archive*

The shocking truth about Wake's future was driven home when Aichi D3A carrier attack bombers from the carriers *Hiryu* and *Soryu* struck the island for the first time, on December 21, 1941. The shock wasn't so much in the damage they caused as in the determination they represented to win Wake. D3As served throughout the Pacific War, from land bases as well as carriers, and though they were eventually eclipsed by the Yokosuka D4Y, they went to battle until the bitter end. *National Archives & Records Administration*

On December 23, 1941, all U.S. Army forces on Luzon were ordered to fall back on the Bataan Peninsula, comprising the northern arm of Manila Bay. The USAFFE headquarters was to move to Corregidor, a rockbound island fortress in the bay, and the 4th Marines and 1st Separate Battalion were ordered to move with it after they had destroyed Olangapo Naval Station. All Marine units were reunited at Mariveles on December 22 and through the night. Bombing attacks against 1/4 on December 24 killed two Marines and wounded three. Olangapo was blown to pieces on Christmas Day by a 4th Marines demolitions party, and the facilities at Cavite were destroyed by elements of the 1st Separate Battalion (which would be redesignated 3d Battalion, 4th Marines, on January 1). Marines began the displacement to Corregidor after dark on December 26, and there were quartered in barracks in the area known as Middleside. At 1154 on their first day ashore on Corregidor, the Marines were bombed in the first air attack against the island. Although the bombing was protracted and vicious, and material damage was comprehensive, there was only one fatality, and only four Marines were wounded. Shortly after the December 27 bombing attack ended, the troops were moved to beach-defense positions and ordered to dig in. There they would wait for four months, perfecting their positions at every opportunity.

Left behind on Bataan were 120 Marines organized into two antiaircraft batteries based at Mariveles. The troops from one battery were assigned to provide security for MacArthur's advance headquarters on Bataan, but they were instead co-opted to stiffen and train the provisional naval battalion. It was replaced in the security assignment by a detachment from Corregidor. In the end, fewer than 170 Marines in Bataan were spread thin to man two antiaircraft batteries, serve with the naval battalion as trainers, and provide headquarters security.

The Japanese attempted a landing behind the Bataan main line on the night of January 22–23, 1942. The landing craft ran into trouble, and in the end nearly three hundred troops blundered ashore near Mariveles. Over the next week, Marines from the antiaircraft batteries, sailors and Marines from the naval battalion, and even Army Air Corps pilots and groundcrew serving as infantry ran these tenacious Japanese to ground, then supported U.S. Army and Philippine Scout units that ground them to dust by February 13.

On February 14, the 4th Marines on Corregidor was bolstered by the transfer of 9 naval officers and 327 sailors from Bataan. Shortly, approximately seven hundred Philippine Army air cadets and their officers joined the regiment, to be trained by Marines for use as fillers and reserves. Even though Corregidor was bombed and shelled mercilessly from about that time, the naval troops, air cadets, and even contingents of U.S. Army soldiers were integrated into the regiment and trained to the highest degree possible. These troops were eventually stood up as the 4th Battalion, 4th Marines, Provisional—even though the entire Marine contingent in its ranks stood at six: the battalion commander and five non-commissioned officers. The 4th Battalion was designated the regimental reserve.

Bataan fell on April 9. Among the very few troops to get over to Corregidor during the night of April 8 were the Marine antiaircraft gunners—but not the guns—assigned to Mariveles. These men brought the strength of the heavily bolstered regiment to more than four thousand.

From the moment of the Bataan surrender, Corregidor became the sole target of an immense and even burgeoning artillery force on the surrounding land, and, of course, ceaseless air raids. By May 2, the 1/4 commander reported that his defenses were "practically destroyed." It was much the same throughout the island bastion. That day, 240mm shells fell on the defenses at a rate of twelve per minute. The Marine sector was hit especially hard because it incorporated the lowest point on the island and was thus the obvious target of the main landing force.

Beginning at about 2300 hours on May 5, the Japanese landed in overwhelming force behind a crushing bombardment. As anticipated, their landing craft arrowed directly into the lowest part of the island, directly at 1/4. Resistance was stiff and cool; often it was just plain gallant. But it was doomed. In due course the regimental reserve—the hodgepodge 4th Battalion—was committed to the last man, but the Japanese onslaught never ceased; it only wavered here and there as it overwhelmed one last stand of heroes after another. By 1130 on May 6, only about 150 Marines, sailors, and soldiers under Marine command—many already wounded and all exhausted—stood between the Japanese and Malinta Tunnel, the island headquarters. The troops were willing to defend to the death, but the island commander, Lieutenant General Jonathan Wainwright, saw no purpose in fighting on. All hope had been extinguished. Word was passed to stand down and destroy weapons. Marines burned the regimental and national colors while several other Marines were asked to carry a truce flag into the Japanese lines. A Marine bugler sounded off, the flag was carried forward, and the surrender process commenced. Shortly, all the guns went silent.

Midway Atoll from the air on November 24, 1941. The airfield is on Eastern Island and most facilities are on Sand Island. Note the darker channel cut through the coral to Eastern Island's seaplane ramp. By June 1, 1942, the islands were chock-a-block with troops, coastal and antiaircraft guns, and aircraft from three services. *Official USMC Photo*

Bomb damage on Midway's Sand Island on June 4, 1942. Note the density of the tents and buildings. Note also that the observation tower is camouflaged from view from the air. *Official USMC Photo*

Throughout its fight in the Philippines, the 4th Marine Regiment, including the 1st Separate Battalion, lost 315 officers and men killed, 357 wounded, and 15 missing in action. Most became casualties in twelve hours of intense combat on Corregidor. It is probable that the number of non-Marine dead, wounded, and missing during service with the 4th Marines will never be known; certainly it numbers in the hundreds.

THE ONSET OF WAR SUDDENLY MADE THE U.S. JOINT CHIEFS OF STAFF RALLY TO ITS obligation to bolster the American line of fixed bases extending southward and westward from Hawaii. A flurry of activity ensued as the direction of the American line of communication and supply across the Pacific was bolstered, expanded, filled in, and shifted southwestward toward Australia from its original westward orientation toward the Philippines.

There was no way the Marine Corps could handle the array of vital basing requirements, so in very short order, the Army stood up a new infantry division in Hawaii, dispatched an existing infantry division to Australia, established base-defense forces on Canton and Christmas islands and in the French Society Islands, and reinforced a New Zealand ground garrison in the Fiji Islands. In March 1942, an Army divisional task force occupied New Caledonia, and then Army garrisons moved to Efate in the New Hebrides and Tongatabu in the Tonga Islands.

The cornerstone of the air and sea route to Australia remained Samoa. On December 7, American Eastern Samoa was held by the 7th Defense Battalion and a small local Marine

Corps Reserve battalion. It was obvious early on that this meager force could not possibly hold such a large and vital base in the face of a determined invasion effort, so within days of the Pearl Harbor attack plans were put forth to man a complete Marine brigade for service in American Samoa.

The 2d Marine Brigade, built around the 2d Marine Division's 8th Marine Regiment, sailed from San Diego on January 6, 1942. The completion of the barely started Tutuila airdrome was deemed so vital that the brigade took with it $200,000 worth of engineering equipment purchased on the civilian market.

The only attack against American Samoa occurred on the night of January 11, while the 2d Marine Brigade was still at sea. A Japanese submarine shelled the naval station, caused light damage, lightly wounded two sailors, and withdrew.

The reinforcements reached Samoa on January 19 and went straight to work, around the clock, to install comprehensive defensive positions and complete the air base at Tutuila. It took three months to get the job done.

Marine Douglas SBD Dauntless dive-bombers going out on a mission. This photo was taken later in the war, probably in 1944, but the scene is close to the single Midway mission, where six Marine SBDs flew their service's first mission of the war. The SBD was a two-place scout bomber, with pilot and radioman-gunner. The nimble light bomber was armed with two cowl-mounted .50-caliber machine guns and a .30-caliber dual mount facing rearward. SBDs carried either a 500-pound or a 1,000-pound mounted on a centerline yoke that swung the bomb beyond the propeller arc. These late-version SBDs also are equipped with rocket rails.
Official USMC Photo

The occupation and defense of Eastern Samoa was fine as far as it went, but British Western Samoa was vital to the successful defense of the island group. Only 157 New Zealand troops held the British islands, so diplomatic arrangements were quickly set in motion to facilitate the basing of yet another Marine brigade there and on Wallis Island, a French possession that shielded the western approaches to Samoa. As soon as permission was in hand, a detachment of the 7th Defense Battalion moved to Upolu Island in Western Samoa, and the 1st Marine Division, in North Carolina, was ordered to stand up the 3d Marine Brigade, which was built around the 7th Marines. Shortly, the 8th Defense Battalion was stood up around the 7th Defense Battalion detachment at Upolu, and fresh troops for both units were sent from the States (in most cases directly upon completing boot camp). Thus, by early June 1942, the Fleet Marine Force had invested more than ten thousand troops in the defense of Samoa—including most of the Marine Corps' meager store of banana wars veterans, who volunteered in droves when the two brigades were stood up.

A crash building program brought the Tutuila airdrome—only 10 percent complete when the 2d Brigade arrived—to operational status on March 17. On March 19, an advance detachment of MAG-13 arrived from San Diego with only VMF-111, in F4F-3s, under its control. Marine Observation Squadron 151 (VMO-151), in obsolete Curtiss SBC Helldiver *biplane* scout-bombers, arrived with the 3d Marine Brigade, and a Navy amphibian bomber detachment, based in American Samoa before the start of the war, came under MAG-13 control as it was advanced to operate from Upolu.

A Vought SB2U Vindicator dive-bomber, in this case a Navy carrier bomber serving with the Atlantic Fleet in February 1942. By June 1942, only Marines flew SB2Us in combat, and they did so only at Midway. *Official USN Photo*

Wallis Island was occupied by a reinforced battalion of the 3d Marine Brigade and bolstered by Navy amphibians, which served as advance scouts to the extremity of their range.

The defenses in Samoa and on Wallis were never tested; there is no telling how they might have fared in the face of a determined attack. Samoa served throughout the war as an important aviation way station, naval staging base, and training ground for American fleets and ground units heading westward into the war.

As early as March 1942, Pacific Fleet intelligence officers warned the new Pacific Fleet commander in chief, Admiral Chester Nimitz, that the Japanese might be staging for an invasion of Midway, perhaps as the first step for an invasion of Hawaii. Then and there, without certain knowledge, the offensive-minded Nimitz decided to gamble on a massive response if the perceived threat reached fruition. In short order, the precise Japanese plan was recovered from coded intercepts and confirmed by a singular radio-intelligence ruse that pinpointed Midway as the objective. Nimitz immediately put his plan into action and even visited lonely Midway on May 2—just as the Coral Sea battle was about to get under way in the South Pacific, between New Guinea and the Solomon Islands. Upon his return to Pearl Harbor, Nimitz freed up whatever land-based aviation units he could find. There wasn't much to be had, but it all went to Midway, as did a large contingent from the 3d Marine Defense Battalion (including a light tank platoon) and about half of the 2d Marine Raider Battalion. VMF-221 was beefed up with seven Grumman F4F-3 Wildcat fighters, and VMSB-241 received sixteen SBD-2 dive-bombers.

The first inkling of battle came from a report from a Navy PBY at 0900 on June 3. Eleven ships, no doubt carrying Japanese ground troops, were east of Midway and closing at 19 knots. These ships were attacked by nine Army Air Forces (Army Air Corps until March 1) Boeing B-17 Flying Fortress heavy bombers based at Wake.

At 0430, the Japanese carrier fleet launched thirty-six Aichi D3A dive-bombers, thirty-six bomb-armed Nakajima B5N torpedo planes, and thirty-six Mitsubishi A6M carrier fighters against Midway. As far as the Japanese knew, the only opposition would be land-based fighters and antiaircraft guns; they knew nothing of the American carrier task forces Nimitz had placed northwest of the target area. The carrier aircraft were spotted by a Midway-based PBY at 0545, just 150 miles from the atoll. All hands were called to general quarters, and every available fighter was alerted. Ten minutes later, the 6th Defense Battalion's and the naval station's own radars picked up "many planes" on their scopes. Every Marine plane on the atoll was aloft within ten minutes—SB2Us, SBDs, F2As, and F4Fs. The fighters beelined to intercept the attack while the dive-bombers flew east to await instructions.

Major Floyd Parks, the VMF-221 commander, was the first to spot the Japanese. It was 0616 when the two forces met 30 miles from Midway. Twelve Marine F2A and F4F pilots pitched in, but the nimble, deadly Zeros were better aircraft, flown by veterans. Nine of the twelve Marine fighters were quickly shot down, but the survivors reported several kills for their side.

Next up were thirteen F2As under Captain Kirk Armistead. Somehow this wave of fighters fared better than Major Parks'; only one F2A went down.

The Japanese carrier bombers reached Midway at 0630. There they were faced by antiair-craft fire that downed two, but twenty-two others unloaded their bombs, as did eighteen bombers in the second wave. Bomb damage was moderate to heavy and included several impor-tant facilities—a power plant and a 6th Defense Battalion sector command post. Zeros strafed behind the bombers and left. This sole raid on Midway during the battle was over by 0700.

As the Japanese attack formations returned to their ships—the *Kaga* and the *Akagi*—one of the formation leaders radioed a report that recommended a follow-on strike. This recommendation—coupled with an attack on the Japanese flagship by four torpedo-laden Martin B-26 Marauder medium bombers and six Grumman TBF Avenger torpedo bombers—set in motion a series of events that led to the destruction of *four* of the six Japanese carriers that had taken part in the Pearl Harbor attack and run roughshod over

VMSB-142's Second Lieutenant Daniel Iverson, back from the clash over the Japanese fleet carrier *Akagi*. Iverson's SBD was hit by 249 machine-gun rounds and shrapnel shards in its brief flight over the Imperial battle fleet, including one that clipped off the pilot's throat microphone. Danny Iverson went on to gallant service over Guadalcanal until he was severely wounded during a night bombardment of his base (named Henderson Field after the downed VMSB-241 squadron commander, Major Lofton Henderson). *Official USMC Photo*

The heavy cruiser HIJMS *Mikuma* a day after the dive-bombing attack led by VMSB-241's Captain Richard Fleming on June 5, 1942. Difficult to see or out of view in this June 6 photo are hundreds of Japanese sailors seeking cover at the bow and stern of the, by then, sinking ship. *Official USN Photo*

Allied navies from Hawaii to Ceylon and as far south as Darwin, Australia. Basically, the Japanese intended to look for American carriers, and had armed their planes to do so, but the land-based torpedo attack caused them to rearm for another attack on Midway. It was while these aircraft were being rearmed and refueled that American carrier strike groups found and attacked the Japanese carriers.

After it flew to safe airspace at the start of the attack, VMSB-241 was vectored out after the Japanese carriers. The sixteen SBD crews, commanded by Major Lofton Henderson, had their first look at the carriers from 9,000 feet at 0744 hours. Before the attack formation could reach the carriers, it was assaulted by Zeros and D3As. No bomb hits were scored, and Henderson's and seven other SBDs were shot down.

Fifteen B-17s were next to attack the Japanese carriers. Claims were high, but there is nothing in Japanese records to back such optimism. As the B-17s recovered toward Midway, eleven VMSB-241 SB2Us under Captain Benjamin Norris arrived on the scene. Zeros deflected the Vindicators from the carriers, so Norris headed toward an accompanying battleship, and several of his pilots settled on a second battleship. Three SB2Us were lost with their crews and no hits were scored.

The Marine aircraft were all back on the ground by 1100 hours. Losses were two F4Fs, thirteen F2As, eight SBDs, and three SB2Us with their pilots and crews. Also, twenty-eight Marines were killed by bombs on Midway.

Marines played no other role in the immense strategy-altering battle that engulfed both carrier fleets over the course of June 4, but at 1900 hours Captain Norris led six SBDs and five SB2Us in a vain effort to locate a damaged Imperial Navy carrier. Nothing was found, but Norris and his radioman-gunner were killed in a landing accident.

Six SBD crews under Captain M. A. Taylor and six SB2U crews under Captain Richard Fleming played a role as the Japanese armada retired. The target was a surface battle flotilla composed of four cruisers and two destroyers spotted by an American submarine at daybreak. Two of the cruisers had already been damaged in a collision; the heavy cruiser *Mogami* had damage around her bows, and the heavy cruiser *Mikuma* was trailing an oil slick. The Marine bombers took off at 0700 and found the ships at 0800 as they cruised 170 miles west of the airfield. Taylor's SBDs went after the *Mogami* and Fleming led his SB2Us after the *Mikuma* through intense antiaircraft fire. The SBDs scored six near misses that caused visible damage. Captain Fleming's plane was mortally damaged on the way down, but he maintained sufficient control to crash it into one of the *Mikuma's* after gun turrets. No bomb hits were scored, but both heavy cruisers suffered sufficient damage to further slow the flotilla. The *Mikuma* was sunk on June 6 by carrier planes, and the *Mogami* was additionally damaged and kept from sea for two years. Richard Fleming was awarded a posthumous Medal of Honor, the first of the war to a Marine Corps Reserve officer.

In all, forty-nine Marines died in the Midway battle, and fifty-three were wounded. Marine pilots and aircrewmen were credited with downing forty-three Japanese aircraft (undoubtedly an exaggeration; postwar estimates account for no more than seventeen

Surviving pilots and radioman-gunners from VMSB-241 were photographed on July 5, 1942, shortly before these airmen were evacuated to Hawaii. The entire squadron was replaced at one time. *Official USMC Photo*

VMF-221 survivors of the Midway battle were evacuated to Hawaii on June 22, 1942. Many of the survivors never flew in combat again, so deep was their trauma. On the other hand, several Midway veterans excelled, none more than Captain Marion Carl, seen here at the far left of the group. Carl was credited with downing one Zero and damaging two others near Midway on June 4, 1942, and by the end of his one combat tour at Guadalcanal he had an official tally of 18 1/2 confirmed kills and three damage claims, for which he earned a Navy Cross. He set many world flying records after the war and ultimately retired from the Marine Corps as a brigadier general after commanding an *infantry* brigade in Vietnam. *Official USMC Photo*

confirmed kills, two probables, and four damaged, which still might be high), and antiaircraft gunners were credited with ten.

THE WESTERNMOST MARINES DEPLOYED TO THE SOUTH PACIFIC THROUGH JULY 1942 were based in the New Hebrides Islands. In March, the 4th Defense Battalion, 950 men strong, and MAG-23's VMF-212, in F4F Wildcat fighters, were dispatched from Hawaii to Tongatabu but then diverted to bolster a 500-man U.S. Army garrison recently advanced to Efate in the New Hebrides. There the Marines assisted in the construction, defense, and manning of an airfield at Vila.

In little more than a month, Japanese naval forces occupied Tulagi in the Solomon Islands and shortly thereafter began to build an advance bomber base at Guadalcanal, only 700 miles from Efate (but not quite within the operational range of their land-based bombers).

The Army next advanced a 500-man garrison to Espiritu Santo, 150 miles closer to and within bomber range of Tulagi, in May 1942. An attempt to build an airfield fell afoul of poor site selection; then a second attempt was rushed through to support a prospective assault on Tulagi. On July 15, a strong detachment from the 4th Defense Battalion was moved to Espiritu Santo to both defend the base and help to complete the airstrip.

A Marine Observation Squadron 151 (VMO-151) Curtiss SBC Helldiver scout-bomber off Samoa in early 1942. VMO-151 was the first Marine bombing squadron to reach the South Pacific, on May 9, 1942. The unit was eventually reequipped with SBDs and saw service into 1943 at Wallis Island. *Official USMC Photo*

Finally, on July 12, VMO-251, in F4F-3 photo-reconnaissance fighters, arrived in Nouméa aboard ship. On July 28, as soon as the airfield at Espiritu Santo became operational, the new unit and VMF-212 were ordered to take up residence.

THE JAPANESE NEVER PROMULGATED PLANS TO SEIZE SAMOA OR WALLIS, BUT THEY might have in due course, for as the Samoa defenses were being built up in the first half of 1942, Japanese advances through the Solomon Islands and plans to advance into the New Hebrides and on to Fiji certainly placed Samoa on an extended path of conquest. What saved all the garrisons in Samoa, Wallis, and the New Hebrides from a test of arms was a test of wills in the Solomons. By July 1942, the United States finally had the means in place to stand up to the Japanese juggernaut, in both New Guinea and the Solomon Islands.

A VMO-251 F4F photo-reconnaissance plane on Espiritu Santo in late 1942. As in mid-1942, the stripped-for-speed VMO-251 photo planes carried no guns; they had only their speed and ability to climb to very high altitude to carry them from danger. Overall, this is an excellent study of the F4F Wildcat. *Official USMC Photo*

CHAPTER 4

GUADALCANAL

AUGUST 7, 1942–FEBRUARY 9, 1943

The six-month-long Guadalcanal Campaign was by far the longest and most complicated operation Marines faced in the Pacific War. It started on the fly, when the Japanese were found to be building a bomber base on the northern coast of Guadalcanal near Lunga. An attack against the potential fleet-size anchorage at nearby Tulagi had been discussed, but planning quickly turned to Guadalcanal as well as Tulagi and a seaplane base set on several small islands near Tulagi.

The 1st Marine Division (less the 3d Marine Brigade, in Samoa) happened to be landing in New Zealand for advanced training when the decision was made, and it was selected to seize the new objectives in early August. To replace the division's missing troops, the 2d Marine Division's reinforced 2d Marine Regiment (2d Marines) was added to the 1st Division roster as a reserve force. As things developed, the 1st Marine Raider Battalion also was in the Pacific for training, and it was added to the invasion force. The 3d Defense Battalion was added as a base force, and finally the incomplete 350-man 1st Parachute Battalion was attached to the landing force.

The 1st and 5th Marines were assigned to land on Guadalcanal to seize the airfield and several key terrain features; the 1st Raider Battalion and 2/5 were to seize Tulagi; and the 1st Parachute Battalion was to seize the seaplane base on Gavutu and Tanambogo, just off Tulagi. The 2d Marines was the force reserve; it was to roll up outposts on Florida Island, then sail to occupy the Santa Cruz Islands.

After the invasion force stopped in the Fijis to rendezvous with all the attachments and a naval covering force incorporating three fleet carriers, the division undertook a massive

This aerial view of Red Beach on August 7, 1942, belies the serious shortcomings of the landing effort. The front-line troops were put ashore without much difficulty, but unmapped terrain amid a coconut plantation caused monumental problems in moving and storing goods, then transporting them toward the objective. Moreover, the 1st Pioneer Battalion was inadequate for the task, and drafts of bluejackets from the transports were untrained. Goods were either dumped willy-nilly along the beach, or landing craft faced schedule-busting delays awaiting clearance to land. The largest and first modern amphibious assault to that date was nearly an abject failure and would leave great privation in its wake. *Official USN Photo*

The seaplane base at Gavutu and Tanambogo was struck by carrier planes from the USS *Wasp* and then assaulted by the tiny 1st Parachute Battalion. In a precursor to assaults in the central Pacific, the landing was violently opposed, and it took help from two battalions of the 2d Marines to secure both islands.
Official USN Photo

The first flag raising of the Pacific offensive occurred beside the captured Lunga runway on August 9, 1942. It is possible that the Marine third from left with the halyard in hand is the 1st Marine Division commander, Major General A. A. Vandegrift.
Official USMC Photo

landing rehearsal of such ineptitude that it only served to worry the leadership. The reinforced division sailed in time to reach Guadalcanal on D-day, August 7, and undertake the landing. The airfield was seized without a fight and named after the martyred Midway dive-bomber commander, Major Lofton Henderson. Tulagi was seized following a brutal fight, and so were Gavutu and Tanambogo, with the help of the 2d Marines.

On the night of August 8–9, a Japanese surface battle force attacked the anchorage off Guadalcanal, mixed it up with screening warships, sank four heavy cruisers, and fled without losing a ship. Coming as it did on the heels of an announcement by the carrier commander that he was pulling out to refuel on August 9, the defeat at sea so unnerved the transport commander that he also pulled out on December 9, leaving the Santa Cruz–bound 2d Marines on the beach and taking with him more than half of the landing force's supplies, heavy weapons, and equipment, including engineering equipment needed to complete Henderson Field.

In one swoop, the Guadalcanal campaign was recast as a defensive effort barely bolstered by inadequate air and naval support. The 1st Marine Division was pretty much on its own, beyond the range of fighter support and served by naval covering forces that tended to cower out of range of Japanese warships and bombers.

The nearest Japanese fleet and air bases were 600 miles northwest of Guadalcanal, at Rabaul, on New Britain Island. The Marine Lunga Perimeter on Guadalcanal was just inside the operational range of Japanese bombers and fighters based at Rabaul, and the Japanese were not afraid to send warships down from Rabaul to bombard Lunga or attack American warships and transports that sneaked in from more secure bases at Nouméa and the New Hebrides.

Looking northward on Henderson Field, Bloody Ridge, which the Japanese assaulted in September and October, is the bare high ground just to the south of the airfield. *Official USMC Photo*

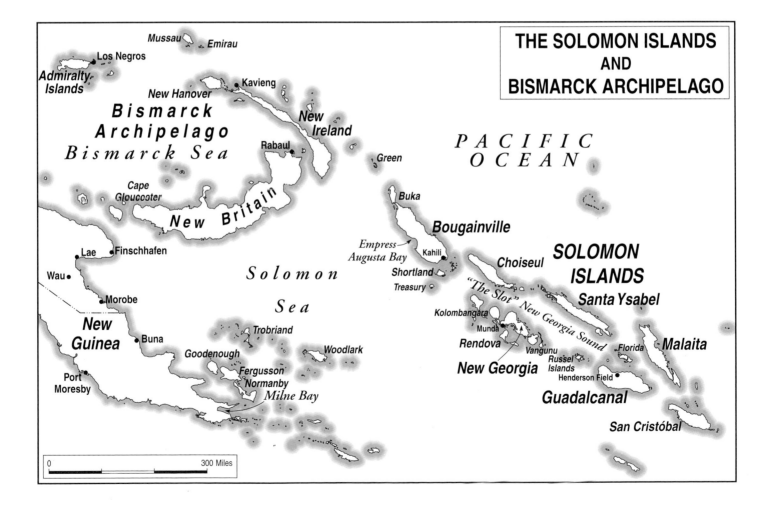

THE SOLOMON ISLANDS
AND
BISMARCK ARCHIPELAGO

A Marine infantry patrol wades across a lagoon in the Matanikau River as it patrols the rainforest west of the Lunga Perimeter. Often, an advance along waterways was the easiest way to get around in the otherwise dense and choked forest terrain. *Official USMC Photo*

Higher-level command posts were necessarily set up in the safer rear areas, giving many headquarters personnel access to various amenities not available to front-line troops. Nevertheless, given the constrained circumstances of life around Lunga, a perverse democracy of adversity brought the highest nearly to the level of the lowest. This sparsely appointed tent was the sole personal abode throughout the campaign of Major General Vandegrift, the Marine commanding general. *Official USMC Photo*

A line of bombs walks across the terrain adjacent to Henderson Field. Weather permitting, bombing attacks against the air base were almost a daily occurrence, one of the chief characteristics of the fighting. They abated somewhat after the arrival of Marine and Navy Wildcat squadrons, but the Japanese kept them up regularly into November. Most bombing attacks were the work of Imperial Navy bomber groups based in Rabaul, but Japanese carriers took part on several occasions. *Official USMC Photo*

Uncontested bombardments from the air and sea characterized the early phase of the defense of the Lunga Perimeter.

The Marines got patrols out early to mop up Japanese troops and laborers who had fled the invasion. A patrol led by the division intelligence officer was ambushed by a small Japanese force fresh from Rabaul, and nearly all hands perished. In response, in the largest combat initiative undertaken by Marines since World War I, a retaliatory assault incorporating three infantry companies was sent in, with limited results.

On August 20, the Lunga garrison was bolstered by the arrival at newly operational Henderson Field of VMF-223 in F4F Wildcats and VMSB-232 in SBD Dauntlesses. Thus the Lunga garrison had the means to at least begin staving off nearly daily aerial attacks.

On the night of August 20, a freshly landed Imperial Army regiment, goaded into action when it was discovered by a Marine patrol, attacked the eastern side of the perimeter. One Marine infantry battalion held against repeated vicious assaults, and the Japanese force was nearly annihilated by a counterassault thrown in by a second Marine battalion. The so-called Tenaru River battle was by far the largest land victory scored by the United States to that point in the Pacific War. It was made sweeter by a victory of American carriers over a Japanese carrier force on August 24. Moreover, the utterly outnumbered Marine fighter pilots began

As soon as it arrived at Lunga and set up, the 3d Defense Battalion carried the brunt of defending Henderson Field against aerial assault. Shown here are (a) a .50-caliber machine gun in an antiaircraft mount and (b) a 90mm antiaircraft gun in action. The 3d Defense Battalion also fielded coastal guns for use in an antiboat role. As seen here, the antiaircraft guns were set up on high ground when that was possible. *Official USMC Photos*

scoring victories on August 21, and Marine SBDs took part in sinking a number of troop transports and destroyers bound to Guadalcanal from Rabaul.

In mid-September, the 1st Raider and 1st Parachute Battalions held a ridgeline (dubbed Bloody Ridge) just to the south of Henderson Field against a brigade-size infantry attack. A week later, the 3d Marine Brigade (the 7th Marines and support units) arrived from Samoa and immediately opened a series of offensive patrols east of the perimeter. Successes alternated with defeats, but slowly the air contingent operating from Henderson Field and newly operational Fighter-1 wielded more weight and authority in response to an ongoing, almost daily aerial assault from Rabaul. There was also an important naval victory one night in mid-October that put the Japanese naval flotillas staging through Rabaul on notice that Lunga was no longer a free ride.

This bombproof shelter was no doubt constructed near the airfield or a headquarters for use by pilots or senior officers. All of the sandbags and rope coils shown were from Japanese stocks captured when Lunga fell to the Marines. The entire structure is probably above the ground due to severe drainage problems throughout the perimeter. *Official USMC Photo*

Fighter-1 was little more than an improved, mown pasture. For a very long time, the Japanese failed to recognize the modest airfield for what it was. But it lay on the direct route to Henderson Field, so Japanese bombers under attack from Fighter-1-based F4Fs often salvoed their bombs early and thereby hit Fighter-1. Nevertheless, the fighter strip was rarely bombarded by Japanese naval surface forces that routinely struck Henderson Field at night. *Official USMC Photo*

In late October, following a long build-up accompanied by vicious and protracted air and naval bombardments that very nearly swamped Henderson Field, Marine and newly arrived Army battalions turned back massive infantry assaults at Bloody Ridge and on the western side of the perimeter, along the Matanikau River. A carrier battle fought on October 26 turned back Japanese carriers bound to strike the Lunga Perimeter (and, incidentally, caused the Imperial Navy to withdraw its carrier fleet from action for twenty crucial months). For several days in mid-November, the Japanese once again attempted to wear out the Lunga defenders by air and naval bombardment as they landed yet more reinforcements. Bolstered by carrier-based air, the Lunga-based fighters and bombers fought the reinforcement convoys to a standstill, and then in separate actions on the nights of November 12–13 and 14–15, U.S. naval surface task forces turned back two surface bombardment flotillas and sank two battleships—and other ships—in the bargain. U.S. naval losses were high, but the victory, known in history as the Naval Battle of Guadalcanal, was so resounding that the Imperial Navy never sent its battleships into action again in any meaningful way.

Defeated on land, at sea, and in the air, the Japanese thereafter merely attempted to hang on to what they could, to perhaps use it as a springboard for some later assault on Lunga. The Americans never looked back. The 2d Marine Brigade (the 8th Marines and

The successful defense of the Lunga Perimeter in late August and most of September 1942 lay largely in the hands of these three Marine Wildcat pilots: Major John Smith, the commanding officer of VMF-223; Major Robert Galer, the commanding officer of VMF-224; and Captain Marion Carl, one of several Midway defenders who served with VMF-223. During the Guadalcanal Campaign, Smith was credited with 19 confirmed kills, Galer was credited with 14, and Carl was credited with 17 1/2 (plus 1 at Midway). Shown here, the three have just had Navy Crosses pinned on by the Pacific Fleet commander in chief, Admiral Chester Nimitz. The two squadron commanders were later awarded Medals of Honor for their leadership role and, in Smith's case, for developing the tactics that cost the Imperial Navy so many of its airmen. In all during the Guadalcanal Campaign, the Imperial Navy lost a staggering six hundred aircraft to American guns. *Official USMC Photo*

This rather odd photo was taken in the Henderson Field dispersal area, probably in September 1942. The bombers are U.S. Army Air Forces B-17s that sometimes operated off Henderson Field when they needed extra range for patrols and attacks up the Solomon chain. The infantry company transiting the area is clad in decent uniforms, so it might be part of the 7th Marines, which arrived from Samoa in September—or a U.S. Army unit that arrived in October. And the pony was no doubt captured by Marines from among those left behind when the coconut plantation at Lunga was abandoned in mid-1942, as soon as the Japanese arrived in the Solomons. *Official USMC Photo*

A Marine infantry company rests while on patrol in the hills west of the Lunga Perimeter. Relatively neat uniforms suggest that this is a fresh unit, possibly part of the 7th Marines shortly after its arrival in mid-September, but it is equally probable that these men belong to the 6th Marines, which arrived in January. Heavily forested in low areas, Guadalcanal offered many clearings and open terrain on higher ground, as shown here. *Official USMC Photo*

support units) was shipped in from Samoa, two U.S. Army infantry divisions replaced the tired and ill 1st Marine Division, the weary 2d Marines were evacuated in due course, and the 2d Marine Division's 6th Marines arrived in early January. The Japanese shipped in reinforcements through January, and a naval surface battle off Guadalcanal was decided in their favor, but the tide had clearly turned against them. A steady American offensive squeezed them back toward the western end of Guadalcanal, and then the last of them were evacuated. The Guadalcanal Campaign officially ended on February 9, 1943—a complete victory for the United States and a singular if hard-won achievement for the Marine Corps.

At Guadalcanal, Marine commanders learned to fight with increasingly larger groupments of troops—multiple companies, then multiple battalions, and finally multiple regiments working together. Marine Air, which contributed the most to the Guadalcanal air effort, came to the fore during the campaign and carved out an enduring niche for itself alongside the Fleet Marine Force. Nearly a loss and quite somber while it was happening, Guadalcanal taught Marines how to fight the next phase of the Pacific War.

The "heavy artillery" of Marine infantry battalions throughout the war were 81mm mortars. Shown here, an 81mm mortar squad, no doubt accompanying a battalion-size patrol, has set up its weapon. Rounds are being broken out for a fire mission as the gunner locates the target on his map. The casual demeanor of these troops and the state of their uniforms indicate they have been ashore for a while. *Official USMC Photo*

A Japanese soldier lies dead where he has been caught by Marines on patrol or advancing west from Lunga. Nearly as many Japanese soldiers starved to death as were killed in action on Guadalcanal. *Official USMC Photo*

The results of naval bombardment, though not as frequent as aerial bombardment, were often staggering in scope and destruction. This photo was taken during the run-up to the immense October offensive that nearly brought the aviation community based at the Henderson Field complex to its knees. *Official USMC Photo*

This airplane has taken a direct hit, either from an aerial bomb or from a naval shell fired at the Henderson Field complex from just offshore. *Official USMC Photo*

As much as aircraft or men, air and naval bombardment went after facilities, chiefly the Henderson Field runway itself. In an extreme case, Marine SBDs lifted off from the runway after dodging shell holes during the take-off run. Shown here is damaged Marston matting, a type of pierced steel planking set out to smooth the runway and stabilize the boggy ground for use by heavy bombers and other heavily laden aircraft. This photo was taken on October 14, 1942, at the height of Japanese bombardments. *Official USMC Photo*

The Imperial Army's October 1942 land offensive kicked off with a premature tank-supported infantry assault across the mouth of the Matanikau River, at the western extremity of the Lunga Perimeter. As soon as the tanks cleared obscuring trees, they ran afoul of several 37mm antitank guns dug in to guard the ford at the river mouth. This gun, backed by other 37s and several 75mm antitank guns mounted on halftracks, was able to penetrate Japanese tank armor. *Official USMC Photo*

These Imperial Army tanks were stopped cold by Marine antitank guns at the mouth of the Matanikau River in October 1942. *Official USMC Photo*

Several battalions of 75mm pack howitzers fired by crews from the 11th Marines also weighed in when the Japanese attempted to cross the Matanikau in November 1942. In addition to interfering with the tanks, the howitzers sealed the battlefield and bombarded a follow-on infantry force. *Official USMC Photo*

Japanese infantry units advancing through the forest and along the beach in the wake of the armor vanguard were pulverized by Marine artillery and mortars. An estimated six hundred Japanese were killed in this single action. Note the destroyed tanks in the background, closer to the river mouth.
Official USMC Photo

Marine defenses were often set on the high ground and became extremely well developed as time passed. This .30-caliber light machine gun position is probably set up on Bloody Ridge, just south of Henderson Field. If so, in late October it was of importance in beating back the largest and fiercest infantry assault of the Guadalcanal Campaign.
Official USMC Photo

The massacre before Bloody Ridge. A line of Marines, barely visible in the smoke- and fog-shrouded air, stands before the killing ground where two Imperial Army regiments were ground to dust in back-to-back assaults on the nights of October 24–25 and 25–26, 1942. The Japanese never recovered from the defeat, and Marines and U.S. Army soldiers went over to relentless offensive operations that eventually led to total victory on Guadalcanal. *Official USMC Photo*

The 1st Marine Division was relieved at Guadalcanal by Marine and Army reinforcements through December 1942 and the first week of January 1943 and sent to Australia to recuperate and refit. A large percentage of the evacuees had to be treated for or even sent home because of a variety of tropical diseases exacerbated by malnutrition and unsanitary conditions on the island. Nearly a year would pass before the blooded division again saw combat. *Official USMC Photo*

The unimproved 1st Marine Division cemetery at Lunga was modestly dressed up as the division was evacuated from the island, but note the makeshift nature of the grave markers and the unadorned simplicity of warriors' graves in a battleground setting. *Official USMC Photo*

Following the grim but decisive October battles, Marines and their U.S. Army comrades routinely crossed the Matanikau River in force, following a period of months in which the waterway was the Lunga Perimeter's hostile western frontier. Improvements such as this engineer-built ferry, and eventually permanent bridges, were installed after American combat units took up permanent possession of the west side of the river and drove the Japanese farther and farther to the west. *Official USMC Photo*

As long as there were Japanese ahead, Marines advancing westward along Guadalcanal's northern shore never stopped probing the defenses with combat patrols, and apparently never stopped using shallow waterways to circumvent dense rainforests. This patrol, probably from the 6th Marines, is accompanied by island scouts serving under British command. *Official USMC Photo*

And as long as there were Japanese ahead, Marine units advancing westward along Guadalcanal's northern shore never stopped taking casualties. This litter team carries Second Lieutenant Baine Kerr, of 1/6, to the rear after the platoon leader was slightly wounded. Kerr later served with an infantry company at Tarawa. *Official USMC Photo*

CHAPTER 5

TRAINING

Once it had some real war experience under its belt, the Marine Corps was able to standardize its training of recruits and specialists for the war in the Pacific. Already fabled for its toughness, the training programs at the Parris Island and San Diego recruit depots naturally took on new purpose and a tougher aura when the first drill instructors who had been battle-tested in the Pacific reported for duty, bringing a most serious intent to the process.

Recruit training was designed, first and foremost, to submerge the recruit in an environment of adversity in which everything came from the troop leaders and the only society of trust was the peer group—the unit. This extremely pressured and largely hostile environment was meant to approximate the stresses of combat and a solution for survival—an us-and-them world of stark contrasts. But boot training was a crash course in physical and mental conditioning, a hell of Pavlovian-style obedience training, and a leveling device aimed at knocking down the mightiest and building up the lowest. Many boots enjoyed their first experience of three square meals a day at boot camp, or the use of their first toothbrushes or regular bathing.

And they all learned to fire rifles. It was a matter of special pride that every Marine recruit passed through the crucible to rifle training, no matter what job he filled after boot camp. Every Marine *was* a rifleman.

Following graduation from boot camp, the new privates (and a small number of meritoriously promoted privates first class) were scattered to the winds. The new Marines were assigned out randomly (it seemed) to fill slots in special schools or sent in drafts to replace riflemen in combat infantry units, or to help form new infantry units.

"Every Marine a rifleman" has been the credo of boot training from farther back than living memory. By far, most Marine recruits had never touched a rifle before they set hands on the one they fired in boot camp. Here, a boot loads a five-round clip into a Springfield M1903 rifle. The bolt-action '03 was replaced in late 1942 by the semiautomatic Garand M1, which featured an eight-round clip.
Official USMC Photo

The training shown here was known as "combat conditioning." It's not clear if it was meant to provide tools for real hand-to-hand combat or to provide yet another means for physical conditioning.
Official USMC Photo

While it was difficult to re-create realistic combat conditions without bloodshed, Marine Corps training during and after boot camp did its best to familiarize Marines with battlefield conditions and simulations—experiences they could draw from and build on in real combat.
Official USMC Photo

While the toughest training of its kind in the U.S. armed services was behind them, Marines never really stopped training, whether they stayed in until wounded or killed, survived three or even four island invasions, or made a life-time career after the war. Marines trained for war or trained others for war for as long as they were Marines.

THIS PAGE AND FOLLOWING PAGE: Following graduation from boot camp, new Marines were selected to attend the numerous special schools required to support a modern military force. There is no empirical evidence to suggest that the skills and talents of any given Marine were matched to the job to which he was assigned, and by the time a Marine had completed boot training his attitude was such that no job beat trigger-pulling. *Official USMC Photos*

The majority of Marines went from boot camp to infantry units. Here, under the guidance of officers and noncommissioned officers, California-based Marines enhance their rifle training with additional marksmanship training, with M1 rifles. *Official USMC Photo*

As well as rifle training, Marine infantrymen never stopped training in basic combat skills or undergoing physical conditioning. This California-based Marine infantry platoon is probably part of a new infantry unit that was stood up at Camp Pendleton. Note the mix of weapons—mostly M1 rifles, but the front center Marine is armed with a Browning Automatic Rifle (BAR), there is a Thompson submachine gun right behind him, and another Tommy gun in the hands of the Marine to his left. *Official USMC Photo*

A Marine BAR-man fires his weapon. It's rather odd that this Marine, who is wearing all of his field gear, has on a green woolen service uniform rather than the herringbone utilities normally worn in the field. *Official USMC Photo*

This is serious hand-to-hand combat training. The Marine at left has an unsheathed K-bar knife in his right hand. *Official USMC Photo*

The 3d Marine Division trained rigorously on Guadalcanal in the mid-1943 run-up to the Bougainville invasion. Here, a member of the division keeps his head down in a deep, commodious foxhole.
Official USMC Photo

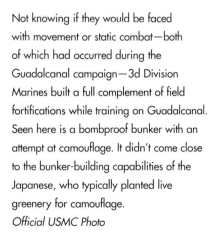

Not knowing if they would be faced with movement or static combat—both of which had occurred during the Guadalcanal campaign—3d Division Marines built a full complement of field fortifications while training on Guadalcanal. Seen here is a bombproof bunker with an attempt at camouflage. It didn't come close to the bunker-building capabilities of the Japanese, who typically planted live greenery for camouflage.
Official USMC Photo

These 3d Division Marines, probably combat engineers, advance during field training on Guadalcanal. Seen here are two flamethrower teams, whose first use by Marines in combat was on Bougainville. *Official USMC Photo*

Training never ceased. Either veterans trained to keep their skill level high, or replacements were taken in hand by troop leaders who had weathered combat and knew well the advantages of well-honed combat skills. This July 1944 photo was taken of 1st Marine Division troops between the New Britain and Peleliu battles. The fact that only carbines are shown suggests that this is a combat-support unit, not infantry.
Official USMC Photo

CHAPTER 6

THE CENTRAL SOLOMONS

NOVEMBER 1942–NOVEMBER 1943

T HE SOLOMONS AIR CAMPAIGN—AS DISTINCT FROM THE GUADALCANAL AIR campaign—began on November 23, 1942, after the close of the decisive Naval Battle of Guadalcanal of November 13–15. The opening round was an attack by six Marine SBD dive-bombers against Japanese base facilities newly discovered at Munda on the island of New Georgia.

Although nobody had actually thought it through as such, the early Pacific War immediately shaped up as a jockeying for air bases. Pete Ellis, early in the twentieth century, had foreseen the strike-and-counterstrike tempo of the war, but he and everyone who followed had been thinking of mutually supporting naval bases within the range of warships. What actually happened, beginning in earnest in December 1941, was a jockeying for mutually supporting *air* bases within the *operational* range of fighters. (Operational range is something less than half the actual range—to allow for getting to the target, completing a mission, and getting home. The focus on fighters lay in the emerging truth that bomber formations were not all that good at defending themselves en route to or over a target.)

When, in the years leading up to the Pacific War, the United States and Japan thought about filling in their respective lines of communication across the Pacific, they looked for naval bases. But when it came to actually filling in the line, they looked for naval bases within the operational range of fighters, then simply for air bases that could be supported from other air bases. The foundation for the Guadalcanal campaign was the acquisition of the Japanese bomber base at Lunga, and every step that was contemplated and taken by either side through the end of 1943 was to support or expand a line of air bases in the Solomons.

The Japanese made the first moves after the Guadalcanal air base was seized in August 1942. First they planted an auxiliary field on Buka, just north of the large island of

In a scene emblematic of the Solomons air offensive of November 1942 to November 1943, Marine SBDs fly northward to deliver bombs against Japanese air bases, naval bases, or ships. *Official USMC Photo*

Bougainville. This was expanded as the Guadalcanal air battles wore on; then a rush to build new bases took place. The problem the new bases took care of was the range—600 miles—between the Japanese airfield complex at Rabaul and Henderson Field. Japanese Zero fighters could reach Lunga from Rabaul, but there was little margin for loitering or fighting over the target, and damaged or malfunctioning fighters had no safety margin. Buka alleviated some of the stress, but new bases were needed for bigger and better air operations. Although the Japanese plan was to step south from Buka to southern Bougainville and the Shortland Islands, and then on down the central Solomons, they first took one giant step to Munda and built a bomber base in secret. But for chance discovery by an alert pilot who saw "something" through elaborate camouflage, Munda might have gone into offensive operations before Americans knew it was there.

In late 1942, Americans knew little about the art of supporting ground troops from the air. Thus, as the Japanese scaled back from operations over Guadalcanal beginning in November 1942, the multiservice air task force known as Aircraft, South Pacific

Marines of the 3d Raider Battalion steal ashore from rubber boats in the Russell Islands, February 21, 1943. The Japanese had no troops in the Russells, so the landing was bloodless.
Official USMC Photo

(AirSoPac), had little work on its plate. When photographic analysts literally put Munda Field on the map, underutilized aviation units at Henderson Field and its two satellite fighter strips put in a bid for the contract on Munda. The longer-ranged B-17s that worked out of Henderson also resumed their efforts against the Japanese intermediate base at Kahili on Bougainville, and on November 28 they attacked a Munda-bound convoy off western New Georgia. By then, AirSoPac wasn't just replacing worn units at Guadalcanal, it also was being built up to something quite large and powerful.

While AirSoPac reached north to hit Japanese air bases, it remained the first line of defense for the expanding American holdings on Guadalcanal. The Japanese had not yet thrown in the towel, a fact that was demonstrated on December 7, 1942, with the discovery of an oncoming troop-laden destroyer-transport convoy. Thirteen Marine SBDs attacked the eleven-ship convoy at 1635 hours, scoring three ships damaged for one SBD and its crew lost.

On December 9, B-17s attacked Munda Field, and on December 10 the heavy bombers attacked a harbor in the Shortland Islands. And so forth. These modest showers of bombs morphed into a mighty torrent, but very slowly. By the time the Guadalcanal campaign was concluded in February 1943, the eyes of the regional commanders were fixed on the problem of interdicting the string of Japanese air bases that ran through the Solomons—and to rolling it up or at least putting in a competing line of bases.

THE AIR WAR WAS THE ONLY WAR IN THE SOLOMONS AFTER FEBRUARY. MARINE AIR, acting within the multiservice and U.S.-New Zealand AirSoPac command, played a key role and carried a substantial burden. Marine F4F fighters were not as long-legged as the

Although Guadalcanal was no longer the scene of a land operation after February 9, 1943, the Henderson Field complex continued to be harassed incessantly by Japanese bombers, especially at night. Overhead cover was never far from living quarters and work areas around the airfields. This photograph was taken in March 1943. *Official USMC Photo*

newly operational Army Air Forces P-38s, but there weren't many P-38s in the theater, so F4Fs dominated, especially in defensive work over Guadalcanal. The Japanese mainly harassed the American bases there with pinprick strikes, mostly at night.

VMF-124, the first Marine unit equipped with the new Vought F4U Corsair fighter, reached Espiritu Santo on February 11, 1943. Twelve VMF-124 pilots and Corsairs reached Guadalcanal the next day, and all twelve made their combat debut—and the Corsair's combat debut—on a bomber-escort mission to Kahili on February 14. The Japanese opposed the attack in force—the first time they appeared in large numbers over Kahili—and two of the VMF-124 novices were lost with their airplanes against the first three Zeros ever shot down by Corsair pilots. In a day of firsts, the February 14 Kahili mission was the longest undertaken to date by any Marine fighters, and it put the Japanese on notice that the air war in the Solomons had entered a new phase.

The first new step up the Solomons chain was taken on February 21, when the 3d Marine Raider Battalion and U.S. Army troops bloodlessly seized the Russell Islands, 45 miles northwest of Guadalcanal. The plan was to turn one of the principal islands into an advance air base, but the vaunted American ability to develop new airfields in very little time had not yet matured, and work proceeded at an agonizing pace. Nevertheless, as February progressed, the newly invigorated and enlarged AirSoPac combat commands ranged farther and wider along the Solomons chain to interdict the newly invigorated

From February through early June 1943, the best defense against attacks on Henderson Field remained trusty Marine F4F Wildcat fighters such as this one, which is scrambling from Fighter-1 in response to a warning that enemy aircraft are on the way. *Official USMC Photo*

Japanese effort to fortify the central and northern Solomons against the assumed Allied offensive from Guadalcanal toward Rabaul.

Also on February 21, AirSoPac stood up the subordinate Aircraft, Solomons (AirSols) command to oversee front-line operations in the battle zone. Like its parent, AirSols was a multiservice and international organization commanded and staffed by officers from all the component services, including the Royal New Zealand Air Force. Marine bombing squadrons equipped with Grumman TBF Avenger light bombers and Douglas SBD Dauntless dive-bombers were the backbone of the AirSols Strike Command, more numerous than an aggregate of all other bombers, and Marine fighters prevailed in the AirSols Fighter Command.

The build-up and intensification of the Solomons air effort burgeoned. On March 12, in the New Hebrides, VMF-213 became the first F4F unit in the war zone to transition to F4Us. On March 20 an advance ground detachment from Hawaii-based MAG-21 disembarked in the Russells to prepare to support the group's three fighter squadrons at Advance Base Knucklehead, as the new air base on Banika Island was known.

On the night of March 19–20, in the first operation of its kind, forty-two Marine and Navy TBFs each laid a 1,600-pound antishipping mine in the Buin–Tonolei area of southern Bougainville. The mines were dropped by parachute from altitudes of 800 to 1,300 feet. This feat was repeated the next night by forty Navy and Marine TBFs.

Farther afield but technically within the South Pacific Area, in anticipation of an eventual offensive in the central Pacific, six VMF-441 F4Fs were advanced on March 22 from Samoa to a new base at Funafuti in the Ellice Islands. Eventually, heavy bombers

VMF-221's First Lieutenant James Elms Swett was awarded a Medal of Honor for downing 7 Imperial Navy dive-bombers off Guadalcanal on April 7, 1943, even though his F4F had been damaged by friendly antiaircraft fire. Ordered back to the United States to receive his award, Swett refused on grounds that he had just arrived in the Pacific and wanted to put his training to work. He received the award at a special parade on Henderson Field and went on to down 3 G4M bombers, 2 1/2 Zeros, and 2 more D3A dive-bombers in the tour. In 1945, he flew Corsairs off a carrier near Okinawa and downed another dive-bomber, for a total of 15 1/2 confirmed kills and 4 probable kills. *Official USMC Photo*

operating from Funafuti would be able to reach the Japanese-held Gilbert Islands, 700 miles away. At 1115 on only March 25, a VMF-441 F4F pilot shot down a Japanese reconnaissance bomber over the new base. All of VMF-441 displaced to Funafuti on March 31, as did part of an Army Air Forces heavy bomber group.

On March 28, in the United States, the U.S. Joint Chiefs of Staff formalized thinking about an advance on Rabaul when it issued a directive aimed at coordinating efforts between the Navy-dominated South Pacific Command and the Army-dominated Southwest Pacific Command.

THE JAPANESE SAT ON THEIR HANDS FOR SEVERAL MONTHS AS THE RANGE AND BREADTH of AirSoPac and AirSols operations grew, but they struck back on April 1. Fifty-six A6M Zero fighters organized in two waves swept over the Russells, where they were engaged by twenty-eight Navy and Marine F4Fs, eight Marine F4Us, and six Army P-38s, most of them scrambled from Guadalcanal in response to radar sightings. Between 1100 and 1132 hours, VMF-124 F4U pilots and VMF-221 F4F pilots shot down ten Zeros and a D3A dive-bomber, and Navy F4F pilots downed eight Zeros. Losses were five Marine fighters and one Navy fighter downed, and three pilots killed.

Another massive attack—67 D3As and 116 Zeros—went in against Allied shipping off Guadalcanal at 1400 hours on April 7. Thirty-six Navy and Marine F4Fs, 9 Marine F4Us, and 30 assorted Army fighters got into the air, but the Japanese managed to sink an oiler, a U.S. Navy destroyer, and a New Zealand corvette before F4F and F4U pilots from VMF-213, VMF-214, and VMF-221 downed 12 D3As and 15 Zeros.

VMF-221's First Lieutenant James Swett, whose F4F was damaged early on by friendly antiaircraft fire, single-handedly downed seven of the D3As before crash-landing in the water. This was the single most successful combat flight of any Marine pilot, ever. Swett was awarded a Medal of Honor for this stunning achievement.

The Bent-Wing Bird. Marines started flying the powerful, modern Vought F4U Corsair in combat as early as February 1943, but it took until June before all Marine front-line squadrons were equipped with Corsairs. This photograph shows an F4U as it buzzes Henderson Field in June 1943. *Official USMC Photo*

On April 18, Army Air Forces P-38 pilots, acting on intelligence tips, shot down a pair of G4M land attack bombers over southern Bougainville. Killed at the controls of one of the bombers was Admiral Isoroku Yamamoto, commander in chief of the Imperial Navy's Combined Fleet. Little known outside a small circle of planners is that the chief architect of the Yamamoto mission was Major John Condon, a Marine aviator.

On April 21, the Marine Corps stood up Marine Air, South Pacific (MASP) to oversee and facilitate logistical and personnel operations for the 1st and 2d Marine Aircraft wings in the South Pacific Area. Fresh Marine air units of all types that continued to arrive in the war zone kept the contribution of Marine Air to the AirSols effort higher than the aggregate of all the other component services. For all this, however, the war, including the air war, had entered a period of relative inactivity. Blows were swapped, but even the far stronger AirSols effort was limited to pinprick attacks on a broad range of targets—not enough to disable any given Japanese base for any length of time. Although planning was under way for an assault on New Georgia aimed at capturing Munda Field, even Munda—the closest Japanese base to AirSols bases—was barely touched until well into June.

Marines of the 4th Raider Battalion navigate a trackless rainforest on their way to Viru from Segi. The 4th Raiders actually invaded New Georgia eight days before the main invasion was set to begin. The very long shoulder weapons carried by two of the Raiders are British-made Boys antitank rifles purchased by the Marine Corps before the war.
Official USMC Photo

The 4th Raiders honor their fallen comrades following the successful attack on the Imperial Army patrol base at Viru. Note the mix of solid-green herringbone utility uniforms and the new camouflage utilities. *Official USMC Photo*

It is the Japanese who struck the boldest blow of the period—on June 7, after they received news that an invasion force was assembling at Guadalcanal. Ten Nakajima B5N torpedo bombers escorted by 102 Zeros struck at shore facilities and shipping at about 1115 hours, and in a forty-five-minute melee, 20 Zeros were shot down, of which 8 fell to Marine F4U pilots. Four F4Us also were shot down. A follow-on strike by 50 Zeros on June 12 was met at 1030 hours over the Russell Islands, and Marine F4U pilots scored 6 of the 28 Zeros credited to Allied fighter pilots.

In the early afternoon of June 16, 24 D3As and 70 A6Ms attacked the Guadalcanal anchorages again. By the time the Japanese reached the target area, 104 Allied fighters were up, and ships speeding around the anchorage had launched a veritable curtain of antiaircraft fire. At a cost of 6 AirSols fighters and 5 pilots, the Japanese force was virtually annihilated. This was the last daylight attack the Japanese ever launched against Guadalcanal.

MARINE CORPS INVOLVEMENT ON THE GROUND DURING THE CAMPAIGN TO SEIZE MUNDA Field occurred in four acts. In Act One, about half of the 4th Raider Battalion was landed from destroyer-transports in the dead of night on June 21, 1943, to secure a possible airfield site at Segi. The Segi airfield plan had been ongoing, but the Raiders were precipitously thrown in because a large Japanese infantry force at nearby Viru Harbor seemed about to attack the Allied coastwatcher base at Segi.

Segi was secured and bolstered without incident; then the Raiders split into two forces for the attack on Viru. It was very hard going in the rainforest following a ride in war canoes to an intermediate location, and there was action along the way. With an assist from Marine SBDs, Viru was taken on July 1 in a coordinated assault, and the recently formidable Japanese garrison fled.

The second half of the 4th Raiders was sent on June 30, also on virtually no notice, to bolster an Army infantry battalion that was to land at Vangunu, where a small outlying force of Japanese was in a position to report on shipping that plied between the Russell Islands and the primary Allied invasion site, on Rendova Island. The night landing went off without serious mishap, the assault force regrouped, and the attack was driven against the Japanese early on July 30.

American casualties in both operations were light, all objectives were secured, and the 4th Raider Battalion was withdrawn to Guadalcanal.

In Act Two, the 9th Marine Defense Battalion went ashore on Rendova close behind the June 30 invasion and set up 90mm, 40mm, 20mm, and .50-caliber antiaircraft guns to defend the vast dumps on the island that were to support the Army's drive on Munda Field. The battalion also landed its eight modern 155mm field guns—now the standard Marine Corps coast-defense weapon. The 155s were sited both for antiboat defense and to support ground troops on the way to Munda. Deep, viscous mud made setting up a horrible, exhausting experience for the Marines, and then the battalion's tracked artillery prime movers were called on to help move Army field artillery units into place.

Marine air operations in support of the New Georgia invasion force were intense on June 30, and Marine F4U pilots helped beat back a strike by Imperial Navy Zeros and G4M land-based bombers. On July 1, Marine light bombers attacked Viru as well as the nearest Japanese air base, Vila, on Kolombangara. On July 2, after the Allied fighter

A Marine TBF bores through the Solomons sky on July 10, 1943, to deliver supplies via parachute pack to Marine Raiders at Enogai. Marine TBFs typically served as light bombers with a capacity of two 1,000-pound bombs or four 500-pound bombs carried in an internal bomb bay. *Official USMC Photo*

umbrella had been withdrawn from over Rendova due to bad weather, the Japanese went after the dumps with an estimated eighteen G4Ms, escorted by twenty Zeros. Many of the bombs landed short, directly on the 9th Defense Battalion or on a dynamite cache behind a Marine 155mm gun battery. In all, fifty-nine Americans were killed on the ground, many of them Marines. (Later in the New Georgia campaign, 9th Defense Battalion Marines, mostly machine gunners eye-to-eye with the enemy, helped beat off a Japanese ground assault that carried well into the rear of Army ground units.)

IN ACT THREE ON THE GROUND, THE HEADQUARTERS OF THE 1ST RAIDER REGIMENT AND the 1st and 4th Raider battalions were to have landed in northern New Georgia on July 5 to attack a strong Japanese force at Bairoko Harbor, north of Munda. It was felt—and this turned out to be the case—that Bairoko would provide the Munda defenders with a back door for movement of supplies and reinforcements from bases farther to the north. When the 4th Raiders was grabbed up to secure Segi, Viru, and Vangunu, two green Army infantry battalions were precipitously placed under the 1st Raider Regiment command.

The American Northern Landing Force, as it was dubbed, landed at Rice Anchorage on July 5 without incident, and the Raiders secured the Japanese patrol base at Triri on June 7 at a cost of four killed. The much larger village of Enogai—a good base site and jumping-off point just two miles from Bairoko—was to have been attacked on July 8, but a company of Imperial

One of eight 9th Defense Battalion 155mm seacoast guns deployed to guard the many dumps on Rendova Island that served Army units on New Georgia. The Marine 155s fired almost every day in support of the advance on Munda. To set in and bear on targets on New Georgia, the 155 crews in Battery A alone had to cut down more than six hundred palm trees. *Official USMC Photo*

Navy bluejackets charged with retaking Triri plowed into the 1st Raider Battalion, which was strung out on several trails. The Raider regiment headquarters and two Army companies counterattacked, killed fifty Japanese, and drove the rest off. Nevertheless, a larger Japanese force attacked an Army blocking force, and the Raiders had to drive it away.

Enogai was finally taken on July 10 by direct assault following a two-day battle. This gave the Raiders a base from which Bairoko could be attacked, but the two Army battalions failed to block vital trails, and the attack on Bairoko remained stalled for a week. Finally, on July 18, the 4th Raider Battalion landed at Enogai to help matters along.

All the Raiders and one Army battalion assaulted Bairoko on July 20 after an air attack failed to materialize. The intricate plan quickly devolved into a frontal assault that the Japanese first stalled and finally held completely at bay. The Americans traded numerous casualties for very little progress, and the Japanese even mounted a counterattack that was barely beaten back. The two sides fought almost to a standstill during the long afternoon, but the Japanese had ample artillery support, while the Americans could call fire from just one U.S. Navy destroyer. Twenty-two Army Air Forces B-25s, 170 sorties by AirSols light bombers—mainly Marine TBFs and SBDs—and fifty AirSols fighters dumped 132 tons of bombs on Bairoko, but the effort had little effect on the front-line fighting. Finally, the American commanders decided to withdraw. The Japanese were too exhausted to follow the retreat to Enogai, but the battle for Bairoko was nonetheless the soundest defeat administered to U.S. Marines during the Pacific offensive.

Marine Air was of some assistance to the Northern Landing Group. Bairoko was bombed on July 9 by eighteen Marine SBDs, and on July 10 Marine TBFs dropped supply

Marines of the 1st Raider Battalion and 1st Raider Regiment headquarters fought their way into Enogai on July 10, 1943, but they bogged down there for ten days. Shown here are Raiders manning a captured Japanese ship's glass to monitor activities at Bairoko, a mere 2 miles away. *Official USMC Photo*

Marine Raiders load wounded comrades aboard one of several Navy PBY patrol bombers that landed just off Enogai with supplies. Enogai was open to the sea, but it was too close to coastal batteries at Bairoko to be serviced by ships. *Official USMC Photo*

Marine M3 light tanks from the 10th and 11th Defense battalions proved to be invaluable in the jungle flats leading to Munda. Here, a platoon of Marine tanks assists an Army infantry company on a narrow forest track.
Official Signal Corps Photo

bundles to the American troops at Enogai. On July 15, thirty-six Marine SBDs attacked Bairoko again; and on July 19, eight Army Air Forces B-25 medium bombers, nineteen Marine TBFs, and eighteen Marine SBDs did the same. The activity over Bairoko on July 21 did little good, but thirty-seven Marine TBFs and thirty-six AirSols SBDs accompanied by forty Army Air Forces fighters visited the Japanese base again on July 24. (Bairoko fell only after its defenders withdrew in the wake of the fall of Munda Field in August 1943.)

IN ACT FOUR ON THE GROUND ON NEW GEORGIA, MARINE M3 LIGHT TANK CREWS FROM the 10th and 11th Defense battalions provided yeoman service to U.S. Army infantry units bogged down along miles of narrow, twisting trails on the way to Munda. A whole new book on tank-infantry cooperation was written on New Georgia as Marine tankers and Army infantrymen alike learned how the two must remain in extremely close contact while advancing against enemy forces in close-in terrain. Often the tanks were employed as mobile pillboxes whose 37mm guns could be brought to bear effectively against the coral-and-log or earth-and-log pillboxes the Japanese set up on and between the hills the Americans tended to climb for better vistas and defenses than they could find in the forested lowland. Once committed on July 16, Marine light tanks were at the front until the capture of Munda Field on August 5.

NO MARINE INFANTRY DIVISIONS, OR EVEN STANDARD INFANTRY REGIMENTS, WERE available in mid-1943; they were either recuperating and reequipping after Guadalcanal or, in the case of the 3d Marine Division, not yet ready for first combat. The disparate assortment of Marines who fit into the otherwise all-Army New Georgia show acquitted themselves well and, indeed, took part in operations that had a great positive effect on the outcome.

Likewise, Marine Air functioned well throughout the campaign as AirSols' largest component. It was underutilized in support of the ground battle, but that was because air support had never really been integrated into ground operations—and would not be for more than another year. A mission on July 13 was of particular note as the first mission of its kind in the Pacific Theater: Twelve Marine SBDs bombed Japanese ground positions within a thousand yards of U.S. Army units advancing on Munda. Missions to New Georgia through August 5 included participation in softening the defenses close around Munda Field in anticipation of the final ground drive on the strategic objective.

THE AIR CAMPAIGN AGAINST TARGETS NORTH OF MUNDA HEATED UP IN MID-JULY, WITH numerous attacks on an array of air, naval, and supply facilities, mainly in southern Bougainville and the Shortland Islands. The Japanese were able to mount several significant air attacks of their own, but only an attack against Rendova at 1700 hours on July 21 by sixty Imperial Navy fighters and bombers actually breached the AirSols fighter umbrella.

The first American aircraft to be based on the rehabilitated Munda Field were Corsairs from MAG-14's VMF-123 and VMF-124. The first MAG-14 fighter to land on Munda Field was this one, on August 14, 1943. *Official USMC Photo*

Japanese ships were also prominent targets during the period, and several were sunk outright by aerial bombs.

Munda Field was declared operational for emergency use on August 5, only two days after its capture, and engineers swarmed over the base to bring it on line for use in the ongoing offensive. On the night of August 12–13, Army troops seized a toehold at Barakoma, a prospective airfield site on Vella Lavella Island. On August 13, four Army Air Forces P-40s used Munda Field as a fuel stop on their way to targets farther north. On August 4, Aircraft, New Georgia, was stood up at Munda under Marine command, and several Marine F4U squadrons and the MAG-14 headquarters were ordered to base there. On August 15, Barakoma was reinforced, and engineers soon began laying out the new airfield. Barakoma became the V-ring for a series of intense, prolonged air attacks—some of which were effective—but a spirited AirSols fighter defense aided by the guns of the 4th Marine Defense Battalion scored many victories over the attackers and ultimately prevailed.

And so it went; almost daily the power of AirSols increased in small ways—more aircraft employed in attacks, and more range acquired by way of new facilities. Japanese bases formerly beyond the range of Allied fighters and single-engine bombers slowly came under attacks that would eventually overwhelm the Japanese fighter defenses. As it was, the toll exacted from the Imperial Navy fighter force by aggressive, far-ranging AirSols fighters was nearly unsustainable, and often no Japanese fighters challenged AirSols bombing attacks and fighter sweeps.

Looking ahead at a new strategic target, AirSoPac on September 1 stood up Aircraft, Northern Solomons (AirNorSols), under Marine command; it was to plan the air campaign that would support the upcoming invasion of Bougainville. Indeed, the air campaign had begun, if not in name, with increasing weight given to neutralizing Japanese air bases along the shipping route to central Bougainville. Among the targets were Kahili and nearby Ballale to the south of the projected invasion site, Kieta to the east, and Buka and Bonis to the north. Also, farther out, the Army Air Forces New Guinea–based Fifth Air Force intensified its long-range bombing campaign against the huge Japanese air-base complex and anchorage around Rabaul. Closer in, Vila Field on Kolombangara Island was slated for liberation, and its defenses were worn down by steady aerial bombardment. Marine Air carried a significant burden in all these operations.

On September 10, Marine Night Fighter Squadron 541—VMF(N)-531—displaced to Advance Base Knucklehead to begin operations over the central and northern Solomons. The experimental unit was equipped with Lockheed twin-engine PV-1 Ventura light bombers that had been reequipped as radar-carrying night fighters. It would be November before a VMF(N)-531 crew scored the Marine Corps' first night kill.

Barakoma Field was declared operational on September 24 and used in an emergency landing that very day. And during the night of October 2–3, the last Japanese troops on Kolombangara were secretly evacuated, thus clearing the way for the bloodless occupation of Vila Airdrome on October 6. Thereafter, the intense campaign to neutralize the Japanese bases on and around Bougainville became even more intense, with daily attacks that exhausted the Imperial Navy's ability to mount a coherent defense, much less interdict the invasion of Bougainville at Cape Torokina, set to commence on November 1. AirSols—and particularly Marine Air in the Solomons—had gained air superiority and was on its way to gaining air supremacy in advance of the invasion. By November 1, Japanese air bases ringing the Bougainville invasion objective would be unserviceable.

THE LAST UNDERTAKING BY A MARINE GROUND FORCE IN ADVANCE OF THE BOUGAINVILLE invasion was a raid by the 2d Marine Parachute Battalion against Japanese bases on Choiseul Island between October 28 and November 3, 1943. Until the Bougainville invasion actually commenced on November 1, several sites on Choiseul seemed to the Japanese to be potential Allied objectives. Mounted solely to draw Japanese attention away from Bougainville, the Choiseul raid sought merely to create excitement; destroy some stores and facilities; and, if things went especially well, draw in reinforcements that would thus be unavailable for Bougainville. The parachutists succeeded in all these things at relatively light cost, but they barely escaped from the island when perhaps too many Japanese responded to several hit-and-run attacks.

The Choiseul raid was the last bit of stage dressing in advance of the Allied leap to Bougainville. Attacking central Bougainville was a bold strategic move, the first phase of the new Allied bypass strategy, and it would bring Rabaul within range of AirSols land-based fighters as soon as new airfields could be installed.

In a scene entirely typical of the Solomons air campaign, Marine SBDs fly over picturesque islands on their way to help destroy Japanese bases. This photograph, taken on August 22, 1943, is of SBDs on their way to attack Japanese barges and barge facilities on the Vella Lavella coast. *Official USMC Photo*

CHAPTER 7

BOUGAINVILLE

NOVEMBER 1, 1943–JANUARY 16, 1944

THE BOUGAINVILLE INVASION, PLANNED AND OVERSEEN BY THE I MARINE Amphibious Corps (IMAC) headquarters, opened on November 1, 1943, when two regimental landing teams of the 3d Marine Division and two attached Raider battalions landed on and to the west of Cape Torokina, in central Bougainville's Empress Augusta Bay. The 9th Marine Regiment (9th Marines), on the division left, landed in rough surf but against zero opposition. On the right, the 3d Marines and the 2d Raider Battalion landed in smoother waters but faced serious opposition in the form of several defensive sectors that consisted of highly motivated troops manning well-camouflaged bunkers, pillboxes, and antiboat guns.

The invasion plan, which depended too heavily on deception as to the landing site, was inadequately supported by advance ground reconnaissance, and it set aside too many combat troops for use as shore party—the wrong lesson from the calamitous shore party plan at Guadalcanal in August 1942. High tide, narrow beaches, and pounding surf played havoc with the boat formations and, indeed, wrecked sixty-four landing craft in two days. Eight of twelve transports and cargo ships were emptied on D-day alone, but fouled beaches and unmapped swamps and other unreconnoitered obstructions just behind the beaches prevented an orderly build-up of materiel. The bulk of what was landed went ashore in the wrong places and was moved to clear the beaches rather than to ensure accessibility. Moreover, the large number of artillery troops sucked into shore party details actually prevented some needed fire missions.

Training won the right flank of the beachhead. Although infantry units were badly jumbled when landing craft were sent off course by antiboat fire and surf conditions, junior

On November 1, 1943, the 3d Marine Division's 3d Marine Regiment (3d Marines) landed on good beaches under heavy fire. Here, landing dryshod, a boatload of Marines rushes inland to overwhelm Imperial Army positions overlooking other parts of the regimental sector. *Official USMC Photo*

On the division's left, the 9th Marines landed in extremely bad surf conditions on beaches fronted by obstructions that caused many Marines to unload in deep water. Fortunately, no Japanese guarded these beaches. *Official USMC Photo*

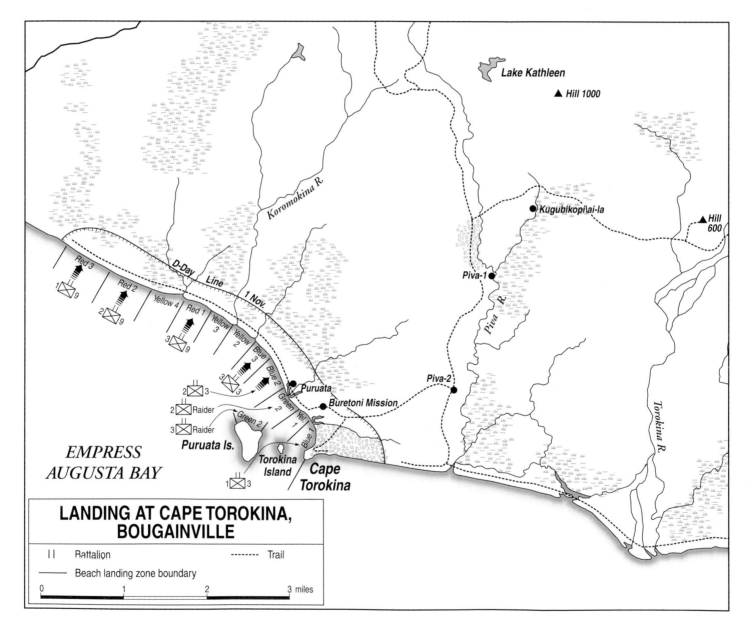

LANDING AT CAPE TOROKINA, BOUGAINVILLE

I I Battalion	- - - - - Trail
——— Beach landing zone boundary	

0   1   2   3 miles

troop leaders pulled together ad hoc assault squads and platoons that fought bitterly to overcome defenses gallantly held by a reinforced Imperial Army infantry company. Similarly, the 3d Raider Battalion, on Puruata Island, faced determined foes who had to be dug out of the dense growth, one position at a time.

D-day air raids against the landing force were held at bay by AirSols fighters that patrolled overhead in dawn-to-dusk relays, and a night attack by a Japanese naval surface force was driven back by Allied cruisers and destroyers. This part of the plan—drawn from experience at Guadalcanal—was nearly flawless.

As Marine infantry deepened the beachhead perimeter over the following week, conditions on the beaches were slowly unsnarled and construction work began on needed amenities. Only two miserable, waterlogged trails leading inland were initially open within the beachhead, and numerous swamps just behind the shoreline broke up the cohesion of the landing force.

Marines from the 2d Raider Battalion hunker down just off the beach in the 3d Marines sector. These troops will shortly advance to help clear stubborn Japanese defenders. *Official USMC Photo*

Although planning had been painstaking, right down to marking landing areas by cargo type (the near banner marks a zone for rations), the rough tide and lack of beach exits resulted in near chaos. Ships were emptied quickly, but supplies were landed wherever they could be dropped, and movement inland was slow because many pre-selected dump sites turned out to be on swampy ground. *Official USMC Photo*

The only reliable means for moving goods, heavy weapons, and troops along submerged roadways and trails was amtracs. Only twenty-nine were allotted to the 3d Amphibian Tractor Battalion, but more were shipped to Bougainville posthaste. The highest count during the entire Bougainville campaign was sixty-four, and that was just for one day. Wear and tear caused many amtracs to be cannibalized to keep others going. *Official USMC Photo*

Marine war dogs were first used by Raiders on the trails leading out from the Cape Torokina perimeter. One of the two dogs seen here on November 3 has alerted its handlers that something or someone is farther down the trail, and Raiders have been dispatched to investigate. Marine war dogs were Dobermans and German shepherds. *Official USMC Photo*

Inasmuch as the beaches in the 9th Marines' sector were subjected to the worst surf conditions, the regiment was drawn to the right, toward Cape Torokina, to make for a more efficient defense and a safer expansion inland. Within a few days, one battalion of the 3d Marines was withdrawn from the line to serve as a reserve force. Likewise, the 2d and 3d Raider battalions were pulled off the line to serve as a reserve force under the command of the 2d Raider Regiment headquarters. Two 75mm pack howitzer battalions of the 12th Marines also were concentrated in the beachhead rear, and the 3d Defense Battalion was landed to provide antiaircraft and seacoast defense.

As soon as they landed, the 3d Engineer Battalion and two Seabee battalions were put to work developing a lateral road, building causeways from the narrow beaches to deeper water, waterproofing the inland trails, and extending dry ground via swamp drainage. Despite feverish road-building activity, only the fully tracked amtracs could reliably carry supplies and move artillery pieces inland. Shortly, every available amtrac in the theater was sent forward to Empress Augusta Bay. And, as soon as possible, construction of a fighter strip commenced right on Cape Torokina.

Final resistance adjacent to and within the perimeter was overcome on November 3, but due to the horrendous terrain handicaps, it was November 6 before the 3d Marine Division rear echelon, including two battalions of the 21st Marine Regiment, could be accommodated inside the beachhead.

A force of Imperial Army troops blundered ashore on the night of November 7, 1943, within sight of 3/9, which anchored the Cape Torokina line at the Korokomina River. Here, Marines from 3/9 hunker down at the edge of the forest, defending their line toe-to-toe against the Japanese. *Official USMC Photo*

Marines tread carefully across marshy ground as they advance to extend the Cape Torokina perimeter. There was so much swampy ground in the area behind the beaches that Marines took to calling the areas between the swamps "dry swamp"—because it often disappeared underwater when it rained or the tide came in. *Official USMC Photo*

When advancing Marine battalions hit high ridges with dry ground, it was often difficult for engineers to push roads all the way to the front. Marines of every calling were pressed into humping food and ammunition to the advancing troops. *Official USMC Photo*

A MIXED BATTALION OF IMPERIAL ARMY TROOPS WAS DISPATCHED FROM RABAUL ON THE night of November 6–7 to mount a counterlanding northwest of the Bougainville perimeter. Through ill calculation and ill luck, not to mention the severe tidal conditions that had plagued the 9th Marines, a number of the Japanese landing barges were tossed up on the beach within eyeball range of Marines of 3/9 who held the perimeter line along the Korokomina River. Following a brief period of uncertainty with respect to whose landing craft they could see, the Marines fired artillery, antitank guns, and even 90mm antiaircraft guns at the barges and the nearest landing site.

The Japanese force was scattered over several miles of beachfront, but those nearest to 3/9—those under fire—had no choice but to retreat or attack on a moment's notice. Fewer than a hundred attacked, thus precipitating a three-day battle royal that involved three Marine infantry battalions, artillery, and air. The Japanese force, estimated to be 850 strong, was annihilated.

ON THE NIGHT OF NOVEMBER 5–6, MARINES OF THE 2D RAIDER BATTALION HOLDING A blocking position on the Mission Trail, several miles inland from Cape Torokina, were probed by a Japanese advance guard that arrived on the scene from eastern Bougainville. The Raiders had been probing forward for several days, intent on blunting an expected counteroffensive from the other side of the island. Their objective was a junction of three trails: the Piva and Mission trails, originating near Cape Torokina; and the Numa Numa Trail, which ran inland.

Two initial probing attacks were beaten back with ease, the 3d Raider Battalion moved up to support the trail block, and it remained quiet until the early afternoon of November 7. The Japanese attacked into the night, until beaten back. The next morning, the 3d Raiders moved into the trail block itself in time to help defeat an even larger Japanese assault. The Marines held the only dry ground in the area, and the only way for the Japanese to reach it was directly down the narrow trail. They kept attacking into the teeth of the Marine defenses, and they kept losing. Raiders attempted a counterattack toward the trail junction, but the same swampy ground that had channelized the Japanese stalled the Raiders.

On the morning of November 9, with ample artillery support and the addition of light tanks and 75mm halftracks, the Raiders attacked directly up the trail—right into a Japanese blocking position whose flanks rested on swampy ground. The fight was toe-to-toe and quite brutal. A Japanese counterattack was forestalled, and then the Raiders began to slowly advance. The Japanese crumbled at 1230 hours, and the Raiders reached the junction of the

Being wounded at the front began a harrowing chancy process of evacuation. First, front-line wounded had to be extricated, often under enemy fire, by corpsmen and fellow Marines. *Official USMC Photo*

After clearing the front, the wounded Marine often had to be carried back to the nearest serviceable road, which might be miles away across high ridges and intervening swampy ground. At minimum, it took eight to twelve able-bodied men, working in backbreaking shifts, to move just one litter case to the rear. Trails often were marked by little more than communications wire strung to the front line. *Official USMC Photo*

Taking a lesson from the oft-bombarded Lunga Perimeter at Guadalcanal, the 3d Medical Battalion dug deep at Cape Torokina. The atmosphere in this hospital ward is palpably claustrophobic, but it was safe and only temporary, for the next step was quick evacuation to Guadalcanal for additional surgery and the beginning of recuperation. *Official USMC Photo*

Piva and Numa Numa trails by 1500. There they dug in. The next day, following air and artillery preparation, two battalions of the 9th Marines attacked through the Raider position and advanced unopposed through Piva Village and out along the Numa Numa Trail toward the Piva River.

THE BUILD-UP OF THE CAPE TOROKINA PERIMETER CONTINUED ON NOVEMBER 8, WHEN the advance guard of a Munda-blooded U.S. Army infantry division landed and began to relieve Marine units on the perimeter's left flank. This allowed the 3d Marine Division to close up to the right and thus provided many more troops for the thrust toward the center, in search of suitable airfield sites.

The road to Tokyo was lined with front-line graves such as this. Often, it was too demanding to evacuate the dead, so they were buried by their buddies. A grave as elaborate as this certainly shows that this Marine, who must have been shot in the head, was highly regarded by the men with whom he served. Most of these front-line dead were disinterred and laid to rest in the division cemetery near Cape Torokina. *Official USMC Photo*

Allied planners had learned a lot since the precipitous thrust to Guadalcanal fifteen months earlier, and their vision of warfare in the region had matured. Rather than attempt to drive many thousands of Japanese from Bougainville or seize established airfields guarded by thousands of troops, the South Pacific command was content to land in an out-of-the-way place, lightly defended and far from the centers of power, to build their own airfields. All that mattered was that the airfields lay within the operational range of AirSols land-based fighters attacking Rabaul and that the defensive perimeter be far enough out to protect the airfields from being overrun. Moreover, the Marines were seen as being an assault force, amply trained and equipped to make the initial landing and thrust out to an early perimeter line, but too specialized and valuable as an assault force to be frittered away on a long defensive assignment. Thus, from planning to execution, the reinforced 3d Marine Division had a limited role of limited duration to play. Army divisions would relieve the Marine division in place as early as possible, and the first move in that direction took place on November 8.

The battles for Piva Forks were supported by light tanks of the 3d Tank Battalion. The M3 shown in this photograph is missing its entire right track. Marine infantrymen and another light tank (looming at the right) advance cautiously to look the damaged tank over and help the crew. *Official USMC Photo*

WHEN AT LAST GOOD GROUND FOR TWO AIRFIELDS—A BOMBER STRIP AND A PARALLEL fighter strip—was located, it was 1,500 yards beyond the Marine front lines. To forestall a Japanese move on the firm, well-drained ground halfway between the Piva and Korokomina rivers, about 5,500 yards inland, a Marine infantry battalion was ordered to advance to outpost the area until the main line could be pushed out.

On November 13, 2/21 ran directly into a Japanese force that already had possession of the junction of the Numa Numa and East-West trails. All evidence points to coincidental moves by both sides to secure the junction.

The Marine battalion was committed piecemeal and without the benefit of reconnaissance to the unexpected battle, divided, and nearly defeated in detail. Nevertheless, in the late afternoon, all units were able to consolidate behind a screen of artillery, and the 2d Raider Battalion was rushed forward to bolster 2/21.

Patrol activity opened the fight on November 14, and eighteen Marine TBFs, each carrying twelve 100-pound bombs, struck the Japanese position—down to within a hundred yards of Marine outposts. The Marine ground attack was delayed by communications difficulties, but it was thrown in at about noon with the help of five light tanks, of which two were shortly disabled. In due course the Japanese position was overrun and mopped up, defensive positions were set near the trail junction, and the next day the main perimeter line was itself advanced right up to the junction.

AS THE MAIN PERIMETER LINE HAD ADVANCED TOWARD THE PIVA–NUMA NUMA TRAIL junction, the storage and movement of supplies had pretty much come unglued. Saddled with an unworkable plan of cutting their own trails and drawing supplies from their own

The 3d Marine Division artillery regiment, the 12th Marines, kept pace with the inland advance throughout the expansion phase. Here, a 4/12 105mm howitzer set for high-angle fire is being reloaded before the smoke from the previous round has dissipated. *Official USMC Photo*

dumps, Marine infantry battalions advancing inland for the first two weeks of the campaign were faced with the choice of advancing slowly to keep supplies flowing, or advancing rapidly without adequate lines of supply and communication. Moreover, using engineering assets to cut and maintain trails slowed the construction of the fighter strip at Cape Torokina. In mid-November, all the dumps in the 3d Marine Division zone were taken over by the division supply section, all supplies were inventoried and constantly rejiggered to meet local needs, and advance distribution points were established in proximity to front-line units. In effect, supply dumps were leapfrogged forward by trucks and amtracs in anticipation of the needs of advancing combat units. The outcome was instantaneous and positive.

Just as the supply situation suddenly improved, the advance Marine battalions leaped forward without much opposition to succeeding lines of defensible ridges. This was both good news and bad news in that the terrain both enhanced defenses and slowed the development of roads and trails, so front-line troops were once again reduced to carrying what

Closer to the front, one of a Marine infantry company's three 60mm mortars has been elaborately dug in. The loader hangs the live round in the gun tube, awaiting the order to fire. *Official USMC Photo*

they could and hoping they might be resupplied in good time. Fortunately, it was easier to build roads on dry, hilly ground than on swampy flat ground.

AFTER THEY CONSOLIDATED POSITIONS FRONTING THE NUMA NUMA TRAIL NEAR ITS juncture with the East-West Trail, several Marine infantry battalions sent probes on November 19 to the nearby Piva River and out along the trails in both directions. The patrols ran into Japanese forces heading toward the trail junction, and a series of fights, large and small, ensued through November 25. Each side threw increasingly larger forces—including more and more artillery—into larger and larger fights over a longer and

Set in on a final defensive line, an infantry battalion .30-caliber medium water-cooled machine gun is manned and ready to fire, as is an ammunition carrier equipped with a .30-caliber M1 carbine and another Marine, perhaps the platoon sergeant or section chief, armed with a .45-caliber Thompson submachine gun. *Official USMC Photo*

longer front. By the time the largest sustained battle of the campaign had ended with a Japanese withdrawal, Marines had crossed the Piva River in force, advanced nearly 1,500 yards, and firmly held several ridges that overlooked all feasible routes of access to the two new airfield sites.

BATTLES ENSUED IN THE HIGH COUNTRY AND THE SWAMPY FLATS IN BETWEEN, THE 3D Parachute Battalion conducted an abortive raid on a Japanese encampment farther east along Empress Augusta Bay, and the perimeter line was pushed out to even safer distances from the new Piva airfields. But the so-called Piva Forks battle of November 19–25 was the last vital action of the campaign. The Japanese mounted a major offensive against the airfields in March 1944, but by then the heavily augmented 3d Marine Division had turned its portion of the perimeter over to a second fresh Army infantry division and

The all-weather coral-topped Cape Torokina fighter strip officially opened for business on December 10, 1943, and immediately became home for a Marine F4U squadron and a mixed squadron of TBFs and SBDs charged with providing air support for the 3d Marine Division. *Official USMC Photo*

withdrawn from Bougainville altogether, beginning on December 27, 1943, and ending on January 16, 1944.

The Torokina airstrip was used for an emergency landing on November 24, but it was not really completed until December 10, on which day VMF-216 landed seventeen F4Us for permanent assignment. A small mixed contingent of Marine SBDs and TBFs flew in on December 10 and 11, and these bombers flew their first direct-support missions for Marine infantry on December 13.

The Piva Uncle bomber strip began landing planes on December 19 and was declared fully operational on December 30. And the Piva Yoke fighter base went into operation on January 9. By then, the strategic purpose of the Bougainville air-base complex was already being fulfilled; AirSols bombers and fighters were regularly attacking the many Japanese airfields and bases in and around Rabaul.

Marine TBFs fly along the Piva River to support Marine infantry pushing outward at the edge of the Cape Torokina perimeter. Although the Marine Corps still lacked a doctrine governing support of ground troops from the air, action on Bougainville represented the Corps' first ongoing experience in coordinating air support from the ground. *Official USMC Photo*

CHAPTER 8

CAPE GLOUCESTER

DECEMBER 1943–APRIL 1944

THE CAMPAIGN BY THE 1ST MARINE DIVISION TO SEIZE IMPERIAL JAPANESE ARMY airfields and bases in western New Britain was unique on several fronts. It was undertaken entirely under U.S. Army command in an area considered the province of the U.S. Army; and it was undertaken entirely without support from or benefit to Marine Air. The Cape Gloucester campaign, in fact, was an offshoot of the New Guinea campaign and not an extension of the Solomons campaign.

The impetus for the landings at Cape Gloucester, New Britain, was the need to deny the Japanese an opportunity to mount air strikes against the open right flank of Australian Army divisions advancing along the New Guinea coast within range of Cape Gloucester. AirSols would be in a position to relieve the New Guinea-based U.S. Fifth Air Force and elements of the Royal Australian Air Force of the burden of neutralizing Rabaul as soon as airfields on Bougainville could be made operational, and those Fifth Air Force and Australian bombers and fighters—including those based at Cape Gloucester—could then assist in speeding the ground advance in New Guinea.

The 1st Marine Division was selected for the main role on New Britain because it had recuperated and retrained in Melbourne, Australia, following its harrowing ordeal at Guadalcanal; it happened to be ready to return to combat at a time General Douglas MacArthur's Southwest Pacific Command needed a fresh, fully trained, and amphibious-capable infantry division for the Cape Gloucester job. Final training and rehearsals took place in New Guinea.

On D-day at Cape Gloucester, December 26, 1943, a flight of U.S. Fifth Air Force B-25 medium bombers passes low over destroyers and landing ships off the smoke-shrouded invasion beaches. *Official USMC Photo*

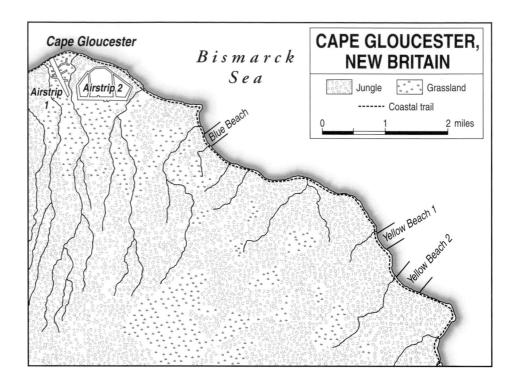

CAPE GLOUCESTER IS AMONG THE RAINIEST REGIONS ON EARTH, AND THE LANDINGS were to take place at the height of the northwestern monsoon. Moreover, as was the case at Cape Torokina on Bougainville, the landing area was filled with swampy lowlands, high ridges, and rugged rainforests with few trails and waterways to aid in movement through the region. On a typical day, temperatures stood at an extremely humid and strength-sapping 90 degrees, and 72 degrees at night.

The key objectives were two airfields just back of Cape Gloucester, but hundreds of square miles of terrain had to be secured to deny access to the airfields by nearly the equivalent of an Imperial Army division deployed in western New Britain, including a depleted infantry regiment in the Cape Gloucester area. Thus, unlike the Bougainville operation, the New Britain operation contemplated the rehabilitation of existing airfields, the development of a thick defensive cordon around them, *and* the pursuit and annihilation of Japanese ground forces across a vast area in which only a few known axes of advance existed. If there were any advantages on the side of the invaders, they were freedom to move amphibiously at the periphery of the area, the deterioration of Japanese command and control following more than a year of war in New Guinea, and the lack of air support on the Japanese side.

THE FIRST MARINES TO GET INTO ACTION ON NEW BRITAIN WERE CREWS FROM Company A, 1st Amphibian Tractor Battalion, who took part in landings at Arawe by U.S. Army troops on December 15. Two of the company's new LVT-2 amtracs took a direct part in overwhelming a Japanese strongpoint.

The net result of the Arawe landing was the dispersal of the Japanese garrison *and* the dispatch of a thousand veteran troops from Cape Gloucester toward Arawe only days before the Marine landings at Cape Gloucester.

THE MAIN PRELANDING BOMBARDMENT WAS UNDERTAKEN BY FIFTH AIR FORCE BOMBERS and fighter-bombers over a period of months under conditions of total air supremacy. The target airfields were not operational by late November, and the garrison was utterly demoralized. At the very end, air sorties were mounted against prepared defenses, which were nearly destroyed.

The landings at Cape Gloucester took place on the morning of December 26, 1943. A reinforced infantry battalion (2/1) went ashore almost without incident to the east of the main beaches, to block trails leading to and from the airdromes. The main landing went straight for the airfields.

The landings were partly screened by heavy smoke from planned fires that Army Air Forces bombers started with eight tons of white phosphorous bombs, but that smoke eventually drifted over the beaches, where it hampered the Marines. The landing force met no human opposition, but a deep, unmapped swamp directly behind the beach and other natural obstacles enhanced by the preinvasion bombardment made for extremely slow progress toward D-day objectives.

Marines of 3/7 hacked through to the coastal trail, and there the right-flank battalion met its first opposition in the form of long-range fire from well-manned bunkers.

Viewed from the bridge of a Landing Craft, Infantry (LCI), the landing is uncontested and routine. Note, however, that the narrow beach is backed by a sight-impeding dense forest that grows out beyond the shoreline. Note, also, the white-water surf conditions.
Official USMC Photo

A file of Marines picks its way through the shell-blasted swamp backing the invasion beaches. A haze is rolling in, the result of deliberately set fires on the high ground overlooking the beachhead.
Official USMC Photo

The advancing infantry was lightly engaged on D-day, and casualties were light. Here, three corpsmen working in a small front-line aid station treat a Marine who has been shot in his left arm.
Official USMC Photo

Bombardment by new 2.36-inch rocket launchers (bazookas) and 37mm guns was ineffective. A follow-on battalion, 3/1, was unable to advance in the face of concentrated fire until an LVT carrying supplies from the beach drove over one of the bunkers and allowed the infantry to penetrate the defensive zone. Thereafter, a platoon of five Sherman M4 medium tanks arrived to help seal the fate of the defenders. The battalion then advanced to its phase line and dug in.

On the left, 1/7 met only light opposition on its way to a feature known as Target Hill. This high ground was seized against light opposition, and 1/7 also dug in.

A pair of Marines carefully inspects a Japanese dugout near the beachhead. The caption written at the time reads, in part: "It's a ticklish job, for the wily Japs remain in hiding for the chance to take an American with them in death."
Official USMC Photo

In the center, 2/7 advanced through an abandoned Japanese supply depot and attacked to its objective through a dense forest in the face of light opposition. During the afternoon, 3/7 advanced through a swamp to its objective and also dug in. Behind this screen of four infantry battalions, 1/1 landed as the force reserve and set up in the Japanese supply depot, and 2/11 set up its 75mm pack howitzers along the edge of the coastal trail that ran through the beachhead. Two other artillery battalions—1/11 with 75mm pack howitzers and 4/11 with 105mm field howitzers—had a much harder time getting ashore over swampy ground. The 75s were moved to dry sites aboard amtracs, but the 105s were too heavy for that. In the end, amtracs blazed trails by crashing through dense growth so that artillery tractors and troops using blocks and pulleys could move the guns, of which only three (of twelve) were set in by nightfall.

Faced with the problem of unmapped swamps sitting on proposed dump sites, the division pioneer battalion (now designated 2d Battalion, 17th Marines) faced problems identical to those encountered at Bougainville for the same reasons, including a 4-foot tidal surge. The landing of supplies became increasingly unglued as the day progressed, and the unprocessed supplies made for a glaring target when eighty-eight Rabaul-based Imperial Navy fighters and dive-bombers attacked in the afternoon. One destroyer was sunk and another was severely damaged, but so many Japanese planes were shot down that the invasion force was never again molested during the day.

The 1st Marine Division command post moved ashore right in the wake of the assault, and it oversaw eleven thousand Marines who got ashore by nightfall. D-day operations—a complete success—cost twenty-one killed and twenty-three wounded. That night, the division commander requested that his force reserve—two reinforced battalions of the 5th Marines—be landed as soon as it could be lifted to Cape Gloucester. The Japanese also sent all available forces toward Cape Gloucester. Most were on the move by the evening of December 26, and at least one major infantry unit arrived opposite 2/7 during the late evening.

As carrying parties maintained a flow of ammunition through the swamp, 2/7 held the counterattack at bay with the use of remarkably accurate fire coupled with iron-willed

Marine 37mm antitank guns were ported directly to the front from D-day onward to fire against prepared defenses. A good or lucky shot through a firing aperture might have taken out a pillbox or a bunker, but most shots did little damage because they hit logs that absorbed the impact. The 37mm guns weighed about 600 pounds, so they could be carried forward by hand if enough troops were available. *Official USMC Photo*

fire discipline—firing only at clear targets and, for the most part, only when fired on. It rained all night, but the rain subsided at dawn, just as Japanese troops assaulted toward a break in the line. At that moment, the troops of a 1st Special Weapons Battalion 37mm antitank battery that had left its guns behind to haul ammunition through the swamp arrived to plug the gap. The day was saved in a heart-stopping seesaw battle in which the Marines finally prevailed. The Japanese left at least two hundred dead on the battlefield and threw in steadily weaker attacks for three days, while the Marines built up their line with all manner of troops. In the tradition of "every Marine is a rifleman," the line in the center of the beachhead was bolstered by 37mm gunners, pioneers, and other special troops acting as infantry.

The 105mm howitzers brought ashore by 4/11 ran into problems immediately behind the beaches. Either they had to be manhandled across swamps—often with the aid of blocks and tackle—to firing positions on dry ground, or the incessant rainy weather turned well-traveled roads to muck. Note that this howitzer's wheels have been doubled up—and how little good that did as the gun shield plowed up the deep mud. *Official USMC Photo*

The artillery workhorse of Marine divisions through 1944 was the 75mm pack howitzer. Its lethality against built-up defenses was limited at range, but it could be broken down to be carried forward by amphibian tractors under any ground or surf conditions, and in a pinch it could be moved by brute human force. This 75mm howitzer has just fired. *Official USMC Photo*

Tanks played a vital role in the advance on the airfields and beyond. The 1st Tank Battalion at Cape Gloucester was the first organic Marine divisional unit to field gun companies equipped with Sherman M4 tanks. This tank is advancing directly up the coastal track on November 27, 1943, and the troops probably are members of 3/1. *Official USMC Photo*

Marine infantrymen and a few jeeps march across one of the two airfields captured at Cape Gloucester on December 29 and 30. Note the wreckage of a Japanese bomber. Both fields were strewn with bomb- and bullet-shattered aircraft. *Official USMC Photo*

In the meantime, with the 7th Marines pinned in the center and many of their own troops committed as infantry, the pioneers of 2/17 cleared the fouled beaches, the 5th Marines was made ready to land at Cape Gloucester, and the 1st Marines (less 2/1, at the trail block) moved on the airfields. Engineers advanced in the infantry's wake to put in roads and drain dump sites all across the perimeter.

The vanguard of the advance on the airfields was 3/1, which moved ahead on the narrow strip of dry land supporting the coastal trail. Progress was orderly and steady behind a fan of combat patrols and on-demand artillery coverage. Tanks aided greatly in overcoming pillboxes and bunkers encountered along the way, and 3/1 advanced five thousand yards on December 27 alone. Ahead lay a belt of bunkers, pillboxes, and trenches centered on a feature eventually dubbed Hell's Point.

Attacking behind a curtain of Army Air Forces A-20 ground-attack bombers and 75mm fire put out by 1/11, 3/1 stepped off toward Hell's Point at 1100 hours and 1/1 cut

Company I, 3/1, conducts an impromptu flag-raising ceremony on Razorback Hill on December 30, 1943. *Official USMC Photo*

The struggle to make a go of the Cape Gloucester perimeter was typified by the struggle to build roads to the front—and keep them in. Here, on December 31, Marine engineers from 1/17 and Navy Seabees from 3/17 lay a temporary corduroy road across a flowing stream to help keep supplies moving toward the airfields. If there was one good thing about operating in a tropical rainforest, it was the bottomless supply of lumber. *Official USMC Photo*

a flanking path through the forest to the left. The battle was joined on the flank when 1/1 ran into the prepared defenses at 1145. At first 1/1 was thrown back, and then the fight developed into a four-hour stalemate. The Marines eventually pulled back for the night to draw ammunition. A stronger attack force that kicked off at dawn on December 29 fell into a vacuum left by the departing Japanese.

In the meantime, 3/1 ground into the main defensive line, right on Hell's Point, throughout the daylight hours of December 28. Rain and dense foliage helped shield both sides from fire, but it also hampered both sides equally. Marine tank-infantry teams went up against defensive positions protected by interlocking bands of fire from other emplacements fielding weapons up to 75mm guns. In some places, Marine medium tanks ran right over pillboxes, smashing them in and exposing the occupants to direct fire. The last bunker was overcome at 1630, its occupants having withdrawn minutes earlier as part of a general retreat. There was nothing left between the Marines and the airfields.

A full battalion of the 5th Marines, most of another battalion, and the regimental headquarters and attachments landed on new beaches just behind the 1st Marines vanguard on the morning of December 29. The rest of the 5th Marines regimental combat team landed farther back and was sent forward as soon as it had reorganized ashore.

Following the fall of the airfields and consolidation of the perimeter defenses, Marine infantry battalions fanned out to run down Japanese units fleeing the Cape Gloucester area or defending other outposts and camps in western New Britain. Here, in January 1944, a tank-supported infantry unit fords one of countless streams cutting through New Britain's interior. *Official USMC Photo*

Air and artillery opened ahead of the 1st and 5th Marine regiments at noon—1/1 on the right, toward Airfield No. 2, and 2/5 on the left, toward foothills dubbed Razorback Hill, which were thought to be the site of a Japanese defensive zone. Attacking in the rain and supported by tanks and 75mm halftracks, 1/1 reached the airfield perimeter against desultory opposition at 1755 hours and was soon joined by 3/1 to defend the area. In the meantime, 2/5 attacked through unexpectedly difficult terrain, found the Japanese hill defenses on Razorback Hill abandoned, and looped down to secure all of Airfield No. 2.

On December 30, the bulk of 2/5 marched across Airfield No. 1 while 1/5 moved up to Airfield No. 2. In going back over Razorback Hill, scouts from 2/5 ran into Japanese troops, possibly an advance guard of a battalion that was to have occupied the vital terrain a day or two earlier. A platoon of Company F, 2/5, was sent to mop up the Japanese, but it was attacked as it reached the summit of one of the hill's knobs. Reinforcements poured in from both sides. The Japanese attacked to dislodge the Marine platoon, but the rest of Company F arrived in time to drive them off. Tanks were called in, the Marine infantry company attacked the Japanese positions, and thirty prepared positions were overcome before noon. More than 150 Japanese bodies were counted against the loss of 13 Marines killed and 19 wounded.

In the meantime, 1/5 ran into prepared defenses east of Razorback Hill, but 3/1 attacked through 1/5 and overcame the defenders. By that evening, the 1st and 5th Marines controlled both airfields and all the important high ground overlooking them.

To keep the perimeter safe, numerous patrols had to be mounted across the deep forest hollows fronting the defenses as far as anyone could walk.
Official USMC Photo

The strategic objectives of the operation were and remained firmly in American hands. An informal flag-raising was held on Razorback Hill by Company I, 3/1, on December 30, and the formal flag-raising was held on the airdrome on December 31.

THE NEW BRITAIN CAMPAIGN GROUND ONWARD INTO MARCH 1944, TAKING ELEMENTS of the 1st Marine Division into several amphibious landings, long trail chases, and a few hard fights as they hunted down Japanese infantry and rolled up bases in the western part of the island. The main purposes of the ongoing and spreading offensive was to prevent

This bearded, pinch-faced machine gunner is coming off the line on January 17, 1944, after nearly three weeks of grinding forward toward the Cape Gloucester airfields and beyond. *Official USMC Photo*

attacks on the air base at Cape Gloucester and to keep the equivalent of a Japanese division from ever taking part in a meaningful operation against Allied forces. These missions were accomplished in spades, and many hundreds of Japanese were killed or dispersed.

Advances in early 1944 by the Southwest Pacific Force in New Guinea and islands off New Guinea were swifter than anticipated in the 1943 run-up to the New Britain invasion, and the importance of the Cape Gloucester air base receded even while the base was being rehabilitated by engineers. Neither airfield was on particularly good ground, and Airfield No. 1 was soon abandoned altogether. The first landing on Airfield No. 2, on January 28, 1944, was that of the personal plane of the 1st Marine Division commanding general. Two Fifth Air Force fighter squadrons were briefly based there, but both were withdrawn when the ground war left them far in the rear.

By the end of April 1944, the entire 1st Marine Division had been relieved by U.S. Army units and withdrawn to a new training base on Pavuvu, in the Russell Islands. A total of 310 members of the division died on New Britain, and 1,083 were wounded in action.

A Marine infantry squad rests on the bank of a stream on January 31, 1944. This unit is now in the position from which it will assault the Japanese base on Borgen Bay, New Britain, one of half a dozen objectives Marines had to secure following the capture of the Cape Gloucester airfields. *Official USMC Photo*

CHAPTER 9

RABAUL

DECEMBER 17, 1943–AUGUST 8, 1945

FROM THE MOMENT ITS VAST HARBOR AND AIRFIELDS WERE SEIZED BY THE IMPERIAL Navy on January 23, 1942, the sleepy former British colonial center at Rabaul became the bustling, burgeoning center of Japanese military power in the New Guinea and Solomon Islands areas. It was the launching point for the Japanese invasion of the Solomons from February to May 1942, and it was the main support base for Japanese moves and defensive efforts in New Guinea for all of 1942 and beyond. During the Guadalcanal campaign, Rabaul was the sole base from which Imperial Navy air and naval forces sought and very nearly won domination. Then, throughout the Allied drive up the Solomons chain, and the slogging campaigns along New Guinea's northern coast, Rabaul remained the vital strategic bastion from which all Japanese efforts in the region ultimately emanated and relied on for support.

Throughout 1942 and 1943, Rabaul's fine harbor, port, logistical facilities, and *five* airfields had been the main goals of Allied efforts in the Solomons campaign. And yet, in all that time, Rabaul had been virtually untouchable. Allied air attacks against Rabaul began with a raid by six Australia-based U.S. Army Air Forces B-17 heavy bombers on February 23, 1942. Thereafter, similar small raids, conducted on the average of one per month, did nothing more than mildly annoy the Japanese.

It wasn't until February 10, 1943, that the Allies produced a clearly enunciated plan (ELKTON, later giving way to Operation CARTWHEEL) detailing the efforts that would have to be made to recapture Rabaul from the Japanese. Those efforts included the seizure of numerous Japanese bases along the 600-mile Solomons chain between Guadalcanal and

Major Gregory Boyington, the commanding officer of VMF-214, was one of the spark plugs of the Marine Air offensive over Rabaul until he was shot down on January 3, 1944. This photograph was taken as he briefed pilots for the December 17, 1943, inaugural AirSols mission to Rabaul. *Official USMC Photo*

Rabaul, and a costly advance by Allied forces along New Guinea's northern coast—for until Rabaul was within range of Allied *fighter* aircraft, there was very little that unescorted Allied bombers could do to smash Rabaul's burgeoning, well-protected, and strategically crucial naval, air, and logistics facilities.

The first Allied fighters over Rabaul were Army Air Forces long-range P-38s out of Dobodura, New Guinea. On October 12, 1943, a total of 349 U.S. Fifth Air Force bombers and fighters (and a squadron of Royal Australian Air Force light bombers) out of New Guinea bases managed to damage several Japanese ships in Rabaul's vast harbor and shoot down four Imperial Navy aircraft—at a cost of five Allied aircraft lost. Thereafter, Fifth Air Force and Australian formations returned to Rabaul on October 13, 18, 23, 24, 25, and 29.

The reason for the wave of air attacks against Rabaul was the upcoming Allied invasion of Bougainville. And the importance of Bougainville was that it was close enough to Rabaul to support its own land-based fighter operations against the Japanese base complex. It was anticipated that the Imperial Navy would mount a major naval and air effort against the Bougainville invasion fleet, and that all possible efforts would be made to prevent the Allies from building any air bases on the island.

And that is what happened. The November 1, 1943, invasion of Cape Torokina, Bougainville, by the 3d Marine Division was met by an all-out Japanese aerial counteroffensive that culminated that very night in the Naval Battle of Empress Augusta Bay, a narrow American victory that deflected the Japanese force from the vulnerable transports. On November 2, a Fifth Air Force bombing mission against Rabaul resulted in two destroyers and eight merchant ships sunk or severely damaged, but also tragic American losses that bloodily confirmed reports of a recent reinforcement of the base via the Japanese base at Truk, in the Caroline Islands. Nevertheless, thirty-one Japanese aircraft were shot down and others were destroyed on the ground on November 2.

On November 5, the U.S. Navy's Task Force 38—including the fleet carrier *Saratoga* and the light carrier *Princeton*—launched ninety-seven bombers and fighters against warships and port facilities at Rabaul. This time, twenty-eight Japanese warplanes were destroyed in the air, but more importantly, the bombers damaged three Imperial Navy heavy cruisers, two light cruisers, and two destroyers. Later, after most of the Japanese planes had departed Rabaul to search for the American carriers, Fifth Air Force B-24 heavy bombers struck the undefended port. The next day, November 6, the Imperial Navy surface force departed Rabaul, never to return. So far, at very little cost in airplanes or men, Americans had achieved a strategic victory of incalculable

Marine light bombers did not get over Rabaul until January 5, 1944, the first day they could stage through Bougainville's Piva Uncle bomber strip. Once in the battle, however, they never left. SBDs from at least two Marine squadrons are shown in this view above Simpson Harbor. *Official USMC Photo*

importance; Imperial Navy surface forces had ceased to be a factor in the final stages of the long campaign against Rabaul. (In fact, the Imperial Navy surface forces turned out to be of no strategic value whatsoever for the remainder of the Pacific War.)

A Marine SBD delivers a bomb on an oil transfer facility near Rapopo Airdrome. *Official USMC Photo*

The Fifth Air Force mounted attacks against Rabaul on November 7 and 10, and then a much stronger Task Force 38—the new fleet carriers *Essex* and *Bunker Hill* and the light carrier *Independence*—returned with a vengeance on November 11 to launch the first phase of what history would call the Battle of the Solomons Sea. In addition to destruction and damage caused by the Navy carrier bombers at Rabaul, U.S. Navy fighters accounted for a staggering 137 Japanese fighters and bombers, both over the target and while fending off a large Japanese attack force over the carriers themselves. (While the Japanese aircraft were chasing the carriers, Fifth Air Force B-24s bombed one of the Rabaul airfields.) And the next day, the Imperial Navy withdrew all the carrier aircraft that had been temporarily detailed to defend Rabaul; too many trained carrier pilots were dying in defense of the land base. Thereafter, Rabaul's port remained empty and its air contingent remained at low ebb, with the result that no American warplanes visited the place between November 11 and mid-December.

Marine TBFs typically delivered four 500-pound bombs or two 1,000-pound bombs each time they struck Rabaul. Here, a 1,000-pound bomb is being positioned beneath an open TBF bomb bay at Bougainville's Piva Uncle bomber base. *Official USMC Photo*

Throughout November 1943, whenever formations of Japanese aircraft based at Rabaul came down to Bougainville to attack supply ships and transports, or facilities ashore, the attackers were routinely knocked down by a virtually around-the-clock fighter umbrella that included Army, Navy, Marine, and Royal New Zealand Air Force fighters flying from numerous airstrips and bases in the Central Solomons. On the relatively few days when the Japanese aircraft appeared, Marine F4U Corsair pilots did about as well as their brothers in other services: five Imperial Navy fighters downed on November 1; two dive-bombers on November 2; three dive-bombers on November 8; a G4M downed by a VMF(N)-531 PV Ventura night-fighter on November 13; six dive-bombers downed by two VMF-221 Corsair pilots on November 17; two fighters downed on November 18; and one twin-engine Imperial Army bomber downed on November 20.

The problem Marine fighter pilots faced was that they had to wait for the Japanese to come to them, and the Japanese were slowly giving up on the notion of doing much damage against Allied forces around Bougainville—because the Allied fighters were taking too great a toll. In point of fact, the large air battles over Rabaul during late October and early November had resulted in aircraft losses—particularly fighter losses—that the Japanese could not immediately replace. The dog days experienced by Marine fighter pilots in November were the result of losses the Japanese sustained at the hands of the U.S. Navy and the Fifth Air Force.

Marine fighter pilots didn't *see* a Japanese warplane within range between November 20 and December 3, when a VMF(N)-531 Ventura night-fighter downed an unidentified airplane at sea. The next encounter was on December 6, when a Marine Ventura downed an Imperial Army fighter.

Throughout the slow waiting days of November, the construction of a fighter strip on Bougainville's Cape Torokina had been nearing completion, and ground was broken for a second airfield at Piva on November 29. Finally, on December 9, the Torokina fighter strip was declared operational. Suddenly Rabaul was within range of land-based Marine fighters—only 255 miles away.

On December 10, the first aircraft to be permanently based at Torokina—seventeen VMF-216 Corsairs—arrived there. Six Marine Douglas SBD dive-bombers and four Marine R4D transports arrived later in the day. For the moment, however, the Marine warplanes were not sent against Rabaul; they were to guard the base and provide support for the 3d Marine Division's efforts to expand and consolidate the defensive perimeter around the new Piva air base.

Interestingly, as Allied air power in the Solomons was being concentrated to begin a strategic air assault against Rabaul, the *apparent* need for such an assault was being removed. Throughout most of 1942 and 1943, it had been an assumption of Allied offensive planning that Rabaul would eventually be recaptured from the Japanese. But even before the Bougainville invasion, the overseers of the Allied Pacific War strategy had decided to bypass the immense base. It was decided that the Allies did not really need Rabaul's facilities to continue with the main thrusts of the Pacific War effort. Rather than mount an assault in which thousands of Allied soldiers might die, it was decided to destroy Rabaul's offensive capability and seal the base off from reinforcement.

The first part of the mission—destroying Rabaul's offensive capability—had been partially completed when Imperial Navy surface forces were permanently withdrawn on November 6. And Rabaul lost its ability to mount strategically meaningful air offensives when the first of the Bougainville airfields was manned by Marine fighters on December 10.

On December 15, U.S. Army troops landed at Arawe, in central New Britain, and the entire 1st Marine Division was going to land at Cape Gloucester on December 26. Later, the Green Islands, between Bougainville and Rabaul, were to be occupied. These operations would seal the air routes to and from Rabaul in three directions, leaving only the route between Rabaul and the Japanese stronghold at Truk.

If Rabaul was going to be bypassed, and if all possible attack routes to vital Allied bases were going to be blocked, then there appeared to be no reason to renew the air offensive against Rabaul. There was no need to soften it up, per se, and throughout World War II, air bases had been notoriously difficult to knock out permanently. Yet, just at the moment when the Allies were attaining and sealing several strategic goals, they were preparing to mount an air offensive with no apparent strategic purpose.

There *were* good reasons to risk the lives of airmen over Rabaul: Japanese warplanes could still fly into Rabaul from Truk or Japanese aircraft carriers, and this posed a direct threat to the upcoming Cape Gloucester invasion. So it was wise, in the short term, to defang Rabaul to provide a margin of safety for the Cape Gloucester invasion force. Because its bases were well within range of Arawe and Cape Gloucester, the Fifth Air Force was given responsibility for supporting and defending those new Allied outposts. This left Rabaul for Allied air units based in the Solomons under AirSols control.

But there was a larger and longer-range strategic imperative behind the new air offensive against Rabaul: the Japanese did not know that their immense base was going to be bypassed. They were prepared to defend it to the last man—as a means of drawing the Allies into a costly and lengthy battle of attrition that might weaken and delay further Allied strikes across the central Pacific. In fact, based on past experience, the Japanese could be *counted* on to relentlessly defend Rabaul against a supposed invasion—certainly against an air offensive that appeared to be softening the place up for an impending invasion.

If the Japanese defended Rabaul "to the last man," it meant they would do everything in their power to move air units to Rabaul via Truk. (In fact, the Imperial Navy was scouring its air establishment for aircraft and flying personnel that could be staged through Truk to Rabaul.) And that was the crux of the new Allied air offensive against Rabaul: drawing Japan's precious few well-trained airmen into the battle for Rabaul, and killing them. If those airmen died over Rabaul, where the Allies were bound to have both the initiative and overwhelming air superiority, then those airmen would not be around to fight later battles as the Allies drew closer and closer to Japan itself. The new air offensive against Rabaul was to be a battle of attrition, and Rabaul was to be the final resting place of meaningful Japanese air power in the Pacific.

The operational plan was straightforward and blunt. Allied bombers were to attack Rabaul's port facilities and airfields, a challenge that was certain to draw Japanese fighters into the air. When Japanese fighters challenged the bombers, Allied fighters would be there to shoot them down. The bombers were bait, and the fighters were executioners. (Of course, no one in authority mentioned this to the bomber crews, who would have been demoralized if they even thought they were being used as bait.)

The first Bougainville-based mission against Rabaul was on December 17, 1943, an all-fighter sweep. This was not in line with the attritional strategy, but the strike was nevertheless mounted to draw Japanese attention away from the Arawe beachhead, and to ease pressure on the Fifth Air Force as it mounted an all-out aerial offensive in preparation for the impending Cape Gloucester invasion.

The first strike force was composed of thirty-one Marine Corsairs, twenty-three New Zealand P-40 fighters, and twenty-two U.S. Navy F6F Hellcats—all of which staged through (that is, refueled at) Torokina from their permanent bases in the central Solomons. Absent a direct threat to their own bases—there were no bombers—the Japanese all but ignored the strike force. The strike commander, Marine Major Gregory Boyington, actually implored the Japanese to rise to the challenge, but only a few Japanese pilots responded, so only a few lost their lives. Low-flying New Zealand P-40 pilots downed five fighters, and one Navy and one Marine pilot each downed one. Three P-40s also were lost, with two of their pilots. When Major Boyington returned to Munda to report, he asked that *fewer* fighters be sent on the next mission—fewer being easier to control and, perhaps, less threatening.

This three-man TBF crew is about to board its airplane at Piva Uncle for the day's trip to Rabaul and back. A TBF crew consisted of a pilot, a radioman-gunner positioned in the upper .50-caliber ball turret, and a bombardier-gunner who manned both the belly bombsight and the lower .30-caliber machine gun. *Official USMC Photo*

But Boyington had missed the point; it wasn't the number of fighters that had kept the Japanese on the ground on December 17, it was the lack of bombers, for only bombers could do Rabaul's facilities and defenses serious harm, and so only bombers were worth the risk of pilots' lives and precious aircraft.

Besides the fighters, Rabaul's antiair defenses were formidable. Eleven operational radar sites were reasonably efficient sentinels, giving the Japanese interceptor force plenty of time to meet incoming aircraft. And there were at least 260 antiaircraft guns arrayed around the harbor area and airfields. Many of these guns, especially the heavier ones (going up to 127mm), were set on high ground, which included three volcanoes, of which one, Vulcan, was still active. Often, bombers approaching at low altitude were below the defensive emplacements. The antiaircraft guns were considered effective, and they forced Army Air Forces B-24s to higher altitudes, which in turn dissipated the effects of the bombs. But damaging Rabaul's military facilities was really only a bonus when it could be done; the real target was the Japanese fighter force, especially the Japanese pilots.

There were four active airfields at Rabaul, and two emergency strips. The Vunakanau and Lakunai airstrips had been captured from the Australians in January 1942, and Rapopo and Tobera had been built by the Japanese. A fifth airstrip, Keravat, had been built, but it suffered from terminal drainage problems and was used only as an emergency runway. An emergency

In early 1944, after the issue over Rabaul had been decided, Marine Air fielded a total of five PBJ squadrons (dubbed VMB) on the fields surrounding the Japanese stronghold. The PBJs were standard North American B-25 medium bombers with a Navy/Marine designation. Marine PBJs were the last aircraft to bomb Rabaul, on August 8, 1945. Here, PBJs over Simpson Harbor are tracked by antiaircraft fire. *Official USMC Photo*

strip on Duke of York Island, at the entrance to Rabaul harbor, was nearing completion when the Rabaul air offensive began.

A strike by Solomons-based Thirteenth Air Force B-24s was thwarted by bad weather on December 18, but fifty Japanese fighters rose to challenge sixteen AirSols B-24s on December 19. Thanks to the typical heavy cloud cover, the large escort was able to down only four of the many interceptors, of which two were credited to Marines from VMF-222.

The next Rabaul strike went out on December 23. This time, AirSols B-24s, escorted by P-38s, went in first to bomb Japanese airfields. As they were withdrawing, before the Japanese interceptor force landed, Major Boyington arrived on the scene at the head of a mixed force of forty-eight Allied fighters. Forty Japanese fighters were engaged, and the Allied pilots claimed thirty of them destroyed. (Marine Corsair pilots from VMF-214, VMF-222, and VMF-223 claimed nineteen victories, of which four were credited to Boyington alone.) Japanese tallies for this and other actions do not come close to agreeing with Allied claims, but it is virtually certain that at least half of the claims throughout the offensive are matched by actual aircraft downed, and this is still a significant number.

There was a B-24 raid the next evening, Christmas Eve, and twenty-six Japanese fighters were claimed, but Marine pilots went scoreless. The next morning, strike aircraft off several U.S. Navy carriers hit the Japanese base at Kavieng, New Ireland, and then Allied fighters from Bougainville swept over Rabaul to keep its air contingent from going after the carriers. Thirteen Japanese fighters were downed over Rabaul, of which eight were credited to Marines from VMF-214 and VMF-223.

While covering a bomber strike on December 27, Marine Corsair pilots from three squadrons staging through Torokina downed fifteen Japanese fighters, and Marine escort pilots from four squadrons claimed twenty-six victories on December 28. The next mission was on December 30. Many Japanese fighters rose to challenge the nineteen B-24s going after shipping targets, and there was a big melee, but only twelve victories were credited, of which only one went to a Marine.

The Navy carriers returned to Kavieng on January 1, where fourteen Japanese aircraft were downed. The third and last carrier strike in the area sought to hit Japanese warships near Kavieng, but to little avail. The result of the three Kavieng carrier missions was that the Japanese were forced to defend the place with fighters they needed over Rabaul.

AirSols B-24s attacked various targets around Rabaul on January 1, and a Marine pilot was credited with one victory. The Japanese also rose to challenge a fighter sweep on

January 2, and Marine Corsair pilots from VMF-211 and VMF-321 were credited with eight victories. And Marines taking part in another fighter sweep on January 3 downed seven Japanese fighters. However, on January 3, Major Boyington and his wingman were shot down during a long chase over the sea. Boyington, who survived and was captured, was seen to down a Japanese fighter, and this tied him—at twenty-six victories apiece—with Marine Captain Joseph Foss, both as the Pacific Theater's high-scoring aces at the time, and as the Marine Corps' all-time high-scoring aces. (After Boyington was released from captivity in 1945, he was given credit for two more victories scored on January 3, 1944, and that made him the all-time high-scoring Marine fighter ace.)

Marines from four Corsair squadrons downed nine Japanese fighters on January 4. And then bombers returned to Rabaul on January 5—Marine bombers. The brand-new bomber field on Bougainville, dubbed Piva Uncle, was used to stage twenty-six Marine SBDs and twenty-one TBF light bombers from their home bases in New Georgia against Rabaul. There were heavy clouds over Rabaul, but the Marine bombers found the briefed target, a radar station. The seventy-two-plane escort scored twelve Japanese fighters, none by Marines.

Marine F4U pilots accounted for two Japanese fighters on January 6 and seven on January 7. Of course, these and previous victories were scored within the context of larger overall losses inflicted as well by Navy, Air Forces, and New Zealand fighter pilots. So far, overall American losses had been quite low.

This photo of Rapopo Airdrome was taken in 1944 from a Marine PBJ. Rapopo was one of five Rabaul-area airfields. *Official USMC Photo*

Once the Marine light bombers could reach Rabaul via Piva Uncle (where they were soon permanently based), life at Rabaul became hellish. Soon, AirSols B-25 medium bombers joined the procession to Rabaul from a new base in the Stirling Islands. Weather permitting, Rabaul was struck almost daily, sometimes several times a day. And almost without fail, the Japanese sent their fighters aloft to attack the bombers—and to be attacked by the increasingly effective Allied escort fighters.

Day in and day out through the balance of January 1944, Marine fighter pilots scored victories over Rabaul as follows: January 9, fifteen; January 11, four; January 14, twenty-six (and three by bomber gunners); January 15, one by a bomber gunner; January 17, ten (and two by bomber gunners); January 18, twelve; January 20, fifteen; January 22, sixteen; January 23, a record forty-five; January 24, fourteen; January 27, seven; January 28, thirteen (and three by bomber gunners); January 29, eleven (and two by bomber gunners); January 30, twelve; and January 31, six. Altogether, in January alone, Marine fighter pilots and bomber gunners were credited with 266 Japanese fighters—not to mention the amount of physical damage Marine bombers inflicted on Rabaul's defenses during the month.

Through January—as the Japanese fed valuable *carrier* aircraft and irreplaceable *carrier* airmen into what even they called "the sinkhole in the Bismarcks"—the Allies developed an effective and deadly modus operandi among their various fighter components. The New Zealand P-40s were low-altitude fighters, so they provided low cover for the bombers. Then the Marine (and one squadron of Navy) Corsairs were stacked to provide medium and high cover. If Army Air Forces P-38s were available, they provided very high cover. The Japanese tried to time their attacks to hit just before the bombers entered the flak belt over any given target, but they were usually challenged by one force of Allied fighters or another. Various ruses were attempted by the American pilots to attack the Japanese fighters as they took off, or even to get them while landing, after all the other Allied aircraft had left the scene, but the biggest dividends came from toe-to-toe brawls in and around the bomber formations. Slowly, the inexorable fall of bombs affected the ability of Japanese ground crews to keep their fighters flying, and the radar early-warning system was slowly depleted by bombs and a general lack of spare parts from outside the battle zone. As regards resupply efforts, Marine bombers sank seven supply ships and an oiler, and badly damaged three supply ships.

The Japanese position at Rabaul was in decline throughout the first half of February 1944, but it is likely the air battles would have slogged on for up to several more months had not the American Pacific War hierarchy decided to end it once and for all with a grand strike—not against Rabaul, but—against Rabaul's only link to fresh supplies and aircraft. In early February, with the successful amphibious leap from the Gilbert to the Marshall Islands, the Pacific Fleet effectively outflanked

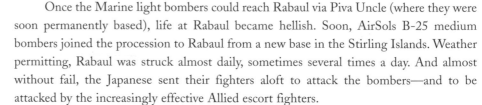

This Marine F4U Corsair was photographed on Green Island on May 1, 1944. Many Marine Corsair squadrons fought elsewhere in the Pacific in 1944 and 1945, but many also flew only over Rabaul for pretty much the rest of the Pacific War. Living was good on the island bases ringing Rabaul, but the work was boring and frustrating. *Official USMC Photo*

the Japanese stronghold at Truk, the only base from which Rabaul could be supported. Thus, for two days, February 18 and 19, nine U.S. Navy carrier air groups pounded Truk nearly to oblivion. Also, on the night of February 17–18, Rabaul and Kavieng were bombarded by U.S. Navy warships. Convinced that Rabaul was about to be invaded, and fearful that the line of retreat via Truk was in danger, the Japanese decided to save all the operational warplanes remaining at Rabaul. As soon as the last Allied escort fighter left the Rabaul area on February 19, the Japanese aircraft were readied for a morning takeoff. Between 70 and 120 aircraft left on schedule, but 30 others were left behind for lack of parts. And that ended the great Allied air offensive against Rabaul. When the Allies' February 20 mission arrived over Rabaul, it was not challenged. On February 21, AirSols bombers sank the ship carrying skilled Japanese aircraft mechanics away from Rabaul.

After the Japanese withdrew their warships and aircraft from Rabaul, there were few targets worth dying over, but the bombing never stopped. Here, Marine SBDs attack a previously sunken cargo ship on August 2, 1944—fifty-three weeks before the last bombs fell on Rabaul. *Official USMC Photo*

In all, Marines were credited with the destruction of 342 Japanese aircraft—nearly all fighters—between December 17, 1943, and February 19, 1944 (and a final 5 fighters in two March engagements). The aerial tally represents 43 percent of the 789 aircraft claimed by all Allied services and nationalities during the entire Rabaul air offensive. Japanese records of the day reveal only about 250 aircraft actually downed over Rabaul between December 17 and February 19. Nevertheless, even if the incomplete Japanese record is correct, the offensive can still be counted a great victory. Far fewer Allied aircraft—151 warplanes in all, including only 25 bombers—were lost, and the Japanese were induced to fritter away vast and valuable resources at a dead end just as the venue of the Pacific War was shifting far and away to the Central Pacific Area, where air opposition was for the time nil. If there were any good veteran Imperial Navy fighter pilots left by November 1943, most of them certainly died over Rabaul.

On March 20, 1943, the new, independent 4th Marine Regiment (formed on February 1 from the four disbanded Marine Raider battalions) landed at Emirau, northeast of Kavieng. There was no opposition, and a new airfield was quickly built.

The heckling of Rabaul's defenders never ended. Once the ring of air bases around the bastion had been forged, Marine Air (for the most part) attacked regularly. In fact, the almost daily "milk runs" to Rabaul became a demoralizing make-work project for Marine Air. Through nearly all of 1944, dormant Rabaul was just about the only target Marine Air had in the war. The last Marine mission over Rabaul took place on August 8, 1945.

CHAPTER 10

TARAWA

Following the bloodless seizure of the Ellice Islands in October 1942, the first offensive in the long-planned, long-delayed push across the central Pacific was in the former British mandate in the Gilbert Islands—simultaneous landings in Makin Atoll by U.S. Army troops and at Tarawa Atoll by the 2d Marine Division. The Gilbert Islands, positioned at the eastern edge of Japanese-held territory in the central Pacific, were selected as targets because the invasion could be supported by long-range bombers operating from the Ellice Islands and would, in their turn, support long-range bombing missions against Japanese-held atolls in the eastern Marshall Islands.

The Gilberts invasion, which opened on November 20, 1943, was the Marine Corps' first "classic" amphibious assault over a reef against a defended beach. As such, it represented the pinnacle of achievement to that time in the practice of amphibious warfare. The invasion of Tarawa was as much a test of the doctrine, training, and equipment of the Marine Corps as it was an example of the bold seizure of a heavily defended island air base.

The U.S. Navy assembled the largest bombardment force seen in the Pacific to that time: several battleships mounting 14- or 16-inch guns, cruisers with 6- and 8-inch batteries, and destroyers with 5-inch batteries for close-in work. A flotilla of aircraft carriers, each brimming with light bombers and fighters, would be on hand to soften the way and provide close air support, which was an emerging doctrine that was itself to be tested fully at Tarawa. So powerful was the bombardment force that very senior Navy officers boasted that the Marines would be needed only to go ashore to pick up the pieces.

The 2d Amphibian Tractor Battalion fielded 125 amtracs on D-day at Tarawa—75 LVT-1s that had been armored and upgunned in New Zealand, and 50 of the new LVT-2 armored amtracs that arrived directly from the United States. Tarawa marked the first real test of the amtrac as an armored assault vehicle. Note the two .50-caliber heavy machine guns on the forward bulkhead of the troop compartment and one of the two .30-caliber light machine guns affixed to the side bulkheads. *Official USMC Photo*

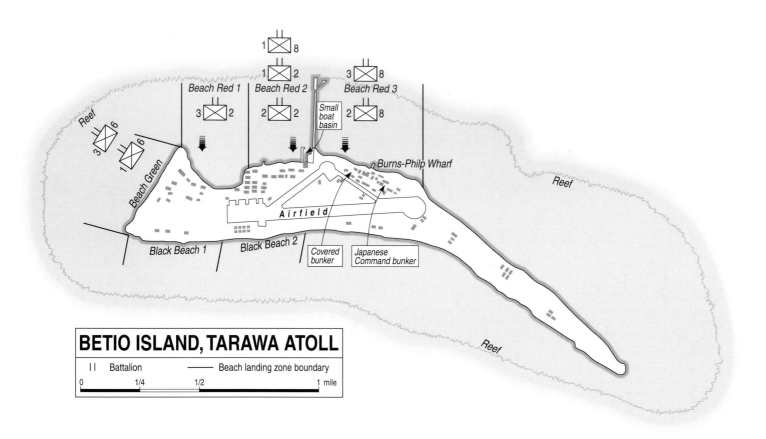

BETIO ISLAND, TARAWA ATOLL

| ǁ | Battalion | —————— | Beach landing zone boundary |

0   1/4   1/2   1 mile

In the two days before the reinforced 2d Marine Division was to land, the battleships, cruisers, destroyers, fighters, and bombers undertook the most massive bombardment any navy had ever hurled at any shore target. The tiny island of Betio, little more than two acres in size, was, it was assumed, pulverized. The five thousand–man Japanese garrison (three thousand naval infantrymen and two thousand construction and base troops) was thought to be destroyed.

The three battalions of the 2d Marines; 2/8; a twelve-gun 75mm pack-howitzer battalion (1/10); a company of Sherman M4 medium tanks; the entire reinforced 2d Amphibious Tractor Battalion; engineers; pioneers; and several special weapons companies armed with 37mm and 75mm antitank guns—about six thousand men in all—were awakened aboard their transports at 0300 on November 20 and launched into a flurry of activity.

It was not yet light as the first landing boats and Marine-filled amtracs swept out of their holding circles and headed toward the unseen beaches. A destroyer raced toward the shore, spewing 5-inch shells as fast as her gunners could reload.

Dawn brought the first great pillars of smoke to the view of the assault companies. Betio was barely four feet above sea level, only ten feet at its highest point. It would not be seen until the landing boats and amtracs had passed through the first reef.

Behind the four infantry assault battalions and their supports, two infantry-reserve battalions (1/2 and 3/8) filed into their landing boats. None of these two thousand Marines

Light, shallow-draft Higgins boats carried the bulk of the assault waves and follow-on units to Betio, but none could get over the reef, leaving thousands of Marines to wade ashore. The tiny objective lies beneath the roiling smoke ahead. *Official USMC Photo*

expected to fight. In fact, 3/8 had been assigned to comb the rubble created by the naval bombardment in search of useful booty and dead bodies to be buried.

Closer to shore, now visible as the minute hand crept toward H-hour and the first wave of amtracs inched across Tarawa Lagoon, Marines in the amtracs could see that the giant battleship shells that were still being fired across Betio were exploding harmlessly over water on the far side. The bravado of the Navy, which included standing close inshore, had rendered most of the noisy two-day bombardment ineffective. Had the battleships and cruisers stood farther out and lofted their shells at higher angles of trajectory, there would have been ample destruction. Hardly any large shells had detonated on the island.

Minutes before the first assault waves were due to arrive, two landing boats swept in toward the head of the 500-yard-long pier that ran from the reef surrounding Betio to a point about midway along the island's northern beach. In one boat was the 2d Marines' Scout-and-Sniper Platoon. In the other was a platoon of assault engineers. Their job was to clear Japanese

There are at least seventeen wrecked or stalled amtracs visible in this reconnaissance photo of Beach Red-1. Nearly all of 3/2 and refugees from fire on adjacent Red-2 were forced by intense fire to close up to the left third of the beach. *Official USN Photo*

machine gunners from the area, for the pier-head was a perfect place from which to sweep passing amtracs and boats with deadly fire. Several Japanese were found, several TNT charges were set, and then the scouts and engineers jumped back into their boats to follow the lead waves to the beach.

Meanwhile, the first troop-laden tractors had swept to within machine-gun range, and the defenders opened fire, killing or severely wounding many amtrac drivers, and causing infantry squads and platoons to become unglued. Many other amtrac drivers swerved from the fire lanes and sought less-contested routes, though doing so destroyed unit integrity.

The worst surprise of all came when the lead amtracs collided with the reef 500

While the sea wall edging the invasion beaches was a refuge for many Marines on D-day and D+1, it was often the site of fierce battles for possession of pillboxes the Japanese built directly into the wall. Seen here, at the far left, is a firing embrasure just above ground level; a second embrasure is two sections to the right. *Official USMC Photo*

A scene of utter horror and chaos greeted most of the troops arriving on Red-3 on D-day and D+1. Here, Marines keep their heads below the level of the sea wall as they strip ammunition and other useful items from the otherwise unattended corpses of their comrades. *Official USMC Photo*

yards from shore. This reef was a known quantity, but it was felt there would be enough water over it to float the assault boats of the following waves. The amtracs crossed the reef high and dry, but there was not enough water to float even empty landing craft.

Navy fighter pilots attempted to suppress the Japanese gunners who were by then pouring an increasing volume of fire into the oncoming amtracs, but there was time for only one pass. Then the first Marine ground troops drove ashore.

Three reinforced Marine infantry battalions landed across three beaches on Betio's northern shore. At no point on any of those beaches was it safe for the troops to disembark. Here and there, brave amtrac drivers drove inland to their objectives, but nearly all of the fifty-plus vehicles in the first wave stopped at the 3-foot-high sea wall; most could not climb over the wall, and where there were breaks, the amtracs were disabled by gunfire. The next two assault waves—seventy-five more amtracs, all there were left in the 2d Marine Division—hit the beach right on time.

As Marine infantrymen immediately vaulted the sides of their amtracs, most were exposed to withering gunfire. Many troop leaders were killed or wounded. Immediately, nearly all the survivors hunkered down behind the sea wall—anxious, confused, leaderless. One of the assault companies of 2/2, which landed on the center beach—Red-2— lost five of its six officers within minutes, and one of its platoons was driven hundreds of yards off course, landing at the extreme western tip of the island, where it joined 3/2 on Beach Red-1. The left battalion, 2/8, landed on Beach Red-3 under just slightly less fire and in reasonable organizational condition, but heavy fire from several bunkers right off the beach held these Marines to zero gains.

Fewer than 1,200 Marines—all infantrymen or engineers—landed in the first three waves. Reinforcements and heavier weapons were desperately needed. They were on the way—three fresh infantry companies, 81mm mortars, machine guns, and hundreds of special troops. But there was no way to tell them that their shallow-draft boats could not breast the reef.

When the first of the landing craft slammed into the reef, Navy boat crews dutifully dropped the steel bow ramps, the only protection the Marines had had against thousands of bullets that were converging on the dozen or so boats. Those who survived the sheets of fire struggled across the belt of coral that had stopped the boats and jumped off into water that was barely waist deep.

There was absolutely no protection for the wading men of 3/2 off Red-1, but most of the men of 2/2 and 2/8 were able to angle toward the pier—which acted as a barrier against most gunfire—and continue on to the beach. There is no way to know how many Marines died in those first shocking minutes after the boats hit the reef.

Here and there, amtracs that had pulled off the beach after delivering the first waves of troops picked up the wounded and carried them to rescue boats beyond the reef.

Other amtrackers stopped to pick up the uninjured living who were ducking fire on the far side of the reef, and these they carried to the sea wall, where hundreds of their comrades had sought cover. Riding an amtrac to the beach was not a free pass, however; dozens more Marines died, and several more amtracs were disabled as they slammed into the incredible volume of the fire the defenders pumped out.

Here and there, small groups of Marines, some led by officers and NCOs, but many led by brave privates and privates first class, took control of tiny patches of ground. Few and far between were the organized squads and platoons that found safe passage to craters as many as ten or fifteen yards south of the sea wall. Most Marines simply huddled behind the sea wall.

This landing of the first three reinforced Marine battalions was, for all the heroic exhibitions of very brave men, an unrelieved disaster. Almost as a reflex to adversity, well within the limits of the prudent plan that guided them, the leaders closest to the scene arranged for the reserve battalion to be landed. This unit, 1/2, was sent to the reef by boat. There it rendezvoused with fewer than a dozen amtracs, all that could be gathered at short notice from the shattered 2d Amphibian Tractor Battalion. Several platoons were quickly broken down into squad elements, filled out with a few engineers and machine gunners, and transferred from the boats to the amtracs. Then the boats, which were by then receiving heavy fire, withdrew to a safer distance while the miniassault headed for Red-2 to bolster the immobile 2/2.

There were casualties inflicted upon these reinforcements, but they landed and re-formed, too weak as yet to have an impact upon the battle but relatively unshaken and, therefore,

Many Marines who did make it across the sea wall on D-day and D+1 had to be hauled back by comrades after being shot. *Official USMC Photo*

of use far greater than the larger knots of men who lay disorganized and disheartened at their feet. The first serious gains were made in a quick series of jabs that led these men and some members of 2/2 to the edge of the Japanese runway that had first marked Betio as a worthwhile objective.

As the first elements of 1/2 struggled across the sea wall, other platoons of the battalion dribbled ashore. Where possible, these newcomers also crossed the sea wall, leading still more Marines from 2/2 southward. As the first series of gains were made, Colonel David Shoup, the commander of the 2d Marines—the man in charge of the assault—landed with his staff and one vitally needed radio, the first to survive the trip to Red-2.

To the right and left, on Beaches Red-1 and Red-3, elements of 3/2 and 2/8 achieved minor gains. Red-1 was isolated from Red-2 by a formidable Japanese strongpoint, and there were not enough Marines on either beach to reduce the strongpoint or to link up. On Red-3, 2/8 was in physical contact with the troops on Red-2, but it also faced an extremely formidable defensive network right at the edge of the sea wall. Gains on Red-3 were measured in feet.

Each of the dwindling number of amtracs that reached Red-2 brought in about a dozen fresh Marines. Of each dozen, an

Despite the known hazards, Marines kept stepping up to the plate. These machine gunners on Red-3 kneel beside—and apparently ignore the fate of—a dead Marine as they await a lull in the fire so they can try their luck, too. *Official USMC Photo*

average of six quickly became casualties or sought cover behind the sea wall. But the remaining six climbed warily over the sea wall and ran, rolled, and crawled across the fine coral sand and mixed debris to holes or the wrecks of buildings and bunkers that could be defended and used as waystations for additional small advances southward.

As soon as Colonel Shoup could make an assessment of the awful situation on the beach, he asked that 3/8 be landed to support 2/8 on Red-3. The fresh battalion was mounted in about a dozen personnel boats and large tank lighters, but no one told its officers about the reef barrier, and no one sent amtracs to meet it. As with the follow-up companies of the lead battalions, the unsuspecting troops of 3/8 were shocked to the soles of their feet when their boats slammed into the reef.

Ramps were dropped and Marines dutifully stepped into the withering Japanese gunfire. Dozens of Marines died in the boats and atop the reef. Hundreds, however, side-stepped to the pier, an angling walk of several hundred yards for many of them. Hundreds of weapons, packs, helmets, radios, and mortar rounds were dropped into the lagoon, the better to gain survival in the waist-deep water.

Several hundred members of 3/8 stopped at the pierhead to catch a collective breath. Hundreds more waded to the beach on one side or another of the pier. Of these, hundreds hunkered down behind the sea wall. And of those few who entered the fight beside the bloodied companies of 2/8, only a few dozen were in gaggles that could be called organized. The first reinforcements from 3/8 to reach Red-3 helped take a little ground, but they had no major impact.

Once inland, troops who breasted the sea wall were often held to modest gains when they ran directly up against defenses they might have been unable to see. This light machine gun team is probably dueling with a Japanese position only a few yards away. *Official USMC Photo*

There was only one uncommitted infantry battalion remaining under the operational control of the 2d Marine Division, 1/8. The 6th Marines was steaming in circles near Betio, but it was the Force Reserve, as likely to be sent to support the Army's bid for Makin Atoll, well to the north of Tarawa, as to Betio. Until the 6th Marines could be released by the force commander, the 2d Marine Division would have to exercise extreme caution in the commitment of its last meaningful asset.

Of the three beaches, Red-1 was the most isolated. The bulk of the 3/2 was probing outward from a small but secure perimeter it had established early around the northwestern tip of the island. It did not seem worthwhile to reinforce Red-1 because the situation was fairly stable and because there was nowhere to go even if the objective were taken.

The surviving portions of 1/2, 2/2, and the regimental headquarters were on Red-2, the center beach. These units had a chance to take ground to the south, so Red-2 seemed a likely place to land 1/8. So did Red-3. The initial assault battalion there, 2/8, was fairly well organized and, though it was meeting fierce opposition, its prospects were fairly bright. One factor favoring a landing by 1/8 on Red-3 was that the 8th Marines headquarters could then control all three of its own infantry battalions in a definable area. Whether for this or better reasons, it was decided to land the 1/8 on Red-3, behind 2/8 and 3/8. But it was not to be. Communications difficulties and an error by an aerial observer kept 1/8 circling offshore all night.

D-day at Betio ended with more than nine thousand Marines committed to the fight. Hundreds had died or been gravely injured just trying to get to the tiny rim of beach. Four 75mm pack howitzers from 1/10 had been landed, as had two 75mm halftracks and four medium tanks. There also were a few 37mm antitank guns ashore. No objectives worth mentioning had been secured.

Most of the men who had survived the trip to the beaches were demoralized, and nearly all of them were huddled behind the sea wall or under cover in shell and bomb craters. For the most part they were unable to organize themselves into combat units and advance.

Ammunition, food, water, and medical supplies were not getting to the beaches, though brave sailors and Marines risked life and limb to run boatloads of goods to the pierhead, which was as close as they could get. There were not nearly enough amtracs left to evacuate the wounded, bring in fresh troops, land artillery, and carry supplies from the pierhead to the beaches. Yet all of these things were done by the incredibly brave amtrackers.

It was finally learned at the 2d Marine Division command post (aboard the battleship *Maryland*) in the wee hours of D+1—November 21—that 1/8 had not yet landed on Red-3. Given this opportunity to rethink his earlier decision, the division commander ordered the fresh battalion to Red-2, the center beach. It was by then clear that the best chance of ultimate success resided there. Before it was decided to land 1/8,

U.S. Navy carrier aircraft had complete air supremacy over Betio, but there weren't many targets they could safely strafe or bomb. Here, two Grumman F6F Hellcat fighter-bombers attack targets beyond the left flank of Red-3. *Official USMC Photo*

Getting ashore was hellish. No matter where on the reef they were dropped, Marines who waded ashore tended to angle toward the relative safety of the pier that ran 500 yards from the reef to the boundary of Red-2 and Red-3. Seen in this reconnaissance photo, in addition to wading troops, are a stalled amtrac and a wrecked Japanese landing barge. *Official USN Photo*

This 37mm crew hauled its gun and ammunition all the way from the pier to the beach by hand. Several brave 37mm crews drove their jeep-attached guns right down the fire-swept pier itself to get into the fight against Japanese pillboxes and bunkers. *Official USMC Photo*

however, the proposition that all the shattered battalions already on Betio be evacuated was debated—and rejected.

For unknown reasons, 1/8 was not informed of the deadly problem at the reef. Nor were amtracs collected to carry the fresh troops in. Well after sunrise, in plain view of thousands of horrified Marines and pleased Japanese, the boats bearing 1/8 slammed into the reef along several hundred yards of frontage 500 yards from Red-2. The boat crews dutifully dropped their ramps, and the dutiful Marines jumped into the water and walked upright across the exposed reef before wading into the waist-deep lagoon. Japanese machine gunners shot 1/8 to ribbons.

The survivors of the battalion (Company A, for example, mustered fewer than seventy effectives on the beach, down from two hundred) formed up on the right flank of Red-2 and, with bits and parts of other units, swung over to the attack. They ground slowly into the clustered bunkers and pillboxes that barred the way to Red-1 and a linkup with isolated 3/2. This single attack by the shattered battalion ranks with the bravest of undertakings in all the annals of all the wars recorded by man—yet few actions have gone so long unsung.

Even as 1/8 was cut to ribbons, what remained of 3/2 attacked southward from its enclave on Red-1. Support was provided by several destroyers standing offshore and two medium tanks, of which only one had a 75mm main gun in working order. In hours of bitter fighting, the battalion reached the southern shore. By clearing the western beach—Beach Green—the attack provided a safe access to Betio.

As 3/2 took ground south of Red-1, elements 1/2 and 2/2 reached the southern beach opposite Red-2. Opposition on the ground between these beaches did not cease, and both flanks remained dangerously exposed, but small groups of Marines were fed southward to secure the large stretches of open ground that provided haven for dozens and perhaps hundreds of Japanese snipers.

There were also modest gains on Red-3 during D+1. A great deal of time and effort went into organizing 2/8's stable line and reorganizing 3/8 from the hundreds of D-day dropouts who reported for duty on D+1. Mostly, the two battalions on Red-3 consolidated

their meager gains and edged closer to several formidable strongpoints the Japanese were doggedly manning within spitting distance of the sea wall. Gains were modest on Red-3 this day, but plenty of Japanese died, and some key ground was taken.

The 6th Marines was released to the 2d Marine Division's operational control late in the morning. It was decided to land 1/6 on Beach Green and send it into the attack down the island's long axis. Meanwhile, 2/6 was to land on the adjacent island, Bairiki, to cut the Japanese line of retreat and provide security for 2/10's dozen 75mm pack howitzers. Once on Bairiki, the howitzer and infantry battalions would have the Japanese on Betio boxed in.

At 1706 hours, November 21, Colonel Shoup was asked by the division command post to file a situation report. His reply was: "Casualties, many; percentage dead not known. Combat Efficiency: We are winning."

It turned out that 1/6 could not be landed on Beach Green until very late on D+1. The division commander therefore decided to delay the battalion's ground attack until daylight.

November 22, 1943—D+2—was the best day the 2d Marine Division had at Tarawa; it was the day the Japanese lost their grip. Mounting its assault down the long axis of the tiny island, the fully intact 1/6 met up with parts of the other units that had struggled inland from

Going the other way, the wounded were taken out by any means at hand. These rescuers are heading toward the reef, where landing craft commandeered for the purpose will run the wounded out to transports designated as hospital ships. The dead were left ashore, to be buried in ad hoc cemeteries. *Official USMC Photo*

Red-2 is at the top of this photograph. The wide-open area in the center is an airfield taxiway (note three log aircraft revetments), and the wide-open area below that is the main runway. To get from Red-2 to the southern beach, hundreds of Marines braved intense fire across both open areas. The distance from beach to beach was 330 yards, the runway was packed coral, and the only waystations were a few water-filled shell craters. *Official USMC Photo*

Red-1 and Red-2 on D-day and D+1. Behind 1/6's steady advance, growing portions of the 1/2 and 2/2 scoured the area between the northern and southern beaches, eradicating Japanese snipers wherever they could be located. At the boundary of Red-1 and Red-2, facing the intensely defended beach-boundary strongpoint, 1/8 was joined by 3/2, and both units pushed slowly into the built-up area. In time, the two weary battalions linked up and pressed upon the strongpoint from three sides.

The two battalions on Red-3 also made significant gains on D+2. The key to the Japanese defense was a huge covered bunker, barely 10 yards south of the sea wall. (If ten yards seems a piddling distance, consider that these two battalions had been crammed into a perimeter seventy-five yards wide by twenty yards at its deepest point for two full days.) D+1 had seen the destruction of several outlying pillboxes and bunkers, but the key to the

It seemed that if just one brave Marine showed the way, dozens and scores followed. Here, a light machine gun squad crosses the sea wall to follow comrades into the teeth of battle. *Official USMC Photo*

Few dead Japanese were seen in the open during the battle. Here, the crew of a stanchion-mounted 13mm antiaircraft machine gun lies dead at its post. The 13mm machine guns were deadly against amtracs and human flesh.
Official USMC Photo

The big covered bunker that was the key to Red-3 finally fell to direct assault on D+2. The organizer and leader of the assault, First Lieutenant Alexander Bonnyman, who was killed as he defended the first foothold atop the bunker, was awarded a Medal of Honor. *Official USMC Photo*

The island command bunker was struck—but not penetrated—by at least two 16-inch shells during the preinvasion bombardment. It took a direct assault on D+2 by Marine infantryman, an M4 tank, and a flamethrower to reduce the largest structure on Betio. *Official USMC Photo*

main bunker was finally turned by a tiny group of engineers and pioneers. A flamethrower fired down a ventilator shaft forced all the Japanese to evacuate the structure. They ran directly into the fire of the last medium tank on Red-3, and nearly a hundred were killed in the open, the most Japanese anyone on Red-3 saw at one time during the entire battle.

The fall of the covered bunker allowed 2/8 and 3/8 to re-form into battalion tactical units. While most of 3/8 cleared ground south of the beach, 2/8 attacked eastward and soon reduced a second huge concrete bunker, the island command post. As soon as the Japanese command bunker fell, 2/8 dug in and sent platoons and squads to the rear to pry out the plague of snipers it had left in its wake.

All through D+2, as the 2d and 8th Marines took ground along the beaches, 1/6 advanced steadily up Betio's long axis against minor opposition. There were a few big fights at several large strongpoints, but casualties were light and gains were substantial. Finally, 1/6 stopped in line with 2/8's farthest advance and dug in for the night. By then, 3/6 had been landed on Beach Green and had come up to support the advance.

The Japanese lost it that night. Although the ultimate outcome of the battle for Betio had passed beyond doubt, grave harm might have been inflicted on the attackers if the defenders had fought the continuing advance from the narrow, relatively untouched eastern tail of the island. But five hundred able-bodied Japanese assaulted dug-in 1/6 during the night. Massed infantry weapons combined with supporting fires from several destroyers offshore and 2/10's pack howitzers on Bairiki doomed the Japanese assault at its outset. The fight was tough, and casualties among the Marine defenders were heavy, but nearly all the Japanese left on Betio at sunset were dead by sunrise.

Betio was declared secure at 1305 hours, November 23, 1943, following a relatively bloodless sweep of the eastern tail of the island by 3/6. Just before this fresh battalion attained its goal, the last organized resistance facing the 3/2 and 1/8 was overcome at the beach-boundary strongpoint. Snipers, many of them badly wounded men in blasted buildings all across Betio, held out for days, taking a toll of combat Marines and the technicians who followed them closely to rehabilitate and expand Betio's airfield.

In just seventy-six hours, almost to the minute, all but 13 Japanese servicemen and all but 134 Korean and Okinawan laborers who had manned Betio were dead. So were more than six hundred U.S. Marines and sailors.

Tarawa was a victory—of that there is no doubt. In the best sense, it was a stunning defeat of unremitting adversity by brave men—a victory at its fullest.

Old Glory was raised on a coconut palm trunk shortly after Betio was declared secure on D+3, November 23, 1943. *Official USMC Photo*

CHAPTER 11

THE MARSHALL ISLANDS

JANUARY 31–MARCH 2, 1944

THE INVASION OF KWAJALEIN ATOLL IN THE JAPANESE-MANDATED MARSHALL Islands was a smash-and-grab operation very much like the November 1943 assault on Tarawa, only easier. After Tarawa and Makin the next logical step toward the goal of mutually supporting airfields across the central Pacific was the Marshall Islands, where ready-made airfields awaited. In addition to a superb fleet anchorage off Kwajalein Island, Kwajalein Atoll—540 miles northwest of Tarawa—had special significance for Marines who recalled that the Japanese land-based bombers that had smashed Wake Island at the start of the Pacific War had operated from Roi Airdrome, also in Kwajalein Atoll.

Following months of staff work, the invasion was set for January 29, 1944. The new 4th Marine Division was to assault Roi and Roi's sandspit-connected twin, Namur; an Army division was to assault Kwajalein Island; and an Army regiment was to seize the largely undefended fleet anchorage in Majuro Atoll. Two main improvements on the Tarawa plan that were to be employed at Kwajalein were longer, harder-hitting naval and air bombardments, and the emplacement of artillery on outlying islands ahead of the main show against Kwajalein, Roi, and Namur. Several neat innovations included the conversion of a flotilla of LCIs—LCI(G)s— to fire 4.5-inch rockets and the inaugural use of amtracs rigged out as armored amphibious tanks—LVT(A)s—each carrying a 37mm gun and bristling with five machine guns.

In December 1943, Army Air Forces bombers based on fields in the Gilbert Islands, U.S. Navy carrier aircraft, and U.S. Navy surface bombardment forces began the systematic interdiction of bases in the Marshalls—both the projected targets of amphibious assaults, and bases from which the targets might be supported, including Wake Island.

Marine-laden amtracs hover off Roi as control boats wrestle them into position. The final prelanding naval fires and air attacks are being mounted. *Official USMC Photo*

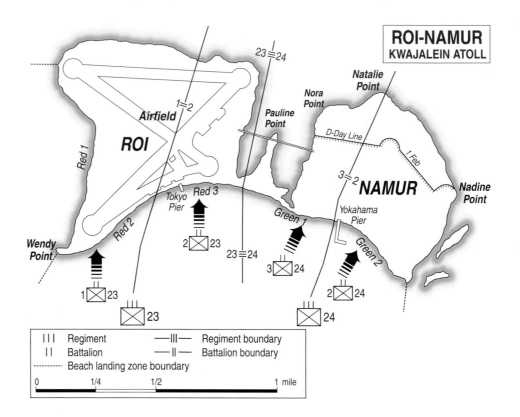

Roi and Namur were thought to be defended by an even greater force than the one that had so bloodily defended Betio, but they were not. Only eighteen hundred to twenty-six hundred combat troops were deployed on the islands, and they manned fewer and less-well-emplaced defense positions.

Marines drop over the side of an LVT-2 and seek cover on Roi's beach.
Official USMC Photo

Beginning at dawn on January 31, the 25th Marines, carried by the 10th Amphibian Tractor Battalion and bolstered by Company A, 1st Armored Amphibian Tractor Battalion, as well as divisional combat support units, assaulted five small islands from which batteries of the 14th Marines would outflank the defenses on Roi and Namur. High winds and heavy seas delayed the assault, but the lead waves carried on with LCI(G)s and LVT(A)s out ahead to deliver final suppressive fires. Carrier fighters also suppressed the defenses until the last possible moment.

At 0952, Company B, 1/25, was the first American unit to land on former Japanese territory, Ennuebing Island. Thereafter, other elements of 1/25 swept over Mellu Island. Thirty Japanese corpses were eventually unearthed, and five prisoners were taken. Shortly, 3/14 landed its 75mm pack howitzers on Ennuebing from LVTs, and 4/14 landed from landing craft on Mellu. Two more artillery outposts were secured by 2/25 during the afternoon, and 1/14 and 2/14 were quickly landed. A fifth outlying island was secured late in the day by 3/25 despite terrible weather-related problems, and an ad hoc gunfire force of five 75mm halftracks, seventeen 37mm guns, four 81mm mortars, nine 60mm mortars, and sixty-one machine guns was set up on the side of the island facing Namur, which was only 400 yards away. The seizure of all five D-day objectives came at the cost of just one Marine wounded by a friendly strafer.

AS AMTRACS COMPLETED THE WORK OF CARRYING THE 25TH AND 14th Marines ashore, they were to climb aboard LSTs for a night refueling. The idea was to use the LSTs to transfer invasion troops from the transports and carry them close to the shore in the morning, then launch them in orderly groups of amtracs. But the D-day operations took longer to complete than was foreseen, so most 10th Amphibian Tractor Battalion amtracs did not get to the LST area until dusk or later. On the one hand, the amtrac crews couldn't find their assigned LSTs, and on the other hand, many picky LST commanders refused to take aboard or refuel amtracs that hadn't been assigned to their ships. The result was chaos and a lot of fuel-starved amtracs that were supposed to lift the 24th Marines to Namur. On top of that, it was extremely difficult and time-consuming to transfer amtracs from an LST's weather deck to the tank deck—which is what most of the 4th Amphibian Tractor Battalion needed to do to get the 23d Marines ashore on Roi.

This Marine 37mm gun crew has moved to the edge of Roi Airdrome to help support the drive by Marine infantry across the vast open space. The G4M medium bomber to the side was destroyed long before any Marines touched down on Roi. *Official USMC Photo*

Advancing across Roi Airdrome was daunting. The flat, open ground was lightly defended, but there was nowhere to hide from Japanese troops emplaced around the periphery.
Official USMC Photo

The schedule suffered. The bombardment of both islands began on time, but the landing operation lost ground. Altogether, twenty-four 10th Amtrac Battalion LVTs couldn't even be located. The 23d Marines conquered its woes by 1100, but the 24th didn't. Then some extra tractors were found, but there were not enough in total for both assault battalions of the 24th Marines—which finally lined up, each at two-thirds of its planned assault strength. And so forth; stuff just kept happening.

The 23d Marines was ready to go at 1100, but the order to land was withheld until 1112, to give the 24th Marines time to catch up. Despite a rain squall that threatened to break up last-minute air attacks, carrier bombers hovering beyond the maximum ordinate of artillery, ships' fire, and rockets were able to deliver pinpoint attacks down to almost the last minute before the first wave of amtracs ground up onto both islands.

Fighting in Kwajalein Atoll produced few prisoners, so the capture of this Japanese soldier on Roi naturally drew a lot of onlookers. *Official USMC Photo*

ROI WAS ALMOST HARDER TO REACH THAN IT WAS TO SECURE. FOUR COMPANIES OF 1/23 and 2/23 landed abreast, with LVT(A)s in the vanguard. The LVT(A)s on the left hit the beach at 1133, and two companies of 1/23 were ashore by 1158. Resistance was negligible in the 1/23 zone, and the first phase line was taken in good order. Medium tanks and

light flame tanks arrived ashore as 1/23 advanced on the airfield.

The action in the 2/23 zone was a little different. The LVT(A)s assigned to 2/23 stopped short to fire at supposed defenses, then the troop-carrying amtracs ran past them to the beach. The infantry landed in some disarray due to alignment problems, but the Japanese were dazed by the heavy bombardment and nearly passive.

Roi was not defended in nearly the strength the planners had been led to believe. There were few formal defensive emplacements. Marine infantrymen were typically cautious, but tanks and armored amtracs advanced without much support, some would say recklessly. This drew the infantry—understandably cautious but dutiful in a pinch—northward in a running effort to provide support for the tanks. The headlong attack was a success even as it drove higher-level officers to distraction because they lost control of their organizations and their plans were rendered obsolete. It took until 1445 to get the tanks back under regimental control, and the infantry followed suit.

These are quibbles. The troops acted bravely and did what Marines are supposed to do if they see the opportunity—which is *seize* the opportunity.

At 1530, the lead battalions opened simultaneous, coordinated advances north along either shoreline. Aided by 75mm halftracks, 2/23 overcame organized resistance in its zone by 1600. On the left, 1/23 was a little slower getting started, but organized resistance in its zone collapsed by 1645. By 1800, the assault battalions were in complete control of Roi's entire shoreline, and 3/23 was at work prying a few defiant defenders from the interior as well as establishing a line to seal Roi from Namur by way of the sandspit that connected the islands.

THE 24TH MARINES HAD PROBLEMS IN SPADES WITH ITS QUOTA OF TROOP-CARRYING amtracs, but four assault companies were launched toward the beach in decent order. The plan was for LVT(A)s to land ahead of the troops and clear routes off the beaches. But the LVT(A)s ran afoul of antitank ditches, trenches, and debris; they could not advance as planned. Initially, they could only support the infantry by fire.

The leading infantry waves became misaligned as they neared the beach because landmarks that were supposed to guide the landing had either been pulverized by the bombardment or were invisible beneath a pall of smoke and dust. The two lead companies of 2/24, on the right beach, became intermingled, but the troops formed into ad hoc assault teams where necessary and racked up some quick advances. The rest of 2/24 landed as amtracs became available, and these troops were fed into a gap that quickly developed in

The battle to take Roi was fierce, but it was relatively light and produced considerably fewer casualties than anticipated. Nevertheless, Marines died and were buried there.
Official USMC Photo

Everything about Namur was more difficult than Roi. Misaligned and misdirected landings jumbled the combat units, Japanese fire was heavier at the outset, a deep antitank ditch stymied armor support, rearranged landmarks caused confusion, and extensive rubble gave the Japanese more defensive options. *Official USMC Photos*

the battalion front line. The deepest penetration in the 2/24 zone was 175 yards, but resistance stiffened appreciably at that point and the troops were pinned down in thick brush.

On the regimental left, 3/24's two lead companies came ashore in better order than the adjacent 2/24 units, and they advanced quickly to the phase line halfway across Namur. The fighting on Namur was trickier than on Roi because Roi was mostly hard-topped runway and taxiways, while Namur was covered with thick growth in which the Japanese could easily hide and dig in. Hard-to-find emplacements were bypassed by the lead units, left to be reduced by the regimental reserve, 1/24.

Only three of five light tanks assigned to support 3/24 landed at 1300. Two bogged down in soft sand, and the third ran into a shell crater. All three were towed free after the two remaining light tanks landed.

One company of 3/24 advanced 150 yards beyond the phase line, but it withdrew when the battalion reorganized.

At 1305, a demolitions team in the 2/24 zone attacked a large concrete bunker with satchel charges and thus set off a huge uncharted torpedo dump. The immense blast leveled the bunker, set off two nearby ammunition dumps, and took down a good deal of the growth and other buildings around it. The multiple blasts killed twenty 2/24 Marines and injured more than a hundred.

Shocked, dazed, and further disorganized by the blast, 2/24 was unable to step off with 3/24 at 1630 for what the commanders hoped would be a final drive to secure the island. But a herculean effort by the 2/24 officers and troops sent the battalion and an array of light and medium tanks back into the advance at 1730.

By late afternoon, elements of 2/24 had driven to within thirty-five yards of the northern shore. The battalion main body could not close on it, so this force was pulled back.

The division commander landed on Namur at 1700 and immediately asked the 24th Marines commander what he needed—which all came down to more troops. A platoon of medium tanks and 3/23 were transferred to the 24th Marines' control and ordered to cross from Roi on the sandspit.

The 3/24 battalion commander ordered the medium tanks to spearhead a new drive as soon as they reached his command post at 1830. This brought Marines to Namur's northwestern point, but low ammunition supplies obliged them to pull back to the 3/24 main body. At 1930, the regimental commander ordered all the troops on Namur to halt, consolidate, dig in, and prepare to make a final sweep at dawn. Fully two-thirds of Namur was solidly in Marine hands when the sun went down.

The Japanese mounted a few desultory attacks during the night, and a lot of Marines fired at spooky targets that were most likely imaginary. Ammunition was distributed to

This Marine light tank, a company commander's vehicle, was assaulted on Namur by Japanese infantry when it became hung up ahead of Marine lines. The Japanese killed two crewmen outright, wounded another, and mortally wounded the company commander before Marine infantry could organize a counterattack. Note that the hull above the track has been breached by an antitank round and that a dead Japanese has been run over. *Official USMC Photo*

Marines with their bayonets fixed rush through a clearing in Namur's otherwise overgrown terrain. Most of the fighting took place at close quarters in sight-impeding woods. *Official USMC Photo*

Many Japanese soldiers on Namur killed themselves rather than be taken prisoner. This suicide, like many others, has shot himself in the head by pulling the trigger with a big toe. *Official USMC Photo*

the troops, but the medium tanks could not access ammunition and fuel stored on Roi, so they pooled what they had, stripping one M4 tank in the process.

Also during the night, Japanese troops located a gap between Company I, 3/24, and Company B, 1/24. They infiltrated in force and launched a counterattack at first light. The four medium tanks and infantrymen on both sides of the gap held the attackers at bay, Marine reinforcements counterattacked, and the action ended in twenty-five minutes. Indeed, tanks and infantry used the opportunity to advance an extra 50 yards.

The attack in the 3/24 zone jumped off on schedule at 0900, and the battalion was in complete control of its objectives by 1215. The attack in the larger right zone was to be undertaken by 2/24 and most of 1/24. Tanks were late getting into position, so the attack jumped off late, at 1006. Light and medium tanks and 75mm halftracks took on a number of blockhouses, bunkers, and pillboxes, and the infantry attacked steadily in good order. Namur was completely in Marine hands by 1215, and the island was declared secure at 1418 hours, February 2, 1944. It took the U.S. Army division assigned to Kwajalein Island until February 4 to secure its larger and better-defended objective.

NEXT UP WAS A BOLD 350-MILE JUMP TO ENIWETOK ATOLL, AT THE WESTERN EDGE OF the Marshall Islands. Eniwetok was one of only a few firm targets developed from a long list of potential bases drawn up before the Marshalls invasion. The seizure of Eniwetok had been penciled in for May, but several factors contributed to an immediate landing in the wake of the Kwajalein coup de main. These were the complete vindication of the tactics of the Kwajalein operation; the ease of the operation; the location of charts of Eniwetok that would otherwise have taken months to compile; and the availability of all the troops, equipment, and ships needed for an immediate invasion.

The fleet elements were drawn from portions of the Kwajalein invasion fleet, and ground troops were mainly the reinforced independent 22d Marines and two-thirds of an Army regiment, both of which had been the Kwajalein reserve; they were all well-trained troops, ready to go.

Planning was done on the fly based on remarkably accurate ad hoc intelligence estimates. As with the use of heavier naval firepower, the landing plan was able to incorporate valuable immediate lessons from Kwajalein.

Three of Eniwetok's four main islands were targeted for amphibious assaults: Engebi and Parry by Marines, and Eniwetok by Army troops. It was estimated that three thousand fresh troops held these islands, about a third of the total on each. Engebi was the site of a newly built airfield, never used by the Japanese; it was the atoll's primary strategic objective, followed by the anchorage.

The 22d Marines had served eighteen months of garrison duty in Samoa and thus was considered well trained and cohesive to the lowest organizational levels. Its organization was a hybrid first fielded by the 2d Raider Battalion: infantry squads were divided into three four-man or four three-man fire teams. This meant that the regiment fielded an extra level of command at its lowest level—corporals and privates first class with hands-on authority that would offset the natural balkanization of infantry units on the modern battlefield.

As at Kwajalein, the decision was taken to land first on several tiny islands from which Engebi—the first target—could be interdicted by artillery fire. Thus, on February 17, 1944, the V Amphibious Corps (VAC) Reconnaissance Company went ashore on five of these islands, and the 2d Separate Pack Howitzer Battalion and an Army 105mm howitzer battalion were emplaced on two of the islands by nightfall. Also on February 17, Navy underwater demolitions teams (UDTs) made their combat debut to examine the beaches off Engebi, and that night the 4th Marine Division reconnaissance company (Company D, 4th Tank Battalion) landed by rubber boat on two more small islands off Engebi to seal the Japanese on Engebi to that island.

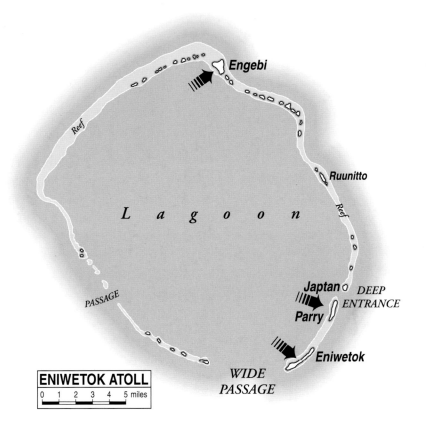

Following a massive artillery, naval gunfire, and air bombardment down to only minutes before the landing, 1/22 and 2/22 landed abreast on the southwestern side of triangular Engebi shortly after 0800 on February 19. The movement to the beaches was so smooth that the final air attacks had to be truncated. Carrying the first waves was an Army amtrac battalion that included a full company of LVT(A)s (which the GIs called amtanks). There were several minor dislocations, but the amtrac crewmen, who had landed at Kwajalein Island, knew what they were about, and organizational mixing was kept to a minimum.

Much of the ground was heavily wooded and quite tangled, but the Marine infantry seized a lodgment and relentlessly worked outward from it. Marine tanks landed in good order, just in time to help the infantry take out Japanese tanks dug in as pillboxes. By 1030 hours, 2/22, on the left, had seized the airfield and all its other objectives except the island's western and northern points.

On the right, 1/22 ran into tangled underbrush that was more heavily defended than the hard-topped airfield. Progress was slower and less cohesive. When a gap in the battalion front developed, a company of 3/22 advanced to fill it. The fighting here was especially difficult, but in the meantime one of 1/22's companies, aided by a pair of Army 105mm self-propelled assault

The 22d Marines, riding ashore in Army amtracs and supported by Army LVT(A)s, took part in all three assaults in Eniwetok Atoll. *Official USMC Photo*

Marines, formed into a skirmish line with bayonets fixed, advance cautiously through dense growth in Eniwetok Atoll. *Official USMC Photo*

guns, overcame the defensive key point in the battalion zone, a cluster of concrete pillboxes on the southern point.

As the heavy fighting in the 1/22 zone gobbled up the regimental reserves, 2/22 took the last defensive positions on its part of the island by 1322. The ground commander declared the island secure at 1450, and at 1456 hours 1/22 overcame the last defensive sector in its zone. Almost immediately, 3/22 and the 2d Separate Tank Company were ordered to reembark to serve as the reserves for landings the next day on Eniwetok Island by Army troops.

EARLY DURING THE ASSAULT AGAINST Eniwetok Island, the Army commander realized that he could not easily take the island with only two infantry battalions. Therefore, 3/22 was sent ashore midway through D-day, February 19, and assigned to sweep half of the southwestern third of the island beside one of the Army battalions. An afternoon attack meant to secure the southwestern part of the island went awry because, depending on who tells it, the Army battalion lagged or the Marine battalion advanced too quickly. Both units advanced after sunset with the aid of artillery illumination, and they lost contact again as they moved ahead at different rates. The Marines reached the tip of the island, assured by their Army counterparts that the battalions were in contact in the center. This proved to be wrong; the Japanese infiltrated the long breach and counterattacked at dawn. Nonetheless, following several heart-stopping assaults by the cornered Japanese, the Americans prevailed. It took almost all of February 20 to scour southwestern Eniwetok, and it took yet another day for the second Army battalion to secure the northeastern half of the island.

TAKING PARRY ISLAND TURNED OUT TO BE QUITE MESSY. THE ARMY AMTRACS WERE facing their fourth amphibious assault since February 1, and it showed; a lot of the Army's equipment was worn or even sidelined, and the troops were physically and emotionally exhausted. The 22d Marines was having problems, too. Its battalions had suffered losses on Engebi and Eniwetok that could not be replaced, only rejiggered, and there were even looming ammunition shortages that had to be factored into the Parry plan. The troops also needed M1 rifles and BARs that many had replaced ahead of the battles with lighter carbines that simply did not have the offensive lethality they learned they needed.

Despite ammunition rationing, the Parry landings, on February 22, pulled down almost too much artillery and naval gunfire support. The invasion beaches on the northwestern coast were so obscured by dust and smoke that many elements of 1/22 and 2/22

Japanese soldiers lay dead outside hard-to-see prepared positions in Eniwetok Atoll. It is difficult to determine if they died where they lay or were pulled out of underground positions by Marines who later mopped up the area.
Official USMC Photo

Fire support while taking Engebi was so intense that ammunition had to be rationed by the time Parry was invaded. The empty cartons strewn around this 60mm mortar position attest to the heavy usage. *Official USMC Photo*

The devastation on all three objectives in Eniwetok Atoll was boggling. Here, a skirmish line of Marines with bayonets fixed sweeps through what must have been fairly dense stands of trees. *Official USMC Photo*

didn't know they had been mislanded and intermingled until well into the action—so much so that gunfire support was mistakenly called on top of friendlies who believed they were someplace else.

Tangled undergrowth and trees, not to mention Japanese troops motivated to fight unto death, made Parry a hell on earth throughout D-day. The plan for postlanding operations was complicated, especially for troops and troop leaders who were emotionally wrung out. After 2/22 had crossed the island, it was to go into regimental reserve. The initial reserve, 3/22, was then to go into the attack down the long north-south axis of the island to the right of 1/22, which had come ashore on 2/22's right and which was to wheel 90 degrees and dress on 3/22's line.

The left battalion, 2/22, took all its objectives by 1400, and 1/22 managed to secure a lot of ground despite heavy casualties. The Japanese bungled their best chance to halt the American advance by withholding their three tanks until American tanks had reached the 1/22 front. A Japanese counterattack employing all three tanks was bloodily repulsed. Remarkably, falling into the vacuum created by the immolation of the Japanese main force, 1/22 secured its entire zone, made the requisite 90-degree pivot, and stood ready to advance down Parry's long axis beside 3/22 at 1330 hours.

Medium tanks made all the difference, as they had wherever they had been landed so far in the central Pacific. By sunset, the regimental front stood 450 yards from the Parry's southern tip, which is to say Marines had secured more than two thousand yards during the day. The attack was halted at sunset to avoid

accidental intramural fighting in the dark, and even though Japanese troops were still out ahead, the island was declared secure.

Snipers engaged the Marines during the night, but casualties were light. The offensive resumed at dawn on February 23, the last defenses were overwhelmed by 0900, and one of the Army battalions, held in reserve, turned to scouring the island for stragglers. The 10th Defense Battalion, which had stood up five ad hoc infantry companies as a force reserve for Parry, remained behind, as did the Army battalions, when the exhausted 22d Marines sailed from Eniwetok on February 25.

THE MARSHALLS CAMPAIGN, WHICH ENGULFED YET MORE ATOLLS OVER SEVERAL MONTHS, painted two bold strokes across the first Japanese mandate to fall into Allied hands. As far as the American Pacific Theater command was concerned, U.S. forces had breached the outer skin of the Empire of Japan and, as such, stood on line to breach a few vital organs.

With two or three assault landings under his belt in only a week's time, this young Marine savors a cup of hot coffee and must be thinking about a shower and sleep, not necessarily in that order.
Official USMC Photo

CHAPTER 12

SAIPAN

JUNE 15–JULY 9, 1944

So far, the Central Pacific drive had been a complete vindication of strategic pronouncements and planning going back to 1913. True, the nature of advancing base seizures had shifted in the main from the consideration of surface fleets to the consideration of air power, but the execution had been nearly picture perfect as based on the vision of Marine Major Pete Ellis and like-minded officers.

Now the tempo was to hit overdrive, for a new paradigm was about to emerge. If a string of advancing fleet bases looked old-fashioned and clunky in just 1942, a string of advancing bases tied to the range of land-based fighters looked even more clunky by the spring of 1944. This was because the Army Air Forces had in its hands the means to strike the Japanese heartland itself from as far away as the Mariana Islands, which happened to be the next logical target of the two-year-old strategy based on the combat ranges of fighter aircraft.

So if the island-hopping basing strategy that had dragged the Allies forward from Samoa to Wallis Island to the Ellice Islands to the Gilbert Islands to the Marshall Islands had made sense in the age of land-based fighters and long-range bombers, the hop from the Marshall Islands to the Mariana Islands made sense in the even higher-level strategic world that could be opened in the emerging age of land-based *very*-long-range bombers, B-29s.

When detailed planning for the Marianas campaign began, the B-29 was still untested in war. There were no bases in the Pacific that could accommodate the giant bombers, and no targets in the Pacific save Japan itself that were worth the effort of building bases for these airplanes. Instead, from early 1944, B-29s were flown to India and China in the hope of striking Japan from that direction, but the B-29 would be able to

Eight Marine battalion landing teams assaulted southwestern Saipan in line-abreast formation. It took four Marine and one Army amtrac battalions to get the lead waves ashore. *Official USMC Photo*

The Japanese put up a stubborn shoreline defense, often employing antiboat guns and plunging fire from heights overlooking the miles-long beachhead. Here, probably in the 2d Marine Division zone, a platoon commander or platoon sergeant rallies Marines prior to leading them inland. *Official USMC Photo*

reach Japan from the Marianas when large islands there could be seized and adequate facilities could be built. Thus, for the time being, the Pacific island-hopping strategy was co-opted by an even higher level strategic requirement for B-29 bases from which the centers of Japanese industrial power, 1,200 miles away, could be reached. Luckily, the program for standing up new B-29 units and the progress of the Pacific War dovetailed perfectly in mid-1944. If the requisite bases fell into American hands, there would be B-29 groups ready to use them by the time runways and infrastructure were in place.

THE ORGANIZATION AND ARMS AVAILABLE to Marine divisions had been in flux since the start of the war. Two factors were in play: needs based on lessons learned that could be projected into the next campaign, and the growing strength of the American industrial base.

In the first case, an ongoing problem that had yet to be licked was shore party support at the beachhead. It was known for an absolute fact that the violence of island warfare could not tolerate the use of combat troops in a supply-handling mode, so the Marine Corps beefed up its pioneer units and drew on Seabee battalions attached to the Marine divisions for beach work, then stood up depot units for overseeing dumps. Too many amtracs were needed for a divisional assault for the divisional organization to handle, so independent amtrac battalions were stood up as corps troops and, in the

wake of the Marshalls operation, the organic divisional amtrac units were reassigned as corps troops. Although trained to build roads and the like, Marine engineer battalions had been used in the assault role—demolitions and flamethrowers—since Tarawa, and this role was beefed up by training and the availability of many more flamethrower teams, so the task of building and maintaining roads fell more heavily on Seabees attached to the divisions as well as on an independent Marine engineer battalion organized for use at the corps level.

More weapons—a cornucopia of weapons—allowed Marine infantry units at all levels to be upgraded and reorganized. All the infantry squads were reorganized into thirteen-man units consisting of a squad leader and three four-man fire teams, and each fire team was built around a BAR. Divisional special weapons battalions were disbanded and regimental weapons companies received additional 37mm antitank guns and 75mm halftracks.

At least five LVT(A)4s have been abandoned on this narrow fringe of beach. No doubt, they were stopped by gunfire or malfunctions. Note, also, the wooden crates that litter the beach. Many troop-carrying amtracs brought battle supplies ashore, but both troops and supplies were simply dumped on the shore as amtrac crews hastily withdrew to evade heavy fire, a tactic that was palpably justified on this stretch of sand. *Official USMC Photo*

The availability of more 105mm howitzers caused the conversion of one 75mm battalion per divisional artillery regiment to a second 105mm battalion, and several independent 105mm and 155mm battalions were added as corps troops. Armored amphibian battalions also were added as corps troops, and new LVT(A)4s, each armed with a short-barrel 75mm gun and a .50-caliber machine gun, replaced most of the older 37mm-armed amtracs.

In sum, each Marine division was about two thousand men smaller than it had been, but each was significantly more lethal. This was a bit of excellent timing, because Saipan, the first objective in the Marianas, was seen as a significantly tougher proposition than any previous objective. At seventy-two square miles, it was much larger than any objective in the Gilberts and Marshalls, yet significantly smaller in land area than any objective in the

A platoon of 4th Marine Division infantrymen and a Sherman medium tank sweep along the railroad tracks that ran north to south along Saipan's coastal plain. Note that an infantrymen is riding behind the turret; his job was to help spot targets in the event Japanese troops opened fire. Tanks and infantry functioned best when they worked together and shared risks. *Official USMC Photo*

Solomons. The problem was that every inch of Saipan was or could be defended in considerable strength by thirty-one thousand troops, so a weeks-long battle of the intensity of Tarawa was foreseen.

Saipan was slated for assault on June 15, 1944, by the 2d and 4th Marine divisions, with an Army division in reserve. Once a beachhead was established, it was felt that at least two and probably all three divisions would undertake a continuous assault to clear the island, then go on to land on adjacent Tinian and do the same. As soon as possible after the landing on Saipan, at least one of the existing airfields would be rehabilitated and improved to provide land-based air support for the ongoing fighting and the invasion of Tinian. Thereafter, the island's air bases would be improved for B-29s and the neutralization from the air of bypassed Japanese bases in the Marianas. Until local air support got up and running, the ground campaign would be supported by carrier air, naval gunfire, and divisional and corps artillery.

The Saipan and Tinian operations would be overseen in their entirety by V Amphibious Corps (VAC), a Marine organization. The Guam operation would be overseen by III Amphibious Corps (IIIAC, formerly designated I Marine Amphibious Corps, or IMAC), also a Marine organization.

BEGINNING AT 0812 ON JUNE 15, 1944, THE LEAD WAVES OF THE 2D AND 4TH MARINE divisions began the final lap of their assault on Saipan's southwestern shore. Each division was led by two reinforced regiments (now known as regimental combat teams), which in turn were each led by two reinforced infantry battalions (now known as battalion landing teams). From north to south, the regiments were arrayed as follows: 6th Marines, then 8th Marines, covered the 2d Marine Division front of 2,400 yards ending at Afetna Point; then the 23d Marines landing south of Afetna Point directly against the sizable town of Charan Kanoa; then the 25th Marines landing on the southernmost beaches from south of Charan Kanoa to Agingan Point. The objective of all four combat teams was to advance a mile or more inland to the day's phase line, then resume the assault all the way across the southern third of Saipan, including Aslito Airdrome. The 2d Marines; 24th Marines; and the independent 1st Battalion, 29th Marines, made a feint toward several beaches in northwestern Saipan. They kept reinforcements

The 2d and 4th Tank battalions were each equipped with a company of flame tanks built on the chassis of M3 light tanks. As the Pacific War progressed, the Marine Corps relied more and more on flame weapons, including several hundred flamethrowers per division at Saipan. Indeed, it was at Saipan that aerial napalm bombs were first tested in combat. *Official USMC Photo*

from rushing south, but they didn't draw any of the southern forces northward.

The landing, beginning at 0843, was marred by ineffective final bombardments and air attacks. There was too much ground to cover. Moreover, the 6th and 8th Marines drifted between four hundred and six hundred yards north of their assigned beaches due to an unanticipated heavy northward current. Defenses at the beach were far heavier and better camouflaged than anticipated, and they were overcome only through sheer determination and a great deal of blood.

The plan of the 6th and 8th Marines was to alight from their amtracs, reorganize, and advance inland on foot. The 23d and 25th Marines planned to advance aboard their amtracs. All the regiments counted heavily on support from LVT(A)4s.

Saipan was heavily cultivated, mostly in sugar cane, and heavily settled by Japanese and native Chamorros. There were many small villages or farmsteads to be overcome and, as seen here, many were burned out on the run.
Official USMC Photo

The 6th Marines, on Beach Red, fought inland about one hundred yards in the face of plunging fire from machine guns, mortars, and artillery emplaced on the ridgeline that was the regimental objective. Several small tank attacks had to be beaten back as well. By 1300 hours, the regiment had suffered losses as high as 35 percent, including the commander of 2/6 and his executive officer. By the end of the day, every available rifleman was on the line, which was 400 yards inland at its deepest point.

Just to the south, on Beach Green, the 8th Marines' two assault battalions had been driven together by the current, and both had landed in the northern half of the regimental zone, albeit with few casualties. The assault battalions quickly sorted themselves out and

The cane fields presented immense danger in that they were typically on flat ground, often under observation from high ground, and were quite dense hiding places for Japanese troops who were highly adept at turning every feature to defensive advantage.
Official USMC Photo

Until Saipan, Marines never encountered anything remotely like the urban-type warfare they faced in Garapan and a number of smaller town centers. Here, a 37mm gun crew searches for a target from behind an abandoned Japanese truck. Masonry and concrete were amply used in the construction of buildings, walls, curbs, and wells, and all were used to advantage by the defenders.
Official USMC Photo

It didn't take much to run a Marine infantry company in 1944—a few good officers and plenty of communications gear. Here, a company commander is on the sound-powered phone, probably with the battalion command post; the Marine at the far left might be an artillery forward observer speaking with a battery fire direction center; and the Marine at the far right is speaking on a walkie-talkie, probably with a rifle platoon commander. City fighting tended to balkanize infantry formations, but good comm balanced out the command-and-control problems imposed by limited vistas.
Official USMC Photo

3/8 attacked inland, as planned. Company G, 2/8, attacked southward toward Afetna Point, using the coastal road as a boundary. By nightfall, the northern half of Afetna Point was in Marine hands and seven of nine antiboat guns in beachside positions had been silenced. The rest of 2/8 advanced toward Lake Susupe but became isolated in marshland and had to withdraw before nightfall. Two reserve battalions—1/8 and 1/29—also landed on Beach Green during the day. Both were broken up to seal various gaps. By the end of D-day, the reinforced 8th Marines was isolated from the regiments on either flank and, stymied by the marshes, had not fully secured its day's objectives. The commanders of 2/8 and 3/8 were wounded in the day's fighting.

The 23d Marines, landing on Beach Green from Afetna Point across Charan Kanoa, faced little opposition at the beach. Still mounted in its LVTs, it reorganized and advanced inland. Troops from 3/23 mounted in eight LVTs and supported by three LVT(A)4s charged straight down the road through Charan Kanoa, all the way to the regimental objective atop Mount Fina Sisu. They were subjected to heavy fire through the day and had to withdraw during the night because no other friendly units could get so far forward. Similarly, troops in three LVTs accompanied by five LVT(A)4s fought through to the 2/23 phase line, but they also were withdrawn in the dark. The same marshes that had stymied 2/8 to the north also stymied the 23d Marines, which came up well short of its D-day goals despite opposition so light that the regimental reserve battalion, 1/23, wasn't even committed.

The 25th Marines, mounted in Army LVTs, landed on Beach Yellow in the standard two-battalion assault. On the left, 2/25, which was supported by Army LVT(A)4s, overcame small-arms fire and advanced through heavy artillery and mortar fire to a rail line that ran diagonally across its front between five hundred and seven hundred yards inland. To the right, the VAC right-flank battalion, 1/25, was stopped cold just inland from the beach, and many

LVTs were forced to retract before supplies and gear could be unloaded. The bulk of the defensive fire was based on Agingan Point, beyond 1/25's right flank. The Japanese constantly attacked northward from the point, but by early afternoon, once 3/25 and a company of 4th Tank Battalion M4s had been committed to support 1/25, the Marines sealed the flank once and for all. Indeed, the 25th Marines was able to conduct a steady advance inland despite the contest on its right flank, and by day's end the entire regiment had advanced to its phase line between seven hundred and two thousand yards inland.

Throughout the beachhead, once naval gunfire observers were ashore, the naval bombardment was highly accurate, as was aerial bombardment guided by observers in the front lines. The pinpoint accuracy of the supporting arms was something of a marvel. And the advances, such as they were, owed much success to tanks and LVT(A)4s, even though many tanks and armored amtracs went astray, were lost in accidents, or were knocked out by enemy fire from the heights. Seven of nine divisional artillery battalions also were landed on D-day, but many of the 14th Marines' howitzers were mislanded, and Japanese mortars knocked out four 4/14 105mm howitzers.

It was later estimated that D-day casualties totaled two thousand killed and wounded,

more or less, but by nightfall the troops had advanced inland from four hundred yards in the north to two thousand yards in the south. Plenty of supplies were ashore, the medical evacuation system was working, and all but two reserve infantry battalions were ashore to plug gaps or await breakthroughs they could exploit. In sum, the beachhead had been well established, albeit at great cost.

The Japanese mounted numerous counterattacks during the night, most heavily against the 6th Marines, where tanks were used. All these attacks were beaten back, some quite easily. As far as the troops were concerned, they would face hundreds fewer dug-in Japanese the next day.

Bazookas came into their own in fighting on Saipan. The shaped-charge warhead of the 2.36-inch model used at the time was dandy for breaching many concrete and masonry walls, or for taking out pillboxes or many of the caves that honeycombed Saipan's jumbled interior. The target here appears to be a small village or farmstead in the smoke-obscured valley below this bazooka team's position. *Official USMC Photo*

The highest point on Saipan, the peak of Mount Tapotchau, was scouted by members of 2/8, then officially seized by 1/29 on June 27. Here, Marines take a welcome break on a ledge just short of the summit. *Official USMC Photo*

DURING D-DAY, THE HIGH COMMAND LEARNED THAT A VAST IMPERIAL NAVY CARRIER and surface armada had been put in motion toward Saipan. There was no great surprise in this; all thinking about a war with Japan had always contemplated a decisive naval battle as its culmination. That the Japanese were making their move at Saipan was no great shock either, as both sides considered the Marianas to be the outer line of the empire itself. The Japanese carriers had not been seen since October 1942, and the battleships had not been seen since November 1942. If they were going to be of some use in the Pacific, Saipan almost had to be the place, and mid-June 1944 had to be the time.

The American admirals reacted by postponing the June 18 Guam invasion indefinitely and ordering all transports and landing ships to sail east, out of range, by the night of June 17–18. Inasmuch as the beachhead was fairly deep by the end of D-day, as many supplies as possible were to be landed in good order as quickly as possible. The VAC commanding general also decided to land two-thirds of the veteran Army infantry division that was his Saipan reserve; the D-day fighting had been heavy enough to warrant the landing of at least a regiment, and nobody knew when the transports might return. No doubt, the GIs would come in handy. Attacks by carrier aircraft were expected, so Army and Marine antiaircraft units also were rushed ashore. The last of all these reinforcements landed after

Marines—*all* infantrymen in combat—habitually dug in as soon as the day's fighting ended. Here, a .30-caliber water-cooled medium machine gun has been brought forward to anchor a line of fighting holes in an area of scrub pines. Note the flash suppressor on the machine gun's muzzle. *Official USMC Photo*

When a combat infantry unit has been worn down to its core of experienced survivors, fewer risks and more steel on target tend to characterize an advance into a suspect area. Perhaps there are Japanese out there, or perhaps these Marines are cautiously employing the essential tricks of their deadly trade, but if they are using hand grenades, then hand grenades are no doubt the best solution to this tactical situation. *Official USMC Photo*

dark on July 17, and the transport fleet sailed east—for a week. By then, Navy amphibian patrol bombers were operating from a seaplane anchorage off the invasion beaches.

THE FIGHTING ON JULY 16 AND 17 WAS HEAVY, AND IT PROVED TO BE DECISIVE. THE 4TH Marine Division and Army troops fought to the edge of Aslito Airdrome, Marines fully secured Charan Kanoa and Afetna Point, and the 2d Marine Division fought inland into the high ground overlooking the northern beachhead. The only delays were in the marshlands around Lake Susupe, but even this vexing terrain was overcome at the divisional boundary on June 17. Moreover, the Japanese mounted a large tank-supported night attack that did little lasting damage and mainly thinned their own ranks. Also, a counterlanding mounted on the night of June 17–18 from the northwestern coast was turned back with heavy losses when engaged by artillery and surface warships. Night attacks by Truk-based torpedo bombers were largely beaten back, but an LCT was fatally damaged, an LST was damaged, and an escort carrier was severely damaged. Basically, these land, amphibious, and air attacks failed to make a dent. With or without its fleet of transports and cargo ships—and even in the face of a massive naval confrontation—VAC was so firmly embedded on Saipan with so many supplies at its disposal that the fate of the invasion was not the least bit in doubt.

During the rush to clear decks for the upcoming naval battle, Marines flying Stinson OY Sentinel observation planes came ashore from escort carriers to locate paths to and around Japanese positions and spot artillery fire and air attacks. The OYs, based initially on Beach Yellow and Charan Kanoa, were operated by VMO-2 and VMO-4 and were often flown by volunteer enlisted pilots. (The innovation had originated with an ad hoc 1st Marine Division squadron using borrowed Army spotter planes at Cape Gloucester.)

ELEMENTS OF THE 4TH MARINE DIVISION DROVE TO THE SOUTHEASTERN COAST ON JUNE 18, which cut off the Japanese in southeastern Saipan from the rest of the defense force. The 4th Division next pivoted northeast of Lake Susupe to join the 2d Division on June 21 along a steep, hilly line stretching across Saipan on the southern side of Mount Tapotchau to Magicienne Bay. The unoccupied areas of southeastern Saipan were left to the Army units. It was no romp. Many of the Japanese units were first-rate—well-trained and highly skilled soldiers and naval infantry who sold their lives at great cost. Others were cannon fodder who died in badly conceived counterattacks that accomplished nothing of value to their cause. The terrain was a horrible mix of lowland cane fields on table-flat land dominated by hills or mountains, or the steep-sided, ravine-cut hills and mountains themselves, where Japanese troops lay in wait in invisible dominating positions that had to be torn down toe-to-toe by infantrymen. Moreover, bad planning had denied the Marine divisions replacements, and the fleet's week-long departure added to that miscalculation; Marine unit strength and fighting power had trended downward to the tune of 6,165 dead, wounded, and missing from the first shot onward.

The fleet and light carrier air groups of Task Force 58 tore the heart out of Japanese carrier aviation on June 19 and 20 in the utterly one-sided Battle of the Philippine Sea, the

As the battle advanced northward, the coast rose more steeply on the 2d Marine Division's left flank. The seaside cliffs were often honeycombed with caves that sheltered diehard Japanese soldiers and, often as not, Japanese civilians. Here, a Marine rifleman draws a bead on the mouth of a large cave sitting high over the ocean. The only tactically sound way to approach the cave is from above, but that route is likely overseen by yet other caves. In the end, Marines called on warships to rifle shells directly into any cave that could be reached from the sea. Only then were troops lowered to check the results. *Official USMC Photo*

Marianas Turkey Shoot. It was, as many prewar planners had foreseen, the grand fleet action that doomed one side to certain defeat. Even if Japan no longer had a real hope of winning the Pacific War, the Japanese thought they would never be ready to stop the killing and dying.

Eight Army Air Forces fighter-bombers operating from Aslito Airdrome supported Marine ground units in an all-out attack on June 22. The Marines unknowingly hit the Japanese main line of resistance that day. Determined defenders numbering nearly ten thousand well-led and well-equipped Imperial Army troops and five thousand less-well-equipped naval infantrymen and sundry Imperial Army stragglers held the Americans to half the day's objectives. That night was the first in which there were no significant counterattacks, which indicated that the Japanese commanders had given up on defeating the invaders and were content to fight a battle of attrition.

The worst ground fighting lay ahead as the gallant and determined Marines attacked into determined and gallant Japanese holding high ground in extremely broken terrain. The names that Marines and the GIs who joined them there gave to terrain features say it all: Death Valley, Purple Heart Ridge, and Hell's Pocket.

The Army division went into the line between the two Marine divisions on June 23, and right away there were complaints and retorts that the Army was going too slow or the Marines were going too fast. The Marine VAC commander relieved the Army division commander on June 25 and sparked a controversy that neither service has laid to rest since.

Americans prevailed in the atrocious battles for the northern half of Saipan, but it took thousands of tons of bombs and naval and artillery shells to help them do so. The ground battle was unremitting and exhausting, but the Americans kept going. In the end, the surviving Japanese troops were pushed back into the Marpi Point area, and here Americans saw the true face of the enemy. A mad, useless final "banzai" attack broke the Japanese defensive organization, but Japanese troops continued to hold out unto death in caves that honeycombed Mount Marpi. It would have been one thing if only Japanese troops held out here, but Saipan had been the center of a large, civilian-run sugar-processing industry. There were thousands of Japanese

This Marine is hurling a smoke grenade into an inland cave. The idea is to locate the extent to which one cave is interconnected with other caves or fissures that might be exploited to outflank the whole system. This was brutal attritional warfare, slow and expensive in lives. *Official USMC Photo*

civilian men, women, and children on the island, and they were held in the caves and warrens alongside the troops. As the noose tightened, they were pressed into service to build fighting positions, then they were simply held hostage. They died with the troops. And in the end, they flung themselves from the cliffs into the ocean in front of the eyes of disbelieving American kids who thought until then that they had seen the worst war could expose to them. Mothers took their children with them off the cliffs, and Japanese soldiers who were about to die in useless little rearguard fights used precious bullets on countrymen who could not defend themselves.

Saipan was declared secure on July 9, but fighting persisted for months as the island was scoured for stragglers by its U.S. Army garrison. Some Japanese held out for going on thirty years.

Only a few Japanese civilians—nearly all mothers and their children—fell into American hands alive. Quite often, after using them as laborers and pack animals, Japanese soldiers murdered the civilians with whom they were holed up as either they reached the point of starvation or were about to be overrun. While this mother's face is quite gaunt, the toddlers seem to be unusually well fed.
Official USMC Photo

CHAPTER 13

TINIAN

THE INVASION AND CAPTURE OF TINIAN WAS THE INEVITABLE EXTENSION OF THE Saipan battle for airfield sites from which the B-29 assault on Japan could be mounted. Following a brief rest and reorganization on Saipan, the 4th Marine Division was launched ashore on J-day, July 24, behind a massive land-based artillery bombardment that had blanketed northern Tinian for days. The invasion beaches were in northwestern Tinian, directly opposite the airfields numbered 1 and 3, which were well within range of the Army-Marine artillery groupment set up in southwestern Saipan.

The 2d and 8th Marines also were offshore Tinian as the landing force reserve as well as to undertake a feint toward beaches in southwestern Tinian. As at Saipan, the feint was realistic enough to pin Japanese forces to the threatened sector but not enough to draw troops away from the real invasion beaches. Apparently it was good enough to cause the Japanese sector commander to believe that his shore guns had repelled an invasion attempt, and, indeed, a battleship and destroyer were struck by shells that caused numerous casualties.

At 0747, three companies of the 4th Marine Division landed abreast on beaches dubbed White-1 and White-2. Although White-1 was only wide enough for four amtracs to land abreast, it was to support the entire 24th Marines landing in column of battalions, each in column of companies. White-2, twice as wide, was set aside for the 25th Marines, landing two battalions abreast in columns of companies.

The defense of White-1 was negligible but determined, and relatively difficult to overcome due to the narrow landing area. Nevertheless, the opposition was overwhelmed

The 4th Marine Division landed about half an infantry company per four-amtrac wave on J-day at Tinian. The amtracs shown in this photo are new LVT-3s, each with a rear ramp. The white areas seen at the top edge of this photograph are Airfield No. 1 (left) and Airfield No. 3. A close look at the beach reveals how sharply the shore rises on either side of the landing zone. *Official USMC Photo*

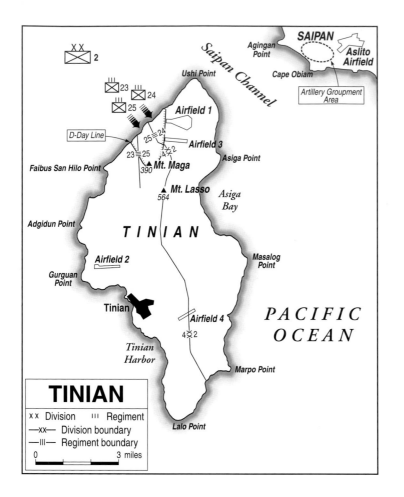

TINIAN

x x — Division   ııı Regiment
—xx— Division boundary
—ııı— Regiment boundary
0   3 miles

in short order. Behind the beach, 2/24 was harried by mortar fire and Japanese troops holed up in caves, but both types of defenses were smothered by fire, and the advance picked up speed in the direction of the day's phase line. The 1st Battalion, 24th Marines, which began to arrive ashore at 0846, spread left, and 3/24 began to land at 0855 as the regimental reserve.

White-2 was better defended than White-1, and the defenders were ready for battle within two pillboxes and outlying positions that had not been badly mauled by virtue of a prelanding bombardment plan that prized surprise above obliteration. The real surprise, however, was that the initial waves of the 25th Marines landed on rocky ledges bordering White-2, and not on the beach itself. This counterintuitive maneuver caught the Japanese off guard and allowed the entire 25th Marines to get ashore by 0930 without encountering a heavily mined sector at and behind the beach.

Inland, 2/24 easily advanced 1,400 yards to its objective, a line at the edge of Airfield No. 3 that also cut the road to Airfield No. 1. To 2/24's left, 1/24 ran into strong defenses based in caves and dense brush about a thousand yards from White-1. The hitherto rapid advance in the 1/24 zone stalled, but LVT(A)s still in the water fired on the caves, and several flame tanks strove to burn off the underbrush. Thereafter, gun tanks were sent up from the beach as they landed. At 1630 hours, 3/25 was moved up from White-1 to close a 400-yard gap that had opened between 1/24 and 2/24, and 1/8 was landed to serve as the 4th Marine Division reserve while the 23d Marines was held offshore as a floating reserve.

On the 4th Division's right, the 25th Marines faced stronger opposition and higher elevations beyond its right flank, from which Japanese observers and artillery had a clear view of the White-2 area. The entire regiment came up well short of its objectives, which were on the first shelf of high ground overlooking the division area.

White-2, which was heavily sown with mines and covered by a relatively strong defensive zone, was left to follow-on troops. As soon as the mines were cleared, the 23d Marines was ordered to land on White-2 as proof against an expected counterattack: 2/23 went into the line to the right of the 25th Marines; 1/23 went into a line behind 2/23; and 3/23 was put in division reserve with 1/8.

Advances throughout the beachhead were voluntarily halted at about 1630 to give all the troops time to dig in for the night, and 37mm antitank guns and 2.36-inch bazookas were rushed to the line to be emplaced along likely routes of approach that tanks might use. The entire 4th Tank Battalion—in forty-eight M4 gun tanks and fifteen M3 flame tanks—was ashore by the late afternoon, its tanks fed into the lines as they arrived.

In some areas inland from the beach tangled brush required the use of flamethrowers and flame tanks to open routes of advance or uncover hidden Japanese positions. *Official USMC Photo*

By nightfall, all the tanks ashore had been integrated into the defenses that figured so heavily in the J-day planning. Four 75mm pack howitzer battalions (1/14, 2/14, 1/10, and 2/10) and the division's entire complement of 75mm halftracks also were landed on J-day. Indeed, counting units attached from the 2d Marine Division, the 4th Marine Division had more than 15,600 troops ashore by nightfall on July 24.

DURING THE FIRST NIGHT ASHORE, THE MARINE LINES were attacked by three large Japanese forces. In the north, at 0200, an estimated six hundred troops from a naval guard force blundered into the defensive line held across the beach by 1/24. The well-prepared Marines opened fire before the Japanese could deploy, and a three-hour blood bath ensued. The next day, 476 Japanese dead were counted in front of the 1/24 line.

In the center, a crack 900-man infantry battalion infiltrated toward the Marine lines from central Tinian and attacked behind artillery and several tanks pretty much at the juncture of the 24th and 25th Marines, which was inadequately outposted and undermanned. The Japanese attack was easily driven off and thus thought to be a feint. But a second attack on this front made a beeline for Battery A, 1/14, which had to defend itself with its howitzers and machine guns. A company of 1/8 and a tank platoon counterattacked at 0400 and drove off the surviving Japanese. A third attack into the 25th Marines rear fared no better. In all, an estimated five hundred Japanese died in these attacks.

On the far right, at 0330, the 23d Marines was assaulted directly up the coastal road by six tanks carrying infantrymen,

These dead Imperial Army troops are probably victims of reckless assaults on Marine lines during the first night of the Tinian operation. The Japanese mounted useless counterattacks from start to finish on Tinian, but they killed few Americans while hastening their own defeat. *Official USMC Photo*

followed by many more infantrymen on foot. In the light of star shells fired by American ships, 75mm halftracks, 37mm antitank guns, and bazookas in the lines of 2/23, directly astride the road, quickly destroyed five tanks and killed the crews and all the infantrymen who rode on them. The sixth tank fled. For all that, veteran troops from three crack infantry battalions assaulted on foot directly into the lines of 2/23 and 2/25—where they were shredded by Marine infantry bolstered by canister-firing antitank guns. After dawn 276 Japanese corpses were counted across the 4th Marine Division's left flank, and in all the Japanese wasted 1,241 of their troops that night, including nearly 700 of their very best.

THE 8TH MARINES, 2D MARINES, AND 2/6 LANDED ON TINIAN ON JULY 25, AND THE rest of the 6th Marines was slated to land on July 26. This was by way of preparation to open a two-division advance down Tinian's long axis as soon as the 4th Marine Division had crossed the entire northern part of the island.

The 4th Division attack on J+1 achieved all of its objectives in the north. On the division's far left, 1/8 attacked northward along the beach, overcame several blocking

The airfields, particularly Airfield No. 1, were strewn with concrete storage bunkers and shelters, but they fell almost without a fight because the Imperial Navy troops who had manned them were either technicians or had gone down fighting in an abortive counterattack the first night of the operations. Marine veterans of earlier fighting took no chances and checked every possible burrow that might shelter snipers or stragglers. *Official USMC Photo*

The earliest use of rockets by Marines took place on Saipan, when the truck-mounted 1st Provisional Rocket Detachment went into action with the 4th Marine Division. As shown here, the detachment continued to support the 4th Marine Division on Tinian. Each rocket truck appears to be supported by an M3 75mm halftrack. *Official USMC Photo*

The center two-thirds of Tinian was mostly a flat plain planted in sugar cane and other agricultural products. There was nowhere for the Japanese to base a defense, merely holding actions in tall growth. The advance across the Tinian plain by Marine infantry and tanks was the closest thing to mobile warfare Marines encountered in the Pacific. *Official USMC Photo*

The mobile war on Tinian came to a dead halt when Marines faced the abrupt escarpment rising out of southern Tinian. It was difficult even for infantry to find a way up to the high ground. The climb was difficult for these 2d Division Marines, but the top of the escarpment was relatively flat. *Official USMC Photo*

Organized resistance on Tinian collapsed on August 1, and the island was declared secure that day, but the end was a foregone conclusion as early as July 26. This brutal scene resulted from a fight to the death between the occupants of a machine-gun bunker at Tinian's southern tip and impatient Marine veterans who had access to a flame tank.
Official USMC Photo

positions in hard fighting, and stood down several hundred yards north of its starting point. There, 2/8 was fed into the line, facing eastward, to cross the northern reaches of Airfield No. 1 in order to link up with 1/24. The juncture was effected halfway across the airfield. In the meantime, 3/24 attacked eastward against negligible opposition, then turned south to support 2/24 as the latter crossed Airfield No. 3. In effect, the Marine line both pivoted around Airfield No. 1 and expanded to accommodate a zone for the 2d Marine Division to the left of the 4th Marine Division.

In the 4th Division center, the 25th Marines had ended J-day well short of its objectives atop Mount Maga. On J+1, while 2/25 manned a base of fire in the center, the rest of the regiment opened a double envelopment, 3/25 on the left and 1/25 on the right. In the 1/25 zone, the infantry was driven back by heavy fire, but tanks drove to the peak once a newly discovered road was cleared of mines. At first, 1/25 was unable to follow, but in due course the Japanese positions were reduced by 81mm mortar fire, and the infantry joined the tanks in the early afternoon. A seesaw battle ensued as the two sides dueled for the heights, but the tanks prevailed, and 1/25 continued around the mountain to link up with 3/25. For its part, 3/25 faced delay after delay in the face of tough opposition despite reinforcement by tanks and flamethrower teams as well as artillery and naval gunfire support. In the meantime, elements of the 23d Marines came up on the right, took out positions in its zone that had stopped 3/25, and 3/25 leaped forward to link up with 1/25. Indeed, the entire 4th Division achieved all of its goals by 1700 at remarkably light cost to the assault battalions.

Japanese artillery either emplaced on the heights facing the Marine advance, or observed from these heights, was active and accurate throughout the day. A direct hit on

Clearing Japanese holdouts from Tinian's caves required patience and ingenuity. The 75mm pack howitzer seen here was hauled aloft in parts on August 5, reassembled, and lashed down so it could bring its fire to bear on a cave mouth that could not be reached by other means. *Official USMC Photo*

the 1/14 fire direction center claimed the lives of the battalion commander and eight others, and Seabees building a pier at Beach White-2 sustained losses in another shelling. Air strikes, naval gunfire, and counterbattery fire apparently destroyed several Japanese guns.

ON JULY 26, J+2, THE 2D MARINE DIVISION RESUMED control of the 8th Marines and took over a sector to the left of the 4th Marine Division. Also, 1/6, 3/6, the 2d Tank Battalion, and other units came ashore to complete the 2d Division order of battle.

The 8th Marines crossed Airfield No. 1 and stood on the east coast by 1140, then passed into division reserve. To the left, covering Tinian's northern point, the 2d Marines was committed to the fight at dawn, and it reached the east coast by 1230. There it redressed its line to face south in anticipation of a two-division drive down Tinian's long axis. The 6th Marines quietly moved into the southward-facing 2d Division line, tied in on the left with the 2d Marines and on the right with the 25th Marines.

Thousands of Japanese and Korean noncombatants hid out in caves in the Tinian escarpment as Marines cleared the area of Japanese fighters. While more than eight thousand civilians were saved, many, many others were held hostage by soldiers, as they had been on Saipan, and thus thousands also died, many by starvation. Painstaking cave-by-cave clearing operations were conducted by the 8th Marines well into October, but some Japanese troops hid out for as long as three decades. *Official USMC Photo*

On the 4th Division right, the 23d Marines rapidly advanced past Point Faibus San Hilo and stood down to wait for all the other regiments to draw abreast. The 25th Marines, from atop Mount Maga, advanced southward in the direction of Mount Lasso, the greatly feared fulcrum of the island's defenses. Unbelievably, the Japanese had abandoned the strategic heights in the night, so the 25th Marines both occupied the peak and ringed the heights to the south. The 24th Marines was squeezed out of the corps front and placed in reserve. Thus, by the end of J+2, four Marine regiments stood in line completely across the island from the west across Mount Lasso, then northeast and east to Asiga Point.

All of the infantry and support units had entered the fight on Tinian in reduced states because no replacements had been available during or after the Saipan battle, but each was battle-tested, tough, and sure of itself. They had won the strategic battle in only three days. All they had to do from then on was actually clear the lower half of Tinian. To help do this—because Marine gains were running beyond the range of Saipan-based artillery—3/14 landed its 105mm howitzers on Tinian on J+2, and other artillery units on Saipan were told to pack for the same brief ride.

THE VAC ATTACK DOWN THE LONG AXIS OF TINIAN WAS RAPID AND EFFICIENT—COSTLY to the Japanese and much less costly to the Americans. By July 31, Airfield No. 2 and Airfield No. 4 were in American hands, and the two Marine divisions had driven to the high, jumbled plateau that characterized the southernmost portion of the island. The fighting turned extremely tough here, partly because of the steep cave-studded terrain, but also because the defenders had become so concentrated. Great effort was expended to induce Japanese and

Korean civilians to surrender, and more than eight thousand answered the call, thus obviating a repeat of the thousands of needless civilian deaths on Saipan. Here also, for the first time in the Pacific War, significant numbers of Japanese servicemen also surrendered.

The island was declared secure on August 1, but mopping up continued for weeks and even months; the 8th Marines hunted down stragglers until late October. The death toll in the Marine divisions was 317 killed and 1,550 wounded, and an estimated 5,000 Japanese troops died on Tinian.

The 2d Marine Division remained on Saipan, where it made good its losses and was reorganized under a new table of organization. The 4th Marine Division was shipped back to Hawaii for the same treatment. Meantime, Saipan and Tinian were rapidly turned into "unsinkable" air bases. The first B-29s landed on Saipan on October 12, 1944.

It is sometimes difficult to remember that most Marines who shouldered the fighting in World War II were in their late teens and early twenties—just plain American kids who killed because they had to but who reverted to their basic good nature between the gruesome chores of war. *Official USMC Photo*

CHAPTER 14

GUAM

JULY 21–AUGUST 11, 1944

W-DAY, THE INVASION OF GUAM, WAS TO HAVE FOLLOWED THE JUNE 15 INVASION of Saipan by three days, but it was delayed by the Battle of the Philippine Sea, when the U.S. Army division set aside as the reserve for the entire Marianas campaign was sent ashore on Saipan. This forced the commanders to designate part of the Guam invasion force as the temporary reserve for Saipan and to scramble to bring up another U.S. Army division from Hawaii, an operation that took time and involved a well-trained but inexperienced division that was completely unfamiliar with any possible roles it might play in the Marianas. W-day was set back to July 21.

The intervening month was put to good use obliterating targets that could be observed from the sea or the air, including virtually every Japanese fixed artillery piece on Guam. But the focus of the prolonged preparatory bombardments allowed the Japanese to mass at precisely the points at which the invasion forces were to land.

The beaches selected for the landings were not as good as other beaches around the island. Wide reefs rising almost to the surface necessitated the early seizure of suitable port facilities from which the invasion force could be sustained, and the best of these were in a marginal landing area from which the island's main airfield also was accessible. (MAG-21, embarked on escort carriers, was slated to begin flying tactical missions as soon as Orote Field could be seized and rehabilitated.)

In the end, given the relentless factors from which such solutions were derived, the invasion force of five Marine infantry regiments—the 3d Marine Division (3d, 9th, and 21st Marines) and the 1st Provisional Marine Brigade (4th and 22d Marines)—had to be

The high cliffs of Guam's central coast loom ahead of these 3d Marine Division troops on W-day, July 21, 1944. Troops carried to the reef on landing craft had to cross-deck to amtracs in order to reach the shore. *Official USMC Photo*

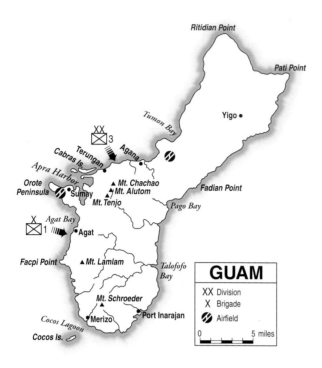

GUAM

XX Division
X Brigade
🔘 Airfield

0   5 miles

A Marine rifle squad leaps from an LVT right at Guam's shoreline. It's difficult to tell if these Marines are under fire or merely eager to find cover and regroup. *Official USMC Photo*

split, and the two forces had to land *five miles apart* on narrow beaches impinged and dominated by high, broken hill country. The main reason for landing the landing forces so far apart also was bound up in the inexorable calculus of war. While the 1st Provisional Marine Brigade and at least one Army regiment went after Orote Airfield, port facilities on the Orote Peninsula, and the southern third of the large island, the 3d Marine Division was to seize the northern two-thirds of Guam. This was because Guam had been selected as a forward base for the B-29 program. Thus the invasion plan for Guam favored the early seizure of suitable sites for three large airfields, and all such sites were in northern and central Guam, in the 3d Marine Division's projected zone of operations. A landing farther to the north would have allowed the 3d Marine Division to employ better landing beaches closer to two of the three airfield sites, but that option was set aside in favor of landing the division as near to the brigade as possible without compromising its strategic mission. Before striking north to seize ground for the B-29 bases, the division was to link up with the brigade along a continuous, defensible front, the so-called Final Beachhead Line. It was anticipated that the linkup and thus the start of the northern drive could be achieved within a day or two. But this did not happen, for the Japanese weathered the ferocious month-long bombardment of the invasion area in much better shape than anyone would have believed.

The final preparatory bombardment of the landing beaches of W-day was ferocious, but flawed; in one sense it worked well, and in another sense it didn't work at all. From close in and afar, dozens of ships, from rocket-firing LCI gunboats to battleships, pounded the cliffs and hills overlooking the landing beaches north and south of the Orote

These 3d Marine Division riflemen have advanced inland and are returning fire from Japanese troops manning a position in the hills. This is a classic study of infantrymen in battle.
Official USMC Photo

Peninsula. The gunfire and bombs from scores and scores of Navy carrier planes scorched the earth and destroyed virtually all—but not quite all—the fixed antiboat defenses that had survived the month-long bombardment that preceded W-day. And the detonations of all those bombs and shells certainly addled the brains of most of the Imperial Japanese Army troops deployed to defend the invasion beaches. But it is doubtful if all that brimstone and fire actually *killed* very many of the defenders, for the month-long run-up to the invasion had given the defenders time to dig secure bunkers and caves on the largely unreachable *reverse* slopes of the many high hills overlooking the landing beaches.

Marines killed in one of the early Japanese night assaults in the 3d Marine Division zone bear grim testimony that the battles in the Pacific didn't all go one way.
Official USMC Photo

What worked is that the landing waves assigned to both sets of beaches got ashore intact and with few casualties. A number of cunningly emplaced and beautifully camouflaged antiboat guns and machine guns destroyed or disabled a significant number of Marine amtracs, which were essential for the landing, for not one landing boat could get across the reef. Most of these weapons were destroyed in short order by hovering Navy fighter-bombers or destroyers and cruisers stationed off the beaches.

The 3d Marine Division landed its three infantry regiments abreast between Asan Point and Adelup Point, north of the Orote Peninsula, on Guam's western shore. And the 1st Provisional Marine Brigade landed its two infantry regiments abreast between Bangi Point and the town of Agat, at the base of the Orote Peninsula. Several amtracs were hit by the antiboat fire, and there were casualties, but most tractors that were lost that morning were put out of commission when their treads were chewed up by the coral.

The lead waves, which were ashore in good order by 0832, formed up, ready to drive on their objectives. But as they did, the defenders shook off the effects of the bombardment, emerged from their reverse-slope burrows, and put up such fierce resistance from the heights that the planned drives to widen the beachhead and link the division with the brigade were stalled in their tracks.

By mid-1944, there were more than two hundred flamethrower teams assigned to each Marine division, thus allowing liberal use of the horrific weapon when it came to clearing vegetation and the well-camouflaged fighting positions it hid. *Official USMC Photo*

In some cases the invaders drove a hundred yards inland from the water line, but no farther.

Already briefed to drive for the heights, 3/3, on the 3d Marine Division's left flank, *had* to do so to save itself from deadly plunging fire. The assigned objective of 3/3 was Chonito Cliff, a high eminence that ran to the water line and thus completely restricted access to the interior as well as the shoreline to the northeast. Fortunately, several companies of 3/3 and several medium tanks were able to advance in the protection of a draw, and the height was in Marine hands by noon. But when 3/3 tried to advance from Chonito Cliff to more distant objectives, it was stopped by fire from a high ridge in the neighboring 1/3 zone that 1/3 could in no way overcome. Indeed, 1/3 was all but pinned by fire from this prickly ridge, and it could not advance without sustaining many casualties.

Having anticipated big problems taking Chonito Cliff, the regimental plan had to be altered on the fly to account for the deadly delay encountered by 1/3. First, 2/3, the regimental reserve, was committed and sent around the Japanese-held ridge, but this did not relieve pressure on 1/3, whose Company A could not advance without drawing withering fire from the heights. In a frustrating second attack that nearly claimed the heights, Company A's Captain Geary Bundschu was killed, and the ridge was named for him.

But the 3d Marine Division's problems did not revolve around one rugged spot. Virtually the entire division was hemmed in by well-defended ridges and hills that utterly dominated most of the packed landing beaches. The day ended with the 3d Marine Division in possession of the beach, Chonito Cliff, and not much else on its list of objectives. Indeed, the 3d Marines was not even in physical contact with the adjacent 21st Marines. Only from the 9th Marines sector, on the division right, was there a report of success: the regiment had landed in good order and taken all its W-day objectives, but at the cost to the regiment of 231 killed and wounded, including a battalion commander wounded and two company commanders killed.

Landing into better terrain, the 1st Provisional Marine Brigade had an easier time getting itself established on or near its W-day objectives, although not without heavy casualties in some units. Despite the brigade's success, the brigade commander decided to draw on his reserve, an Army infantry battalion. Because of heavy losses among Marine amtracs during the initial landing, the Army battalion was forced

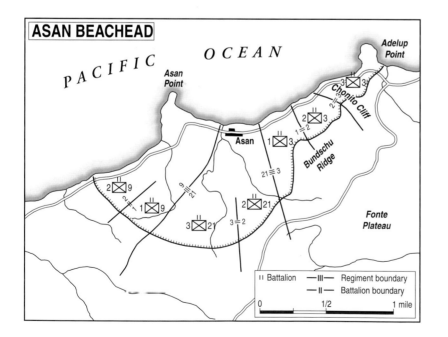

to wade to the beach from the reef. When the brigade commander ordered the rest of the Army regiment ashore late in the day, a series of communications foul-ups kept it from landing until the wee hours, and then it arrived in too disorganized a state to be of any immediate use. There were also problems getting the brigade's artillery ashore.

The bulk of the Japanese infantry regiment facing the brigade mounted an ill-advised, desultory, disorganized, and ultimately unsuccessful counterattack during the night. Hundreds of Japanese soldiers died for no good reason, and any hope the Japanese island commander might have had of holding the brigade to minimal gains were dashed in that foolish act. There were American casualties and other losses, to be sure, but not enough to justify the immolation of two of the three Japanese infantry battalions facing the southern beachhead. Guam's Japanese defenders had gone into W-day facing little hope of turning back the American tide, and they faced their second dawn of battle with *no* hope of holding the island. Thereafter, while the southern half of Guam was not abandoned by the Japanese, it was open for the taking—at a price.

Quite the opposite happened in the 3d Marine Division zone. The Japanese used the night to plug holes and otherwise strengthen their defenses. There were counterattacks here, too, during the night, and several Japanese battalions were chewed to bits, but the majority of the defenders stayed where they were or repositioned themselves to better advantage. The ground favored the defenders, and the Japanese used the ground wisely. And then they used the entire second day, July 22, to wear down the Marines by grinding action.

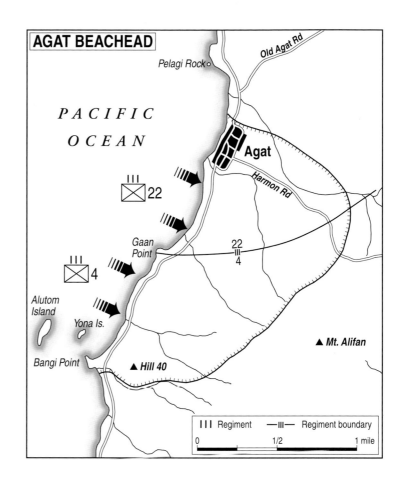

The second day's fighting in the 3d Marine Division zone still centered on Bundschu Ridge, in 1/3's zone. There were many Marine attacks but few gains. Meanwhile, the adjacent 21st Marines had to sit pretty still for most of the day, because an advance in its zone would distort the division's center and expose the center regiment to flanking fire from Bundschu Ridge and other, unreachable heights. The regiment was able to extend its control over a broader reach in some directions, but it was not able to gain direct physical contact with the adjacent 3d Marines because the twisted, hilly terrain was impenetrable beyond imagination. In contrast, the 9th Marines, on the division right, was able to eliminate most of the defenders in its zone and advance to flat ground, but the regiment's progress toward even broader vistas was slowed when the remaining defenders in its zone skillfully stood fast in numerous little ad hoc strongpoints that had to be cleared with painstaking care. At length, 2/9 captured the old Piti Navy Yard, a major divisional objective that was to be rehabilitated to become one of the island's key supply points.

Marines resorted to the liberal use of explosives when clearing otherwise hard-to-reach caves and bunkers. By mid-1944, Marine engineer units had been reorganized to provide demolitions teams down to infantry company and platoon level. *Official USMC Photo*

A wounded Marine is lowered down otherwise impassable terrain by way of a cable trolley installed in the high hills by Marine engineers. Wounded Marines counted on such time-saving evacuation methods to save their lives. *Official USMC Photo*

The 3d Marine Division's plan of action for July 23 was to physically link the 3d and 21st Marine regiments. This plan was immensely aided by fruitless Japanese counterattacks during the night that weakened the defense. One defending battalion destroyed itself making piecemeal suicide attacks that had no effect on the Marines.

On the morning of July 23, the 3d Marines continued to move upon the ridges, hills, and gullies that had all but stymied its planned advance on two previous days. First, 1/3 was reinforced—to an effective strength of 160—and sent back to take Bundschu Ridge behind a massive air, naval, and artillery bombardment. Almost as soon as 1/3 jumped off, and 2/3 also moved on Bundschu Ridge, the objective fell without a fight; the Japanese had abandoned this defensive key point, although the entire day had to be spent cleaning out hot spots on the ridge. Meanwhile, the 3d and 21st Marines attempted to gain firm physical contact in that area, but they could not; the complexity of the terrain simply could not be overcome.

The Japanese put their main effort during the day on keeping 3/3 from exploiting its position on Chonito Cliff. With Bundschu Ridge in Marine hands, the division's left-flank battalion appeared to be free to expand to its next objective, Fonte Plateau. 3/3 managed to advance about halfway to this objective, but at great cost.

The 21st Marines spent July 23 trying to link up with the 3d Marines on its left and attempting to make modest gains in the center, mostly for the sake of tying down Japanese troops who might otherwise have been shifted to the 9th or 3d Marines' zones. Although the defense in its zone was sporadic, the 9th Marines spent the day merely improving its positions. The division reserve, 1/21, was sent to bolster the 3d Marines, and 2/9 was withdrawn from the 9th Marines zone to be the division reserve.

These Japanese tanks were knocked out on July 24 by Marine tanks supporting the 1st Marine Provisional Brigade's drive to seal the Orote Peninsula. The near vehicle was dubbed a "tankette" in that it carried no weapons larger that the turret-mounted heavy machine gun. The rear tank is armed with a turret-mounted cannon. *Official USMC Photo*

Far from internalizing the lessons of the previous two nights—that night attacks made in the open simply fritter away the lives of the troops—Guam's Japanese commander had been planning through the day to mount a major, all-out counterattack that he hoped would drive the vastly stronger 3d Marine Division into the sea. Because the Japanese communications system had been destroyed by bombs and shells, the attacks were fragmented and piecemeal, and they were easily turned back by Marines holding excellent defensive positions as well as by sustained artillery and naval gunfire laid to perfection on known assembly areas and routes of approach. Once again, many Japanese died for absolutely no good reason.

The fighting was heavy in the 3d Marine Division's zone on July 24, but the objectives, and thus the gains, were modest. All three regiments continued to improve their positions as necessary, and 2/21 was finally able to effect an adequate link with the 3d Marines. By 1400, for the first time since landing, the 3d Marine Division held a continuous line, albeit well

Marine infantry and M4 medium tanks advance warily along a trail in the 1st Marine Provisional Brigade's zone. Note that the main guns are swung out to cover both sides of the trail. Tankers hated terrain like this, but they advanced as long as infantry acted as their eyes and ears. Infantrymen hated this kind of terrain, too, so the tanks provided an enormous level of confidence. *Official USMC Photo*

Here, in open terrain, tank-infantry cooperation is even more evident. The tank has just fired at an emplacement pointed out by its infantry escort—an emplacement the infantrymen feel is too dangerous to tackle on their own if a tank is present. In the second photograph, infantrymen firing their weapons move forward to make sure the emplacement has been silenced, something a tank crew cannot do on its own. In the end, tanks were the supporting arm and infantry was the main event. *Official USMC Photos*

short of its objectives for the fourth day on Guam. An attempt also was made by 9th Marines patrols to contact the 1st Provisional Marine Brigade, but the effort fell well short of the objective, although a patrol advanced quite far into a zone that had clearly been abandoned by its defenders.

IN GENERAL, THE 1ST PROVISIONAL MARINE BRIGADE—BOLSTERED TO DIVISIONAL strength with the addition of a U.S. Army infantry regiment on W-day—did better in its zone of action from July 22 to July 24. But the terrain and the circumstances were different, so there is no real point of comparison. On July 22, the brigade concentrated on expanding to the left, toward the base of the Orote Peninsula (and only incidentally toward the 5-miles-distant 3d Marine Division). There were steep, heavily wooded slopes to overcome in some sectors, and the going was slow, particularly as the defense became more concentrated, but the gains were nonetheless substantial. The Army regiment took its objectives on the flat shoreside flank to the south, but 1/4 had a very hard time navigating up the steep, wooded, well-defended slopes of dominant Mount Alifan in the face of plunging fire. In the end, the Japanese abandoned the heights, and 1/4 completed the climb. Also, 3/4 made good its objectives for the day, and the worst problems the 22d Marines faced in its zone to the north was getting enough supplies up from the beach to sustain its advance into jumbled, sparsely defended terrain. Tanks and LVT(A)s had to be employed to help 1/22 advance down the coast, but the defenses there were overcome. In the meantime, most of the III Amphibious Corps (IIIAC) artillery group was landed in the brigade beachhead during the day, as was artillery from the Army division. (The Marine brigade's artillery group had landed on W-day.)

On July 23, the Army regiment reached its sector on the Final Beachhead Line, and the 22d Marines all but sealed off the neck of the Orote Peninsula in the face of a determined, organized defensive effort that inflicted more than a hundred casualties. While these advances were proceeding, the entire Army division, less one regiment held in corps reserve, was landed in the brigade zone. Elements of the 4th Marines were replaced on the inland flank late in the day by elements of the fresh Army regiment, and the 4th Marines withdrew to positions from which it could attack into the Orote Peninsula.

The 1st Provisional Marine Brigade's July 24 attack was preceded by a massive air, artillery, and naval bombardment, especially in the 22d Marines zone across the neck of the Orote Peninsula. When 1/22 jumped off, however, the Japanese responded with heavy artillery, mortar, and machine-gun fire. Marine M4 tanks with the lead company destroyed five Japanese tanks that tried to thwart the attack, and these tanks' 75mm guns also neutralized log and even concrete pillboxes that stood in the way of 1/22's advance. Close-in 20mm and 40mm flanking fire from LCI gunboats also contributed to 1/22's success, as did direct and enfilade 5-inch fire from a destroyer. When 1/22 had advanced well into the Japanese line, 3/22 mounted a

flanking attack that rolled up much of the remaining Japanese defensive position. A major Japanese strongpoint was overcome by 3/22. On the regimental right, 2/22 rolled into its attack late, but it made important gains throughout the afternoon. By day's end, 1/22 and 2/22 were on their day's objectives—the line from which the Orote Peninsula would be assaulted—and 3/22 was nearly there. Also, the 4th Marines, fully relieved by an Army regiment, went into brigade reserve behind or even with the 22d Marines.

THE LAST ARMY INFANTRY REGIMENT WAS LANDED IN THE BRIGADE ZONE ON JULY 24 as the corps reserve. Equally important was the fact that the ship-to-shore movement of supplies into both beachheads was so well in hand as to be characterized as routine, and a major water point was established at a spring in the 3d Marine Division's zone.

Under the original IIIAC plan, the 3d Marine Division and the 1st Provisional Marine Brigade were to have been in contact and in complete control of the corps' Final Beachhead Line by the evening of July 24. By then, however, the brigade was still marginally short of its objective (even after having been reinforced by an Army force greater than its own strength), and the 3d Marine Division was well short of its landing-phase goals.

To the left of Orote Airfield is the town of Sumay and its pier. Marines based on Guam before the war lived in Sumay Barracks, which was surrendered to the Japanese on December 9, 1941. Guam was the first fallen U.S. possession to be liberated from Japan. On July 29, 1944, the 4th Marines objective was the airfield, and the barracks was the prime objective of the 22d Marines. *Official USMC Photo*

The 1926 photograph shows the Marine band at practice on the parade deck adjacent to Sumay Barracks. The July 29, 1944, photograph shows the national colors being run up a makeshift flagpole in front of the same barracks building. *Official USMC Photos*

Moreover, the two beachheads were not yet joined. The brigade was thus given an extra day, July 25, to seal off the Orote Peninsula and prepare for its attack into that well-defended feature, and the 3d Marine Division was ordered to continue its move on the Final Beachhead Line in its zone and to make contact with the brigade. The Army division, which had had no formal objective before landing, was to expand the southern beachhead to the Final Beachhead Line and prepare to extend itself over the southern third of Guam (formerly a brigade objective).

Relying largely on supporting artillery, air, gunboats, and large warships, the 22d Marines advanced into defensive sectors that had clearly been stiffened during the night. (In fact, guns emplaced in the 3d Marine Division's zone had fired on illuminated Japanese landing barges bringing troops to the Orote Peninsula through the night from other areas of Guam.) The 22d Marines did seal off the Orote Peninsula, but it was clear by the end of the day that both regiments of the brigade would be needed to grind into a concentrated defensive zone extending well back into the peninsula. On the bright side, patrols from 2/22 made contact with patrols from the 9th Marines on ground that the Japanese had abandoned. Firm contact between the brigade and the 3d Marine Division could not yet be sealed, but it was clear that joining the Marine commands would not be a major problem once enough troops were sent into the gap.

The 3d Marine Division continued to take ground in its zone, but advances remained limited, in part because of the jumbled terrain and in part because the Japanese put up a lot of resistance on certain features that, as it turned out, they were trying to hold as jumping-off points for an all-out ground offensive the Japanese commander hoped would drive the 3d Marine

Division into the sea. The Japanese did hold these points, but at such great cost as to render some units ineffective in the upcoming attack.

During the morning 2/9 moved into the 3d Marines' zone to relieve 1/3, which was fought out, and secured large parts of Fonte Plateau during the day. Also, Marine tanks were committed for the first time in the division zone, because there was finally ground on the division's front on which they could operate. Their effect on the fighting was profound. For all that, the division's line in the 3d and 21st Marines zones was jumbled and broken by day's end—a factor of the terrain and irregular advances from one battalion zone to the next. The result was that many units had to form battalion-size strongpoints on suitably defensible features. The 9th Marines reached its day's limited objectives on better ground without much trouble, but the regiment was held up by the need to remain in step with the 3d and 21st Marines. Nevertheless, the 21st and 9th Marines had lost contact by nightfall.

The all-out Japanese attack began at 2330 hours on July 25. Its main weight fell precisely on the gap that had developed and remained open between 3/21 and 1/9. The rather fragmented 3d Marines also was hit hard. Artillery and naval gunfire were placed on the advancing Japanese, who nevertheless closed on many Marine positions in the dark. There were some close calls, particularly where the Japanese outnumbered the defenders, but the attack was uncoordinated once it began, and opportunities to overwhelm some Marine positions were lost by the inability of the Japanese to concentrate their forces. Indeed, all the Japanese tanks assigned to the attack became lost, and none reached the front. American artillery and naval gunfire was effective against the Japanese routes of approach and assembly areas, but it could not be fired into areas where the Japanese and Americans were intermingled. Repeated Japanese infantry attacks failed to dislodge any of the Marine units. Marine tanks that had joined the fighting only that day made a critical difference in some zones, particularly in support of 2/9, whose perimeter on Fonte Plateau was strongly attacked seven times during the night. The tanks became particularly effective at dawn, when visibility increased to the decisive advantage of the defenders. Of course, artillery and

The liberation of Sumay Barracks hardly ended the fighting on the Orote Peninsula, which the Japanese had turned into a powerful stronghold with caves such as the one seen here. Moments later, Marine engineers sealed this cave with a powerful explosive charge. *Official USMC Photo*

Two 155mm howitzer battalions took part in the Guam operation as part of the III Amphibious Corps artillery group. *Official USMC Photo*

Partly to protect Chamorros native to Guam, but also for the sake of saving lives of combatants on both sides, Marine psychological operations teams attempted to cajole Japanese troops into surrendering. Results, which were quite good on Tinian, were almost nil on Guam. *Official USMC Photo*

Bad things happened to Japanese troops who failed to surrender. Here, a 37mm gun fires round after round of armor-piercing ammunition (note the pile of empty shell casings at bottom left) into concrete structures in which Japanese troops have taken refuge. *Official USMC Photo*

naval gunfire weighed in with better results as soon as it became light. But the light played in both directions; it actually gave Japanese troops on dominating ground a better opportunity to hurt 3/21, which had held heroically through the night as Japanese advanced into the gap between it and the adjacent 9th Marines. After dawn, the 9th Marines had to withdraw along part of its front to man a counterattack to relieve 3/21. This attack was decisive, and the Japanese overlooking 3/21 were knocked from their perch. Throughout the morning, counterattacks in contested zones pushed the Japanese back from positions they had captured, but at great cost. Among those killed was the 2/3 commander. In the end, it took the commitment of an Army battalion from the corps reserve to man an effective sweeping force against the many Japanese strongpoints intermingled with Marine positions.

But long before the final Japanese infiltrators had been swept up or forced to retire, the decisive battle in the 3d Marine Division zone had been decided in favor of the Marines. There had never been a chance that Guam's Japanese defenders could prevail, but they might have delayed and thus weakened the American B-29 offensive for many weeks had they maintained a cohesive defensive effort in northern Guam. All chances for that were wiped away in the final counterattack on the night of July 25–26. The defense would remain stubborn, and the fall of northern Guam would not be completed until August 11, 1944, but that downfall was assured by Japanese actions on the night of July 25–26.

Likewise, the Japanese defense of the Orote Peninsula was stubborn and often brutal, but a foregone conclusion was reached on July 29, when the 4th and 22d Marines, attacking abreast, reached Orote Point.

Nearly sixteen hundred Marines died to capture Guam, as did 177 U.S. Army infantrymen, and 5,308 Marines and 662 American soldiers were wounded in action. At least eleven thousand Japanese soldiers and sailors died there, too.

The strategic reason for the 1944 battle for Guam came to the fore when B-29s of the U.S. Army Air Forces' Twentieth Air Force began to use the new airfields in northern Guam as bases from which they could destroy war industries and, indeed, whole cities in Japan itself.

This is what the road to victory looks like. Large formations of veteran Marine infantrymen march on Guam's capital, Agana, as signalmen string phone lines alongside the highway.
Official USMC Photo

CHAPTER 15

PELELIU

SEPTEMBER 15–OCTOBER 15, 1944

Aformed FTER THE FALL OF BUNA, NEW GUINEA, IN JANUARY 1943, AND OF GUADALCANAL in February, the course of the Pacific War seemed inevitable throughout the remainder of its days. Allied soldiers, sailors, and airmen pushed their way steadily along the Solomons chain and across the back of New Guinea for all of 1943, and the Americans began their long-awaited and always-preferred Central Pacific offensive at Tarawa and Makin in November 1943.

The logic that guided the advance from east to west and then south to north seemed to be firmly established as it unfolded. After securing eastern New Guinea (Papua), the Southwest Pacific Area forces under General Douglas MacArthur leapfrogged westward from base to base, often avoiding protracted and costly confrontations by landing where the Japanese had no strong fortifications. Likewise, the South Pacific Area forces under Vice Admiral William Halsey. A bypass strategy became firmly embedded in Allied policy wherever Japanese bases, both major and minor, could be evaded and contained. The "bypass strategy" became the favored outlook as the battle lines extended westward along New Guinea's endless-seeming northern coast and across the vast reaches of the Central Pacific. Tens and eventually hundreds of thousands of Japanese defenders on unwanted and unneeded bases were left, as Admiral Ernest King, the chief of naval operations, put it, "to wither on the vine." Of course, where conditions made it impossible to bypass a powerfully defended and needed Japanese base, Allied troops were in no way hesitant to overwhelm them by direct amphibious assault—as at Tarawa, Kwajalein, Eniwetok, Saipan, Tinian, and Guam. But many powerfully defended Japanese bases were bypassed or detoured,

Once ashore in southwestern Peleliu, the landing force sorted itself out to begin the drive inland. Fighting was most intense on the northern beaches, in the 1st Marines' zone, less so in the adjacent 5th Marines' zone, and even less so in the right-hand 7th Marines' zone. *Official USMC Photo*

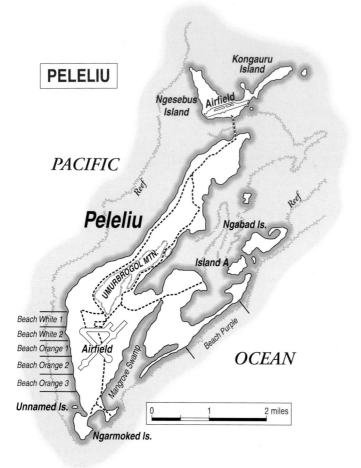

PELELIU

PACIFIC

Peleliu

UMURBROGOL MTN.

Kongauru
Island

Ngesebus
Island   Airfield

Ngabad Is.

Island A

Beach White 1
Beach White 2
Beach Orange 1   Airfield
Beach Orange 2
Beach Orange 3   Mangrove Swamp   Beach Purple

Unnamed Is.

Ngarmoked Is.

OCEAN

Reef

Reef

0   1   2 miles

among them Rabaul, Truk, and numerous locations along the New Guinea coast.

By early August 1944, the twin Allied lines of advance seemed to be converging on the Philippine Islands. MacArthur's forces were in the Schouten Islands, off western New Guinea (Irian), and Admiral Chester Nimitz's advance across the vast Central Pacific had just about taken the Mariana Islands. Acting on the logic and reason that had thus far sustained the brilliantly successful (if often bloody) twin drives, the Central Pacific force would next turn north to jump into the Volcano Islands, a drive that would have taken these powerful amphibious and air forces directly toward Japan, and MacArthur's Southwest Pacific Area forces would have jumped into the southern Philippines, perhaps ending up in Formosa, or even the China coast between Hong Kong and Shanghai.

It was, in fact, the uncertainty of the ultimate goals and true direction of the next series of long reaches that were at the center of a major debate in the highest echelons of the American Pacific War leadership. Serious consideration was given to an invasion of Formosa and a landing at or near Amoy, China. The temptation to turn north from the Marianas toward Tokyo was tempered by a strategic view that pointed to the Volcanoes as well as to Okinawa, through which an entry into the southernmost Japanese home island of Kyushu could be made, rather than a direct assault on Japan's centrally located capital.

Through the summer of 1944, as the Marianas invasion played itself out, and as MacArthur's planners debated alternatives to a slow drive from south to north through the Philippines, a diversion of attention occurred. MacArthur's planners asked, quite rightly, how the Philippines invasion force was to be assured a safe passage from New Guinea to Mindanao if Japanese air bases in the Palau Islands were still in Japanese hands and intact. So far, none of the Caroline Islands—which stretch from Truk in the east to the Palaus in the west—had fallen into American hands. They had been bypassed for better invasion routes to the north and south, but there were still air routes in Japanese hands by which the bypassed (and only partially contained) Carolines bases could be sustained and reinforced. Only 500 air miles from the nearest Philippines air bases, the Palaus were particularly problematic in that they could be reached by air from the Japanese side without problem but were too far from the nearest American base to be powerfully and continuously interdicted from the air (a job for land-based bombers). It was true that the airfields in the Palaus had been raked clean by U.S. Navy carrier strikes on March 31, 1944, and it was further true that the many losses had not been replaced. Nevertheless, the Palaus air bases could be remanned and reinforced with great ease from the Philippines. If that happened, then the direct line of supply and communication running toward the Philippines from New Guinea

As in every assault landing before and after, some troops were happy to be marked "present" while the battle was carried to the enemy by a sanguinary minority willing to risk life and limb in direct, over-the-sights combat. Here, an LVT(A) shields the majority while four Marines atop the huge vehicle duel the defenders eye-to-eye. *Official USMC Photo*

could be attacked with great ease from them or from bases in the eastern Netherlands East Indies, especially in the Molucca Islands.

The reverse also was true. If Japanese land-based bombers could reach the Palaus from the Philippines, then Allied land-based bombers could reach the Philippines from the Palaus. Since the remote Palaus air bases could not be easily bombed into submission from any base in Allied hands at the time, and since Allied bombers based in the Palaus could help prepare the way for the inevitable Allied invasion of the Philippines, it seemed both necessary and useful that an invasion of the Palaus be mounted. (Most of the same holds true in the case of Japanese bases in the eastern Netherlands East Indies, and a parallel plan regarding the Molucca Islands also was set in motion.) A look at a map makes a step to the Palaus appear as half a step backward from either the new Southwest Pacific bases in western New Guinea and the Schouten Islands, or a full step backward from the new Central Pacific bases in the Marianas. But given the ranges and positions of Allied and Japanese land-based bombers, half a step backward or a full step to the side into the Palaus appeared

The first units of African-American Marines to see live combat in any war were depot and ammunition companies at Saipan. Note the yellow discs these Marines on Peleliu have affixed to their field blouses and trousers. These identified them as shore party. Many black Marines at Saipan and later took opportunities to fight the Japanese during supply runs to the front. *Official USMC Photo*

to be altogether necessary and perfectly logical by any measure available to the mid-1944 observer. The Allies knew this to be the case, and believed in it. So did the Japanese. Both sides prepared for an inevitable confrontation over the Palaus.

There were several possible objectives to consider for the projected Palaus invasion. The first, and seemingly the best, was the Japanese airfield complex on Babelthaup, by far the largest of the Palau islands. The second was a lesser air base on Peleliu, in the southern Palaus. And a third alternative was the seizure of an island that had no airfield but upon which a new bomber base could be built quickly. The third was actually the preferred scenario, and it was a proven method by that stage of the Pacific War, but alas, there was not enough time to create an invasion force, seize a suitable island, build a new base, and mount an aerial offensive against the Philippines in time to adequately precede the upcoming invasion of Mindanao. Intelligence in the form of Japanese documents captured on Saipan indicated that Babelthaup was very heavily defended, and it was too big to be taken quickly by any landing force of

The largest tank-versus-tank battle of the Pacific War occurred when a Japanese tank company and infantry charged straight into the teeth of a dozen Marine M4 medium tanks arrayed in the lines of the 5th Marines stretched across the airfield. The action took place on D-day afternoon. *Official USMC Photo*

a size that could be gathered in time. The airfield on Peleliu was smaller and less adequate than the one on Babelthaup, but it could be quickly expanded, and it seemed that it could be seized more easily by the two-division invasion force that could be made available. So, almost solely by a process of elimination, Peleliu was made the chief target of the largely preemptive Allied venture into the Palau Islands.

The Japanese had a special surprise planned for the veteran 1st Marine Division, to which the job of seizing Peleliu was given. Until that point in the war, Japanese defensive doctrine had favored a water's-edge defensive tactic coupled with ongoing massed-infantry attacks against the invading force. Almost without exception in the year-long trek across the Central Pacific, this ironclad rule had spelled doom for the defenders. If, as they always did, the invaders breached the water's-edge defenses, then the landing itself was secure. And if, as they always did, the main body of defenders threw themselves on the guns of the more numerous attackers, the defense degenerated into a series of isolated actions against holed-up survivors.

Under a new formula issued by Imperial General Headquarters during the summer of 1944, the defenders of Peleliu and other potential invasion targets throughout Japan's shrinking Pacific empire were to hole up from the start and fight attritional battles

The airfield—the largest swath of flat ground on Peleliu—fell completely to the 5th Marines attacking in the open on D+1. *Official USMC Photo*

throughout the length and breadth of their island bastions. Japanese ground troops who had done so on their own on Biak, in the Schouten Islands, had delayed an Allied victory far beyond the most pessimistic Allied estimate, and they had killed many more invasion troops than the island was worth.

The troops of the veteran and highly confident 1st Marine Division knew they would be facing more than ten thousand crack, battle-hardened Imperial Army troops on Peleliu; they had no idea, however, that those Japanese would dig in and prepare to defend themselves as had no other Japanese the Marines had ever faced in the Pacific.

PRECEDED BY FOUR DAYS OF VERY HEAVY BOMBARDMENT BY CARRIER AIRCRAFT AND TWO days of very heavy bombardment by all manner of fire-support ships, the lead waves of the 1st Marine Division opened its assault on Peleliu's five southwestern invasion beaches at 0832 hours on September 15, 1944. (A simultaneous invasion was being launched by Southwest Pacific Area troops in the Molucca Islands.) The immediate objective of the Peleliu invasion was the southern fourth of the small island, for that is where the all-impor-

This LVT(A)'s gunner was unable to depress his 75mm main gun far enough to take out a Japanese 5-inch naval gun dug in close to the ground, so the driver rolled over the position, caving in the roof and crushing the entire Japanese bunker. *Official USMC Photo*

tant airfield was located. Peleliu was to be a battle aimed at eradicating the foe, but getting Peleliu-based bombers into operation against targets in the Philippines was the prime strategic objective.

Landing on the division's left was the 1st Marines, whose lead waves made it to the beach without much opposition but that right away ran into formidable defenses on bluffs and other high ground to the immediate left. As more and more defenders recovered from the effects of last-minute bombardments or shifted toward the invaders from deep caves and shelters, the fire intensified against the leading troops as well as successive landing waves.

Charged with sealing a significant portion of the regiment's and the division's far-left flank, 3/1 quickly counted itself lucky merely to have established a beachhead under such intense and dominating fire. Casualties ran very high. Indeed, Company K, 3/1, the division's left flank unit, suffered grievous losses when it impaled itself on the heavily defended promontory upon which the division's left flank was to be anchored. Though Company K won a two-hour-long hand-to-hand struggle, the thirty-two survivors of its two-platoon assault force ended up being isolated from the rest of the division, unable to evacuate its casualties or receive supplies and replacements. To Company K's right, the remainder of 3/1 went to ground in swampy or open ground, and great unbridgeable gaps appeared. In sum, intense fire from hidden defenses caused 3/1 to end its first-day advance well short of nearly all its first-day objectives. On the regimental right, 2/1 ran into less opposition and thus was able to drive to the nearer of its two first-day objective lines. But 2/1's partial success caused it to lose contact with 3/1, so 1/1 and numerous support troops had to be committed to cover the worst of the yawning gaps in the regimental line.

The 5th Marines had a somewhat easier time of it. Its drive toward the southeastern shore was to take place across the open ground of the airfield, so its left flank was entirely exposed to fire from the heights and its advance was contested all along the front by dug-in Japanese. But the 5th Marines faced nothing like the intense fire that had stalled the adjacent 1st Marines. On the regimental left, 1/5 reached its first phase line in good order, but it was obliged to hold there because 2/1, on its left, was held up. So 1/5 and several M4 medium tanks dug in to await developments on its flanks.

To the right of 1/5, 3/5's left company had no trouble landing or advancing, but the battalion's right company had trouble doing both, a situation that became worse when 3/7 landed on 3/5's beach because heavy fire had forced it away from its own beach. Confusion slowed 3/5 at first, and then enemy fire slowed the battalion, but its advance continued at a methodical pace against well-organized resistance that included accurate mortar barrages. At length, 2/5 had to be committed to bolster the advance, which was faltering due to battle and heat casualties. There also were problems maintaining contact with 3/7, on the right.

The 7th Marines landed across the southernmost beach in column of battalions—two battalions, actually, since 2/7 was the division reserve. Japanese fire forced most of 3/7 to land on the next beach to the north, behind 3/5, but the 7th Marines arrived ashore intact and not too badly hurt. There were confusion and delays, but 3/7 sorted itself out

The flamethrower LVT was tested on Peleliu with spectacular results. In this photograph, the flame gun is trained out on a shell-torn concrete structure as the LVT and infantry in its wake move past. *Official USMC Photo*

Vistas in Peleliu's broken terrain were often short, but every once in a while a sharpshooter got in a clear shot over open ground. The long-barrel BAR was a particularly good weapon for scoring single-shot kills over long distances and had been used as a sniper rifle at least as early as Guadalcanal.
Official USMC Photo

and attacked toward the east. The job of the 7th Marines was to drive to the eastern shore and then wheel right to clear the southern portion of the island. Here, Marine tanks played a pivotal role in overcoming Japanese defensive emplacements and facilitating the advance. Terrain along 1/7's front was very swampy, so unit cohesion had to be sacrificed. Opposition was based on numerous strongpoints, each of which had to be reduced as it was encountered. The 7th Marines fought through the day, overcame many obstacles, and advanced deeply, but reached none of its D-day objectives.

Although Peleliu's defenders had built a formidable defense-in-depth and were committed to a battle of attrition from which they frankly did not expect to escape, there was a counterattack plan. There was always some small hope that the landing force could be dislodged early in an amphibious assault, so a company of light tanks and a specially trained infantry unit attacked behind an artillery and mortar preparation at nearly 1700 hours. The attack came across the open airfield, more or less toward 1/5, which had dug in earlier precisely because it was known that Japanese tanks were part of the defensive team. Marine infantry weapons, antitank guns, and as many as a dozen M4 tanks stood off and blasted the Japanese tanks and infantry, which were completely in the open. Several Japanese tanks got into the Marine rear, where they were blown up, and two Japanese light tanks escaped, but the attack was crushed and, in its wake, elements of 2/5 were able to drive to the center of the airfield. Except for a few local forays, the tank attack was to be the only time the Japanese came out of their burrows to fight in the open. After this D-day attack, all the Japanese on Peleliu would have to be pried out of their fighting positions or blown up in them.

By dusk, only two Marine companies had achieved their D-day goals. Though undermanned and isolated, Company K, 3/1, had anchored the division's left, and Company L, 3/5, completely crossed the island to the eastern shore. Otherwise, eight Marine infantry battalions were strewn across the length and breadth of the southern fourth of Peleliu. Heavy counterattacks were expected during the night, but none materialized, which in a way was disappointing because the attack plan counted on the suicidal tactics Marines had overcome all along the way from Tarawa to Guam.

Marine casualties on D-day were heavy: 210 dead and 901 wounded, not including hundreds of heat cases caused by scorching daytime temperatures coupled with inadequate

The .45-caliber Thompson submachine gun was never considered a precision weapon; it had a mean kick to the right and high, and the bullets tended to tumble shortly after being fired. But it was a great area or suppressive weapon at short distances, and tumbling rounds tended to kill rather than wound.
Official USMC Photo

water supplies. There was concern that casualties were so high and that so few objectives had been seized, but everyone was fundamentally optimistic that D+1 would be a much better day, for the 1st Marine Division was firmly established on Peleliu and in possession of enormous offensive strength relative to the living defenders.

On D+1, Marine medium tanks came into their own—as they never had to this point in the Pacific War. The grinding advance across Peleliu probably could not have taken place as well as it did without the incredible bravery and selfless devotion exhibited by the 1st Tank Battalion's M4 crews. They were magnificent. Often as not, despite heavy small-arms fire at every point, tank commanders stood upright in open hatches to see targets in Peleliu's jumbled, closed terrain, and so casualties among tank commanders were very high. Most, perhaps all, of the battalion's mediums were knocked out at one time or another during the campaign, but most were speedily returned to duty by expert, dedicated repair crews. The tanks made all the difference on Peleliu.

The infantry was no less magnificent. It took utmost teamwork and bravery to advance on hidden, mutually supporting bunkers and caves, and these were traits the Marine infantry possessed in abundance. With or without the support of the tanks, the infantry steadily reduced bunker after bunker, cave after cave, defensive locale after defensive locale. The price was exorbitant, but the gains from D+1 onward were often considerable.

On D+1, the two-battalion 7th Marines advanced to the eastern shore in its zone and then wheeled smartly to the south to take on the defenses between the airfield and the southern shore. Both battalions of the 7th Marines had to halt in place at one time or another to await the arrival of fresh water. The heat caused as many casualties as enemy fire, and would do so throughout the battle. Most of the 7th Marines' objectives were taken on D+1, but the regiment was unable to take the last of its southern objectives until D+3, September 18. In accomplishing its mission, the regiment destroyed a reinforced battalion of Japanese infantry amounting to 2,609 known enemy dead, about a fourth of the original defenders. The cost, overall, was 47 killed, 37 missing in action, and 414 wounded.

Also on D+1, 3/1 and 1/1 attempted to attack into the first line of ridges north of the open airfield area, but both battalions were stymied by heavy fire from large numbers of defensive emplacements dug into unbelievably broken terrain. Withal, 2/1 and the 5th Marines succeeded in driving across the entire airfield complex, reaching the eastern shore, and sealing the southern portion of the island from infiltration from the north. The division reserve, 2/7, was landed on D+1, attached to the 1st Marines, and used to bridge a widening gap between the

Molotov cocktails were not part of any officially sanctioned weapons package, but they were lethally effective against caves and fighting holes in cases where a flamethrower was either not available or might have endangered friendly troops caught up in close-terrain fighting. Note, at the center of this photograph—taken on a feature known as Suicide Ridge—that a second Molotov cocktail has already been lighted. *Official USMC Photo*

Tanks were invaluable on Peleliu when they could be driven close enough to the action to lay their main guns on Japanese fighting positions. Note at left the white smoke rising from, presumably, just such a position. *Official USMC Photo*

stalled 1/1 and the advancing 2/1. By day's end on September 16, a continuous if extremely jagged line ran across the entire island somewhat to the north of the airfield and, on the left and in the center, somewhat into the southern verge of Peleliu's central ridge complex, upon which the bulk of the diehard Japanese would be basing their stand.

On D+3, after containing the Japanese defensive zone in the southeastern ridge area north of the airfield, the 5th Marines (less 1/5, in division reserve) attacked into a rather large but isolated eastern extension of Peleliu, almost a separate island adjacent to the main island. Here, and on several small islands in the sector, hundreds of Japanese defenders were killed in their burrows between D+3 and D+8, when the sector was ultimately declared secure.

In stark contrast to the successes of the 5th and 7th Marines in their zones, the 1st Marines (including 2/7) was extremely hard-pressed as it advanced into the well-defended ridge country north of the airfield—the so-called Umurbrogol Mountains. Peleliu is actually centered on a ridge of coral that was driven up from the sea bottom by an earthquake in the distant past. Thus the central ridge is little more than a shattered coral reef thrown into the air. The Japanese had spent months feverishly improving on nature's handiwork, and the result—nature's and the defenders'—was simply awesome, all but impenetrable. Tanks were helpful on the verges, where they could find suitable ground, but they could not get up to the central areas once Marine infantrymen passed beyond range or line of sight. Artillery and air support were ample, but both were largely ineffective. Because the artillery was free to fire at any time, the airplanes could not get low enough to hit individual caves and burrows with any degree of accuracy. And the artillery could not reach the many Japanese hiding holes on the reverse slopes of the craggy, broken coral Umurbrogol Mountains. So the 1st Marines bogged down entirely in the center on D+3 and then had to halt on the left on D+5 to remain in possession of a coherent line. The regiment fought bravely—perhaps too bravely, for it shattered itself in eking out gains that were ultimately too small to justify the loss of so many magnificent troops. In the first three days on Peleliu, the reinforced 1st Marines sustained 1,236 battle casualties, nearly a third its original strength. By D+5, more than 1,500 members of the regiment had been killed or wounded, and this does not take into account a steady, debilitating stream of heat casualties.

On September 20, three of the 1st Marines' four infantry battalions were relieved by 1/7 and 3/7. Attacks into the teeth of Japanese-held defensive complexes continued for

A MAG-11 F4U Corsair based at Peleliu's airfield has just dropped napalm on an otherwise inaccessible Japanese position. *Official USMC Photo*

As in all the island battles, modern heavy weapons were fine when they could be employed, but in the final accounting it took infantrymen armored in cloth shirts to clear the ground with hand grenades, Molotov cocktails, and rifles. *Official USMC Photo*

three more days, but to little avail. Only then did Marine commanders conclude that the strategically vital portions of the island—the airfield, and little else—had been in their hands for nearly a week. Easy pickings to the north still remained to be harvested (by the 5th Marines, in a comparatively bloodless grab that included an amphibious landing on Ngesebus Island), and the Umurbrogol Mountains could be contained from virtually all quarters, leaving the conduct of air operations in virtual peace. By September 22, the bulk of a green U.S. Army division had seized most of neighboring Angaur Island and thus was available to relieve elements of the 1st Marine Division on Peleliu. This was done in a matter of days. (A third regimental combat team of the Army division almost bloodlessly seized Ulithi Atoll between September 21 and 23. (Ulithi was turned into the Pacific Fleet's westernmost anchorage and base for the remainder of the war.)

The decision to contain the Umurbrogols and turn the island over to the Army division took virtually all the pressure off the battered 1st Marine Division. Army troops began to replace the 1st Marines on September 23. Meanwhile, the 5th Marines swept from the eastern side of the island to contain the northern reaches, after which it attacked southward to compress the Japanese central pocket from that quadrant. Japanese resistance ceased in northern Peleliu on September 30, after which an Army regiment relieved the 5th Marines.

By October 7, the 7th Marines had been so weakened by sustained combat that it had to be replaced on the line by the 5th Marines.

Marine infantry battalions rotated in and out of combat assignments until October 12, when the "assault" phase was declared at an end. On October 15, the 1st Marine Division was formally relieved of its combat role in the Palaus, and large elements of the division began leaving Peleliu on October 30. It was not until November 27, however, that the Umurbrogol Pocket was eradicated by Army troops and the island declared secure.

A total of 6,265 Marines became casualties on Peleliu— 1,124 killed, 117 missing, and 5,024 wounded or injured. It is estimated that 10,695 Japanese died on Peleliu, and 301 were taken prisoner.

Development of the airfield—Peleliu's strategic prize—began as soon as the complex fell into Marine hands on D+2. A U.S. Navy carrier bomber was the first American airplane to land there, on September 3, and two VMO-3 OY artillery spotter planes arrived for permanent duty on the same day. An advance flight echelon of MAG-11's VMF(N)-541 arrived on September 24, VMF-114 arrived on September 26, and VMF-122 and the rest of VMF(N)-541 arrived on October 1. All of these Marine aircraft (and others that followed) were deployed at Peleliu to fulfill a tactical role—to support the ground troops—or to interdict bypassed Japanese bases in the western Carolines that were within their range.

The *strategic* purpose for attacking the Palau Islands was to put them at the disposal of long-range bombers that could mount preinvasion attacks against Japanese bases in the southern Philippines. This mission was never accomplished. In the first place, a decision made on September 15—the very day the 1st Marine Division invaded Peleliu—moved the initial invasion target in the Philippines from Mindanao, in the south, to Leyte, in the center. Moreover, the date of the U.S. return to the Philippines was advanced from December 20, 1944, to October 20. The first Peleliu-based U.S. Army Air Forces preinvasion heavy-bomber mission to the Philippines took place on October 17; the invasion of Leyte took place on October 20. At most, a few tens of tons of bombs were delivered from Peleliu before the Philippines invasion began. On October 21, the built-from-scratch runway on Angaur—an island taken at very little cost—was declared operational, and heavy-bomber operations from there commenced within days.

The bold fact, seen so clearly in hindsight, that Peleliu need not have been invaded—that Angaur alone (if any Palaus objective at all) would have sufficed, and at much reduced cost in blood—detracts nothing whatever from the utmost bravery and sacrifice exhibited and endured by the superb 1st Marine Division between September 15 and October 15, 1944. As in the case of Cape Gloucester, the seizure of Peleliu seemed necessary and vital while it was happening. It is ironic and extremely sad that, like Cape Gloucester, Peleliu turned out to be worth almost none of the human lives and limbs expended there. But thousands of brave 1st Division Marines once again did their duty at Peleliu, and nothing can ever detract from that.

CHAPTER 16

IWO JIMA

FEBRUARY 19–MARCH 16, 1945

IWO JIMA WAS IN A CLASS BY ITSELF, THE ULTIMATE EXPRESSION OF DEATH AND MAYHEM FOR the sake of death and mayhem to be found in the annals of the Pacific War. Improving exponentially on a "defend-and-die" concept first encountered by U.S. Army troops on Biak, in the Schouten Islands off New Guinea, and then by Marines at Peleliu, the island commander oversaw the construction of hundreds of concrete bunkers, pillboxes, blockhouses, and other fighting positions as well as multistory underground command centers and underground barracks—as deep at seventy-five feet, and all interconnected by D-day by eleven of a projected seventeen miles of underground passageways. These positions were held by an estimated twenty-three thousand Imperial troops, many of them veterans. The hundreds of mortars and artillery pieces sprinkled throughout the defensive sectors were painstakingly preregistered to cover virtually every square yard of the island. Nearly all the defenders had been bonded into a brotherhood born of the extreme difficulties encountered during the building of bunkers and passageways underground in extreme heat laced with sulfurous fumes. Beyond that, all the defenders took an oath to fight to the death, to give no ground for any reason short of death. All questions of counterattacking the invaders were quelled; except for designated roving assault detachments, the defenders would man their positions unto death.

There was no dead ground on Iwo Jima, not one square yard that could be employed as cover with any certainty whatsoever that it was in fact cover. The only way to find dead ground was to kill for it.

Following a seventy-four-day air and naval bombardment that was felt by its architects to cover all the dangerous ground, two veteran regiments of the 4th Marine Division

These Marine Corsairs from VMF-124 and VMF-213, based aboard the fleet carrier USS *Essex,* were the first Marine aircraft based aboard any carrier in World War II. Pilots from both squadrons were the first Marines to fire their weapons at targets on Iwo Jima. *Official USMC Photo*

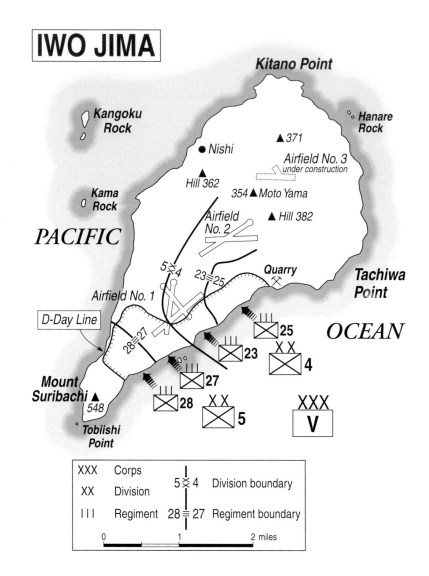

IWO JIMA

Kitano Point

Kangoku
Rock

Hanare
Rock

▲ 371

● Nishi

Airfield No. 3
under construction

▲
Hill 362

354 ▲ Moto Yama

Kama
Rock

▲ Hill 382

PACIFIC

Airfield
No. 2

5 ⊠ 4

23 ≡ 25

Quarry

Tachiwa
Point

Airfield No. 1

D-Day Line

OCEAN

│││
⊠ 25

28 ≡ 27

│││
⊠ 23

X X
⊠ 4

│││
⊠ 27

Mount
Suribachi ▲

│││
⊠ 28

X X
⊠ 5

XXX
V

548

Tobiishi
Point

XXX	Corps		5 ⊠ 4	Division boundary
XX	Division			
││││	Regiment		28 ≡ 27	Regiment boundary

0   1   2 miles

The first waves of eight battalion landing
teams were allowed to come ashore
against almost zero opposition. Here,
keyed-up Marines advance from cover to
cover under an LVT(A)'s 75mm gun while
naval gunfire curtains the beachhead.
Official USMC Photo

landed alongside two regiments of the new 5th Marine Division—eight battalion landing teams in all. Aircraft, battleships, cruisers, and destroyers pummeled ground targets near and far from the landing beaches, and the destroyers established a literal curtain of fire four hundred yards from the front as the first wave of amtracs climbed ashore. LCI gunboats fired hundreds of rockets to suppress fire at the very last moment; then two squadrons of Marine Corsairs—VMF-124 and VMF-213, based aboard the USS *Essex* since December—strafed the ground just behind the beaches at such low altitude that it looked to men on the water as if they were on the ground.

Nothing happened. There was no return fire. No Japanese fired at the ships offshore, nor at the oncoming waves of amtracs, nor at Marines who were surprised to learn as their feet touched down that all of southern Iwo Jima was covered in a thick mantle of black volcanic ash—not simply black sand—that offered no purchase for their feet or their shovels.

Ahead lay another surprise: a fifteen-foot terrace that rose sharply from just in back of the beaches. LVT(A)s that fired as they landed were unable to scale this slippery slope, so many returned to the water and fired on the few suspect features the gunners could see.

Most of the beachhead was shielded by a 15-foot-high terrace of loose volcanic dust. The troops appreciated the cover until tracked vehicles were stalled in the fine volcanic ash and the advance into withering fire had to be made without them. *Official USMC Photo*

This Marine was lucky to have been wounded behind cover, on the beach, and with corpsmen on the spot.
Official USMC Photo

This Marine never had a chance. He was shot through the temple, right through his steel helmet, as he lay in shallow cover he had probably scooped out himself in the black volcanic ash overlooking the beach.
Official USMC Photo

Wave upon wave landed on eerily safe beaches. Three Marine divisions had come to fight for Iwo Jima, and two-thirds of two of them appeared to be getting a free pass.

The descent to hell began as the lead infantry units advanced up the terrace and to points about 500 yards inland. Then the world fell in on them as prearranged fires directed by steady leaders erupted on and around every living man and mechanical aid on the landing beaches. Japanese machine gunners and riflemen hitherto hunkered down in caves or fighting positions opened fire on Marines advancing across open ground.

The Marines fell to the ground, looking for targets or looking after their wounds. Those who tried to dig in found that the volcanic ash could not be moved without moving back. Immediately, a great hue and cry went up: send us sandbags. There was no way to dig in and no means at hand to build shelter. Marines had walked into the kill zone, and they were being killed.

There was mayhem at the beach. Infantry could manage after a fashion; there was always a way to get forward on foot, but anything with wheels sank to its axles, and even

Japanese gunners cannily held their fire until thousands of Marines and vehicles were packed into the beaches. Imagine trying to locate a gun emplacement like this one from hundreds of yards away or even a few hundred feet overhead. The artillery fan on Iwo Jima was nearly perfect when the guns and mortars opened fire on D-day. Note the heavy antiaircraft machine gun on the terrace just over the big gun's barrel. *Official USMC Photo*

A Marine LVT(A) has just taken a direct hit on the beach and explodes, presumably as flames reach its fuel or ammunition. In the murk to the right of the stricken LVT(A) is an overturned wheeled vehicle. *Official USMC Photo*

This scene has a little bit of everything: two blasted amtracs and a tank that has thrown a track after digging into the volcanic ash; and the Marine in the foreground is digging a shelter that is filling itself in only a little more slowly than he is shoveling. *Official USMC Photo*

It was extremely difficult to get 75mm and 105mm howitzers ashore. The DUKW amphibian trucks that brought them ashore could not negotiate the terrace without being winched forward, and then digging the guns in couldn't be completed without sandbags to hold back the shifting ash. And, of course, this was all accomplished under a rain of shells until holes could be made in the artfully overlapping Japanese artillery fan. Note the jerry cans of water in this and other photographs. Iwo Jima had no streams, ponds, or springs—no sources of fresh water at all except man-made catchments for rainwater in the northern third of the island. It took an immense supply of water to nourish more than one hundred thousand invaders. *Official USMC Photo*

the treads on tanks and amtracs slipped and dug into the bottomless ash. In at least one case, the front wheels of a vehicle dug in as soon as they left the ramp of a landing craft, and that pinned the ramp to the beach, preventing the craft from retracting under intense mortar and artillery fire. As the day progressed, a high inshore tide just made things worse, and scores of landing craft broached in the surf and foundered.

At the front, the infantry quickly adapted to the harsh realities of Iwo Jima. Infantrymen always adapt; they are the best adapters in the world, for if they cannot or will not or even do not adapt, they die. They couldn't dig in, and they certainly could not withdraw to the shell-struck mayhem on the beaches. So they attacked. They attacked every fighting position they could both see and reach, and then they went looking for more. In due course, they won ground, killed defenders, and advanced toward their D-day objectives. The reserve battalions were landed and thrown into the fight at the front or cleared bypassed positions behind the front. In due course, tanks, LVT(A)s, 75mm halftracks, and 37mm guns found their way to the front. But it was the brave infantry who took the ground from other brave infantry, all of them heedless of their lives.

At Iwo Jima's narrowest point, two companies of 1/28—a new regiment composed in large part of veteran Raiders and parachutists—drove to the western shore with a costly gallantry that cannot be described in terms that have been invented yet. Both company commanders led small teams of volunteers at the heads of their units, knocked out position after position until one of the captains collapsed from the effects of his mortal wounds and the

This 28th Marines 81mm mortar crew is firing at targets on Mount Suribachi from within a gun pit defined by wooden crates that hold back the liquidlike volcanic ash that covers this part of Iwo Jima. There is *no* cover between this position and distant Suribachi. *Official USMC Photo*

A busy day at the office. These .30-caliber medium machine gunners have fired off dozens of belts of ammunition to suppress Japanese positions that otherwise would have impeded or stopped the advance of their company's riflemen. *Official USMC Photo*

Joe Rosenthal's immortal "Flag Raising on Iwo Jima," a stirring view of American gallantry that the Marine Corps adopted within days as its primary icon.
Joe Rosenthal

The Japanese defenders died in their thousands beneath the ground, rarely exposed to sunlight or scrutiny. High atop Mount Suribachi, Marines gather to stare at the rarest sight of all, a living Japanese soldier in Marine custody.
Official USMC Photo

By only D+4, February 23, Company G, 24th Marines, was down to 40 percent of its original complement. Here, the survivors take a break in a gully beside a disabled tank. Note the eyes of the Marines closest to the camera.
Official USMC Photo

other was incapacitated by merely "serious" wounds. In the wake of leaders like these, Marines who lost track of their own units joined other stragglers to take out fighting positions whose interlocking bands of fire swept over all Marines, lost and found, all along and behind the front. Marine mortars with no cover and just the rounds that could be carried to them were fired directly at targets their crews could see with their own eyes—a situation that was rare on any other modern battlefield.

Six of eight Marine 75mm and 105mm howitzer battalions came ashore in dribs and drabs through the long afternoon. Guns were lost when their conveyances to the beach—DUKWs from two Marine and one Army amphibian truck companies—took direct hits from the pervasive bombardment, or they were hit after they were set in, or they couldn't

Marines break from cover to take new ground. The Marine at the far right, a radioman, has stopped to aim his rifle at something he sees over the horizon. Another Marine is carrying a spool of communications wire.
Official USMC Photo

The flash suppressor of a Japanese heavy machine gun aimed down a narrow vista is all that can be seen *after* this pillbox's firing aperture has been ripped open by the direct hit of a heavy shell. Finding targets in rubble was as hard as finding targets without the rubble.
Official USMC Photo

Several Marine rocket detachments served on Iwo Jima. Rockets are an area-saturation weapon meant to suppress defenses while infantry and tanks move in for the kill. If rockets actually destroy a particular position, it is a matter of luck.
Official USMC Photo

be carried over the terrace to be set in in the first place. But slowly, using coordinates radioed in by aerial observers or forward observers at the front, or anyone at the front who could provide reliable real-time information, the guns in the beachhead took out positions that were holding up the ground advance. The Marine artillery and the mobile naval gunfire also took out Japanese guns, mortars, and observation posts and thus slowly cut ragged holes in the Japanese coverage of the battlefield, created dead ground by creating dead Japanese gunners and dead Japanese mortar and artillery observers.

By 1100, ten Marines from two platoons of Company B, 1/28, joined forces on their battalion's objective, the western beach at Iwo Jima's narrowest point, just 700 yards from the beachhead. Behind these brave but exhausted Marines, the 28th Marines mopped up its zone and established a continuous line across the narrow neck, then faced the southwestern tail of the island, which was dominated by the forbidding heights of Mount Suribachi. To the right, the 27th Marines came abreast, in places only a few yards from the western shore. But farther to the right, the 4th Marine Division was bogged down in line with the northeast-southwest taxiway of Airfield No. 1, which was to have been taken in its entirety by the 23d Marines. And farthest to the right, the 25th Marines advanced nearly to its objective, the island's shoreside quarry, but it failed by hundreds of yards to swing to the objective line anchored by the quarry. Instead of ending D-day on a line running generally east to west across the midpoint of Iwo Jima, the two Marine divisions held a northeast-to-southwest line about halfway across the southern half of the island—less than half the ground they had planned to take. Estimates place D-day casualties at nearly 550 killed and more than 1,800 wounded or otherwise incapacitated.

The 550-foot peak of Mount Suribachi fell on February 23 to the 28th Marines, who raised two flags. It took five days and the commitment in the corps center of most of the 3d Marine Division for the rest of VAC troops to reach approximately their D-day objective line. The fighting was horrendous, and thousands of Marines were killed or wounded. There was no finesse, no elegant battlefield solutions; only sledgehammer tactics worked, only brute force prevailed.

Slow, steady advances over increasingly rough terrain ensued. Two-thirds of Iwo Jima was in Marine hands by March 1. The rough terrain actually made the job easier as firm ground and natural cover became ample, but it also provided the Japanese with ample defensive possibilities. Nonetheless, by then, artillery, naval gunfire, and air support had winnowed the Japanese artillery, mortars, and machine guns and broken unit cohesion. No place on Iwo Jima was ever safe throughout and even after the long, grueling battle, but a lot of the island was safer than it had been in the first week.

Flamethrower operators incinerate
Japanese emplacements at close range. It
is difficult to see how Iwo Jima could have
been secured at a cost of *only* 6,821
dead Americans without the liberal use of
flamethrowers—or the unbelievably brave
men who carried them in range of targets.
Official USMC Photos

As his buddies take a break behind cover, this Marine sharpshooter tests his skills against a target that requires perfect shooting acumen. Note that he is perched on Japanese ammunition boxes.
Official USMC Photo

Well into the northern part of Iwo Jima, with its firm soil and scrub growth, a Marine flamethrower team carries out a sentence of death on the Japanese in this pillbox, which the Marines have approached from a blind side without taking fire from other pillboxes. Most defensive zones are difficult to crack but relatively easy to defeat once experienced combat troops break in.
Official USMC Photo

By March 11, the organized defense had been squeezed into two pockets, then pushed back until the island was declared secure on March 16. Mopping up continued for months, and stragglers and organized assault teams evaded capture and threw in raids where they could.

Killed and wounded numbered 6,821 and 18,070, respectively. Iwo Jima was America's bloodiest Pacific War battle, by far and by any measure.

AIRFIELD REHABILITATION GOT UNDER WAY CLOSE ON THE HEELS OF THE CAPTURE OF Airfield No. 1 in late February. The task was threefold: to base Marine squadrons assigned to help over the battlefield and isolate nearby garrisons; to base long-range Army Air Forces fighters that would escort Marianas-based B-29s over Japan; and to serve as an emergency base for B-29s with malfunctions or battle damage that might not otherwise have been able to get back to the Marianas. In some circles, it is noted that Iwo Jima serviced 2,251 B-29s by the end of the war, and this figure is converted to a claim that the lives of 24,761 crewmen were saved—a number just a little below the number of casualties sustained by VAC in taking the island. Others point out that many of the B-29s that landed at Iwo did so because it was there, not because they direly needed to set down there. A response to that is that Iwo-based fighters operating over Japan saved hundreds of bombers from being shot down there. And so forth.

Taken on its own merits, Iwo Jima was a meatgrinder taken by a blunt instrument at exceedingly high cost. As was the case in every bloody battle in the Pacific and, indeed, in most wars, very little comes between the bravery of men who did their duty and the heartfelt thanks of a grateful nation. Moreover, a single photograph snapped by a civilian war correspondent at the summit of Mount Suribachi on February 23, 1945, has served from that very week onward as a palpably living symbol of the bravery that rose upon every square inch that was touched by an American boot during that bloodiest of Pacific battles— indeed, in all Pacific War battles.

CHAPTER 17

OKINAWA

APRIL 1–JUNE 22, 1945

WHEN TWO MARINE AND TWO U.S. ARMY DIVISIONS LANDED ABREAST ON Okinawa on L-day, April 1, 1945, they faced an estimated one hundred fifty-five thousand Japanese ground, air, and naval troops holding an immense island on which an estimated five hundred thousand civilians lived in cities, towns, and villages. Okinawa was to be, in every way, vast when compared to any other operation undertaken by Allied forces in the Pacific War under U.S. Navy command. Indeed, using mainly divisions that had undertaken island-hopping operations in the south and central Pacific since mid-1942, the U.S. Pacific Fleet stood up the Tenth U.S. Army, consisting of III Amphibious Corps and XXIV Army Corps—the largest land command ever assembled under the direct control of the U.S. Navy.

To those Japanese who thought the war was winnable, Okinawa was the last chance. The island lay within 350 miles—easy flight distance—from the Japanese homeland and was, by American design, to be the base from which the southernmost home island, Kyushu, was to be pummeled to dust ahead of the expected follow-on invasion. Anything short of complete victory over Allied air, naval, and ground forces spelled doom for Japan—and no such victory was remotely in the cards. Thus, by Japanese lights, Okinawa was and could be no more than a delaying battle of attrition on a grand scale. The few Japanese who knew that Japan's war effort was in extremis were content to fight on Okinawa simply for reasons of honor, for all military logic pointed to the same dismal conclusion: Japan was vanquished in all but name as soon as the first B-29s left the ground in the Marianas, as soon as American carrier aircraft hit targets in Japan at will, as soon as

These Marines have just landed on Okinawa and are advancing to contact with an enemy who for now prefers to remain hunkered down in massive fortified sectors far to the south. *Official USMC Photo*

even twin-engine bombers could strike Japanese ports from Iwo Jima, as soon as Japan dared not move a warship or cargo vessel from a port in any part of the shrinking empire for fear it would be sunk by an American submarine. By April 1, 1945, all those events were taking place routinely.

Although the Japanese commanders counted one hundred fifty-five thousand defenders, their forces were of widely mixed abilities, and there were not nearly enough troops in total to cover the ground the way twenty-three thousand troops had covered Iwo Jima. Rather than cover all the ground, the forces on Okinawa were concentrated in a number of sectors that offered the best prospects for a robust, attritional defense. The northern half of the island was virtually conceded, and the south was turned into four extremely tough hedgehog defense sectors. The proportion of artillery and mortars to infantry was the highest encountered in the Pacific War.

The Marine advance across Okinawa's midriff and then northward was so rapid that it threatened to outrun the ability of engineers to widen roads and bridge gullies that would have impeded the movement of supplies and thus slowed the advance. These troops from the 6th Engineer Battalion are installing a prefabricated Bailey bridge over a wide gully. *Official USMC Photo*

The new 6th Marine Division (1st Provisional Marine Brigade plus the 29th Marines and attachments) landed over the northernmost beaches on the western side of Okinawa a little south of the island's midpoint. It was to strike across the island, then turn north to pacify a little more than half of Okinawa on its own. To the right, the 1st Marine Division was also to strike across the island, then turn to as part of the Tenth Army reserve. Two Army divisions that landed side by side in the southern half of the Tenth Army beachhead were to pivot south to cover the width of the island. Also on April 1, the IIIAC reserve, the 2d Marine Division, made a feint toward a set of beaches in southeastern Okinawa. This feint was in line with where the Japanese predicted the main landing would take place, so for once a feint actually held large numbers of defenders in place looking the wrong way. Other units, including the Fleet Marine Force Pacific, Reconnaissance Battalion, were assigned objectives elsewhere in the Ryukyu Islands, most of which were taken or at least assaulted before L-day on Okinawa.

Immediate objectives were Yontan and Kadena airdromes, in the IIIAC and XXIV Corps zones, respectively. As soon as these airfields could be brought to operational status, combat-support aircraft would operate from them. Also, many aircraft carriers would remain on station off Okinawa for as long as their air groups were needed. The land-based component was a Marine command named the Tactical Air Force and consisting of several Marine air groups of fighters and light bombers. Marine fighter squadrons based aboard fleet carriers and several new Marine carrier air groups (fighters and torpedo bombers) based aboard escort carriers would be available throughout the land operation.

The landings were made against zero opposition and with almost no casualties. Far from going into a state of optimism, however, the many veterans in the assault force realized that a very hard road lay before them, that the Japanese had chosen to dig deep and fight on their own terms.

Yontan Airdrome fell by midmorning, after Marines overcame very light opposition along the juncture of the 1st and 6th Marine divisions. Reinforcements moved to fill gaps that developed due to rapid advances by the 22d, 4th, and 7th Marines. Marines of the 1st Division captured an intact bridge across a stream at the IIIAC–XXIV Corps boundary and overcame hastily built field fortifications all across the division front. Divisional and IIIAC artillery battalions landed routinely, and many batteries were providing fire by 1530 hours. The IIIAC advance halted between 1600 and 1700 to avoid more gaps and to help the Marines on the far right maintain contact with the left Army division, whose left flank outpaced the 1st Marine Division right-flank unit by several hundred yards. The halt also gave artillery units outpaced by the rapid advance time to move forward and register night defensive fires.

Basically, all of L-day's headaches arose from the light-to-nonexistent defensive effort, and not the usual spate of battle problems. Both airdromes, Kadena and Yontan, were firmly in American hands by nightfall, and engineers were already at work to get them operational in the shortest possible time.

As the 6th Marine Division rolled northward, the troops got a lift on every available tracked or wheeled vehicle. Shown here are M7 105mm assault gun carriages belonging to the 29th Marines' regimental heavy weapons company. The M7s replaced M3 75mm halftracks. *Official USMC Photo*

These Marines have spotted a cave or emplacement on lower ground and called forward a 2.36-inch bazooka team to knock it out. Note that the Marine next to the bazookaman is holding a Thompson submachine gun equipped with an old drum magazine. Note also the rocket on the ground. *Official USMC Photo*

This 81mm gun pit took a direct round in counterbattery fire. The Japanese on Okinawa massed the highest percentage of artillery and mortars to infantry in the Pacific War. *Official USMC Photo*

While by no means a romp, the days that followed on L-day were nearly bloodless. Enemy troops were encountered here and there as the two Marine divisions swallowed up miles of territory against, at most, desultory opposition. Captives proved to be second- and third-rate troops, mostly technicians and other noncombatants drafted into ad hoc defensive units, lightly armed and miserably trained. Also, many thousands of civilians turned themselves in to Marines, to be passed along to temporary stockades in the safe rear. The most hard-pressed Marine units were engineers, then supply troops. Roads were barely discernible

A Marine swings a deadly satchel charge before hurling it into a cave dug into a coral outcropping. *Official USMC Photo*

Another cave is blasted by a Marine squad that waits pensively for possible survivors to emerge. *Official USMC Photo*

The hardest positions of all to crack were fortified Okinawan burial vaults like these. It usually took artillery or aerial ordnance to get the defenders' heads down, then a demolitions attack from over the top of the vault. In this photograph, Marines are checking the contents of the position as other Marines haul it out.
Official USMC Photo

paths, so they had to be engineered for modern traffic, and many bridges had to be built over gullies and other breaks in the terrain. Even with roads in place, it was difficult to push supplies forward to the rapidly advancing ground units; they moved ahead thousands of yards a day and were constantly on the brink of outrunning their dumps. It was difficult, also, for artillery units to keep pace with the advance, and the infantry had a difficult time maintaining contact with flank units, because the advance tended to broaden an already broad front. By April 3, the Marine divisions were on ground slated to fall on L+15.

As the Okinawa fighting progressed, Marine Air based on the island was able to offer a growing array of services to the ground troops. Here, a VMTB-232 TBM light bomber drops supply bundles to Marines near the front line. Colored panels, seen at the lower right, mark the drop zone and show the preferred approach path. *Official USMC Photo*

A picture slowly emerged from prisoner interrogations. The main Japanese effort had gone into deeply fortifying the southern portion of the island. XXIV Corps ran into the outlying positions on April 4, on the phase line established for L+10. But Marines were oriented east and north, and swallowing miles of lightly defended ground each day. Before the two Marine divisions could join the fight in the south, they had to secure the rest of the island.

By April 4, the 1st Marine Division had completed its cross-island advance and had thus run out of objectives. It turned to scouring land already in its hands and building up its logistical base. By then, cut-off Japanese troops in the IIIAC zone had begun to coalesce into what Marines eventually characterized as guerrilla forces that lived off the land in wild areas and exploited opportunities to attack patrols and rear-area facilities. Such forces also appeared in the rear of the 6th Division. These so-called guerrillas had to be painstakingly tracked by Marine units far more suited for intense modern conflict.

Another new service provided on Okinawa by MAG-31 and MAG-33 Corsairs was the stunning effect of 5-inch aerial rockets fired in clusters of eight, the equivalent of a broadside apiece from two destroyers. Rockets were not precision weapons, but a hit was as good as a kill, and the Corsairs got a lot of steel on target fast. *Official USMC Photo*

Then there was the old-fashioned way to reduce caves and bunkers: direct artillery fire. By mid-1945, all of the Marine artillery regiments retained just one battalion of eighteen 75mm pack howitzers, which were still good to have around when the terrain was hilly. *Official USMC Photo*

Fortunately, though they were well motivated, the Japanese guerrillas also were not trained for such operations and were easily hunted down if they showed themselves. To help quell civilian complicity in the guerrilla operation, several thousand Okinawan males were interned in camps beginning on April 11. Tenth Army eventually clamped down on all civilians and filled eight internment camps in the IIIAC zone with Okinawans of all ages and both sexes. This seemed to end the problem of civilian aid to guerrilla operations, but guerrillas continued to operate in diminished circumstances.

The 6th Marine Division continued to drive north—literally to drive on tanks and other vehicles. One reconnaissance force advanced fourteen miles unopposed, then turned back to the main body. The 6th Engineer Battalion had a tough time widening and improving roads and replacing or bracing bridges at such a pace. On April 9, supplies

Standing on shell-torn ground and taking the time to aim, this Thompson gunner strikes a classic pose of a Marine veteran in battle—unafraid, taking care to score his kill. *Official USMC Photo*

began to come ashore on beaches much closer to the 6th Division front, and the 1st Armored Amtrac Battalion was committed to provide artillery support because the 15th Marines had such a bad time keeping pace with the infantry.

On April 7, MAG-31 began to handle flight operations for its newly arrived squadrons at Yontan Airfield, and MAG-33 arrived on April 9. This relieved some of the ground-support burden on carrier air units, which were increasingly drawn into a battle of attrition with kamikaze units based in Japan and intermediate bases. Indeed, Marine Air became almost wholly committed to XXIV Corps as it hit increasingly stiffer resistance in the south.

It took the 6th Marine Division until April 13 to locate a well-led, competent, and powerful Japanese force—on Mount Yae Take, in extreme northern Okinawa. A four-day battle involving Marine Air and artillery and naval gunfire support reduced the enemy force of fifteen hundred and opened the door for the final northern push, which was completed on April 20. So far on Okinawa, the 6th Marine Division's losses numbered 207 killed, 757 wounded, and 6 missing against an estimated 2,000 Japanese troops killed.

MARINE AIR, AMPLY ASSISTED BY A SOPHISTICATED ARRAY OF MODERN TOOLS SUCH AS search, control, and weather radars; landing force air-support control units equipped with advanced radio equipment; and front-line air control teams played a key role in supporting ground operations *and* forestalling kamikaze and conventional air attacks on the huge fleet that seemed to be a permanent fixture off Okinawa. Indeed, beginning on April 7, MAG-31 and MAG-33 fighter pilots scored hundreds of aerial kills off Okinawa, particularly to the north, toward Japan. These included night kills by Marine squadrons equipped with

In this classic photo, taken in the feature known as Death Valley, Private First Class Paul Ison, a demolitions assaultman serving with the 5th Marines, risks all to sprint from cover to cover. Thousands of statuettes based on this iconic image have been sold to three generations of Marines. *Official USMC Photo*

F6F-5N Hellcat night fighters based ashore. Also, six Marine F4U squadrons were based aboard three fleet carriers, and they provided ground support and fleet cover. Indeed, Marine Corsairs took part in attacks on Kyushu airfields on March 18 and 19 that nearly swept kamikaze and conventional air units from the skies for several days. In return, Japanese aircraft damaged several American carriers, including the USS *Franklin*, embarking two Marine F4U squadrons that saw a total of one day of offensive operations. By April 1945, Marine Air was at the leading edge of technique and technology in support of modern combat operations across all three battle dimensions—land, sea, and air.

A battle-hardened Marine infantry platoon jogs across a broad expanse of open ground, past the body of a fellow Marine who was shot dead on an earlier attempt. The Marine or corpsman at left is carrying a litter. *Official USMC Photo*

XXIV CORPS MET ITS FIRST REALLY STIFF OPPOSITION ON THE SOUTHERN FRONT ON April 6. Thereafter, resistance became more violent and better organized to greater depths almost every step of the way. The defenses extended across the entire width of the island and to an undetermined depth. In fact, it was a concentric defense, complete and pervasive, centered on the town of Shuri. Not apparent at the outset, but increasingly obvious with each passing day, the hard defenses could not and would not be carried by merely two infantry divisions supported by organic and corps artillery, even after the artillery was bolstered on April 7 by IIIAC's three 155mm gun battalions and three 155mm howitzer battalions—not to mention Marine Air based at Yontan and whatever carrier air the fleet had on hand for ground support. Next, beginning on April 9, all four battalions of the 11th Marines and two-thirds of a fresh Army division were sent into the southern line, albeit with little effect. By April 14, XXIV Corps had killed nearly seven thousand Japanese, but it had barely made a dent in the defenses north of Shuri. A corps attack on April 19 supported by 27 artillery battalions and 375 aircraft made negligible progress, then halted as the unperturbed Japanese troops moved back to their positions from underground shelters. The Army divisions advanced only after the Japanese withdrew from the advance defensive line on the night of April 23–24 to a more integrated line to the rear. On April 24, IIIAC was ordered to place one of its divisions in the Tenth Army reserve, and the 1st Marine

A Marine OY observation plane from VMO-6 flies over the Okinawa capital, Naha. OYs were the first aircraft to operate off Yontan Field, but as the campaign progressed they tended to work from roads on which temporary fueling facilities were set up. Many of the OY pilots were enlisted Marines who had earned civilian pilot licenses on their own. *Official USMC Photo*

A 6th Marine Division rifle squad moves up a residential street in Naha. Note that the second Marine in the formation is checking the gateway to his right even though the BARman and the photographer have already safely passed it. This is a sign of battle awareness found only in veteran troops.
Official USMC Photo

This Marine light machine gun squad is set up to cover the advance of a rifle squad or infantry platoon across an open area in one of southern Okinawa's cities or large towns. The gun will follow as soon as the crossing has been cleared.
Official USMC Photo

Division was thus ordered to prepare to return to battle. (IIIAC's third division, the 2d, had been returned to Saipan to prepare for an amphibious assault near Okinawa that never took place.) On April 30, the 1st Marine Division advanced to replace an Army division in the XXIV Corps zone, and that Army division was ordered north to replace the 6th Marine Division so it could enter the southern battle.

THE INFANTRY UNITS THE 1ST MARINE DIVISION REPLACED HAD BEEN GROUND DOWN to regiments little larger than battalions, and battalions little larger than companies. Dead ahead was the bulk of a Japanese infantry division holding a defensive sector the island command had just reorganized to higher levels of lethality. On the division's first full day on the line, the weather turned cool and rainy, a state that would prevail into July.

The division went into the offensive on May 2, the westernmost of three divisions in the attack. The 5th Marines was stymied at the outset, but adjacent 3/1 fell into a gap. The 1st Marines attempted to change direction to exploit the gap, and 3/1 advanced even farther in the rain before nightfall. On the other hand, 1/1, on the division's right, faced fierce opposition, and portions of the battalion that were cut off had to withdraw, after which 1/1 changed direction and won some new ground.

This baptismal day on the southern front was emblematic of the fighting that ensued. The Japanese made excellent use of broken ground and other natural cover, and the Marines were either stymied or fell into dead ground from which they could either advance or from which they had to withdraw to maintain a cohesive line against the uncanny knack the defenders showed for mounting enfilade movements. On May 3, the 5th Marines advanced more than five hundred yards in its zone, but the 1st Marines was pinned down with heavy casualties, so the 5th had to pull back several hundred yards in places. There simply was no point at which the Marines could gain adequate leverage—the same scenario the replaced Army divisions had faced in their battle.

The Japanese had many thousands of first-line troops in reserve. These troops had been tied down defending beaches in southeastern Okinawa for landings that never took place. As the Japanese gained a finer sense of American tactics, it was put to the island commander that an offensive using these fresh, well-trained, and well-equipped troops might chasten the Americans and buy a great deal of time and flexibility. Some of the fresh troops were fed into the defensive sectors to make good the losses of weeks of bitter attritional warfare, but the bulk were held back to cover the suspect beaches or to serve as a mobile reserve. By April 22, the bulk of the fresh force was fed into the Shuri sector to stiffen the defenses. Ultimately, however, a number of senior officers won an argument to launch a major tank-supported counteroffensive, including counterlandings behind American lines, that was to blunt the American offensive and perhaps throw it back.

Preceded by mass kamikaze attacks on rear areas on the island and logistical shipping offshore, the counteroffensive, including counterlandings on both coasts, began after dark on May 3. Artillery fire matched artillery fire at the front, while in the rear, Marines opened fire on Japanese troops coming ashore on the beach on which Company B, 1/1, anchored the entire XXIV Corps line. This was not where the Japanese intended to land and, as at Bougainville, quick reaction by the defenders and confusion among the attackers created conditions for a Marine victory. Many more Marines were fed into the fire-lit battle, LVT(A)s sealed the battlefield, and fresh troops hunted down infiltrators. Forewarned by this landing attempt, Marines quelled other attempts farther up the coast. Army troops also defended successfully on the eastern coast.

At dawn, behind an artillery curtain that never abated during the night and a rolling smoke barrage, the bulk of a battle-hardened Imperial Army infantry division crashed into a curtain of fire erected in front of two U.S. Army divisions by twelve 155mm and 8-inch gun and howitzer battalions and tag-team air attacks that would mount to 134 sorties by the day's end. On May 4, the 1st Marine Division actually attacked in its zone despite the efforts of the Japanese to win through to the east, but the division was stalled several hundred yards short of its objective line.

Far from delaying an American victory, the ill-advised Japanese counteroffensive used up the largest pool of seasoned fighters on the island, of which nearly seven thousand were killed. But other good fighters had remained in their excellent defensive sectors, and they showed no sign of cracking appreciably in the face of inexorable pressure across the entire corps front. In less than a week on the Shuri front, 649 Marines became casualties.

THE 6TH MARINE DIVISION BEGAN GOING INTO THE SOUTHERN LINE ON MAY 7, squeezing in along the coast to the right of the 1st Marine Division, and IIIAC resumed control of both Marine divisions. From that point, despite interesting tactical embellishments, the battle to win Okinawa settled down to become a test of attritional theories, one based on attack and the other based on defense. The Japanese had the troops they had, and relatively few were trained infantry. The Americans had a larger pool of trained infantry,

Lieutenant Colonel Richard P. Ross Jr., commanding officer of 3/1, plants the 1st Marine Division colors atop the ruins of Shuri Castle on May 30, 1945. These same colors flew over Cape Gloucester and Peleliu and were personally entrusted to Ross by the division commander. *Official USMC Photo*

including ample replacements who, in the case of IIIAC, were used as logistical fillers until they were needed in the infantry battalions. Even then, attrition was high among all the American divisions—11,147 replacements were fed into Marine infantry units on Okinawa—but when a Japanese veteran was killed, he could not be replaced.

Deadly combinations of spirited infantry, overwhelming artillery and naval gunfire support, and ample air support were played like a piano to advance American units through the rest of May and most of June. The concentric lines of defense built and held by the Japanese never got easier to reduce, but inexorably the quality of the troops holding them shifted downward, and they fell, one after the other.

The 2d Marine Division's 8th Marines took part in several landings on islands elsewhere in the Ryukyus in late May, then went ashore on Okinawa to fill out the 1st Marine Division for the final assaults of the campaign. An interesting footnote to Marine Corps history came about on June 18 when the Tenth Army commander, Lieutenant General Simon Bolivar Buckner Jr., was shot dead in the 8th Marines line while reconnoitering the front. The next-senior general officer on the scene was Marine Major General Roy Geiger, the IIIAC commanding general. Geiger, an aviator who had commanded the 1st Marine Aircraft Wing at Guadalcanal, IMAC at Bougainville, and IIIAC at Guam and Okinawa, was spot-promoted to lieutenant general to become the first and only Marine and the first and only naval aviator—perhaps the first and only aviator—ever to command an American army in the field.

The Japanese defenses were all but overwhelmed by June 16, and the island command realized that the end was near. On June 19, the island commander dissolved his staff and ordered all available troops to go over to guerrilla operations. On June 21, organized resistance came to an end in the 6th Marine Division zone, which encompassed the southern shore of the island. By then, Japanese troops were surrendering in the hundreds. The 1st Marine Division mounted its final attacks of the campaign, also on June 21, and

A Marine infantry platoon advances up a draw through the smoke of a recent artillery or mortar barrage. Once again, note the telltale signs that these Marines are veterans: they are well spread out and wary in all directions, and each Marine seems ready to open fire at the least provocation. *Official USMC Photo*

reported by nightfall that all its objectives had been secured. XXIV Corps made similar announcements. It thus fell to General Geiger to declare Okinawa secure following a bloody eighty-two-day battle. The final official flag-raising ceremony on a Pacific War battlefield took place at the Tenth Army headquarters at 1000 hours, June 22, 1945.

The battle had been among the most brutal of the Pacific War. The Navy suffered its greatest casualties for a single engagement. More than twelve thousand Americans were killed and a further fifty thousand were wounded. And more than one hundred fifty thousand Japanese—many of them civilians—were killed during the battle.

All hands turned to in order to begin preparations to invade Kyushu. Already, Army Air Forces bomber groups that had been in Europe on V-E Day joined Marine Tactical Air Force units operating from Okinawa's airfields and thousands of American, British, and Canadian carrier-based aircraft in the prelanding bombardment that was to lay waste to the southernmost home island before a contemplated October invasion was set in motion.

Who could have known on June 22, 1945, that only some six weeks separated America's Pacific Warriors from blinding flashes over Hiroshima and Nagasaki that would send the vast majority home to the peace so many of their brave comrades had died to secure.

AND WHEN HE GETS TO HEAVEN,
TO SAINT PETER HE WILL TELL,
"ONE MORE MARINE REPORTING, SIR.
"I'VE SERVED MY TIME IN HELL."*

* An anonymous poem found on a grave marker on Guadalcanal.

BIBLIOGRAPHY

BOOKS

Blakeney, Jane. *Heroes: U.S. Marine Corps, 1861–1955*. Blakeney Publishing, 1956.

Frank, Benis M., and Henry I. Shaw Jr. *Victory and Occupation*. Vol. V, *History of U.S. Marine Corps Operations in World War II*. Washington, D.C.: United States Marine Corps, 1968.

Garand, George W., and Truman R. Strobridge. *Western Pacific Operations*. Vol. IV, *History of U.S. Marine Corps Operations in World War II*. Washington, D.C.: United States Marine Corps, 1971.

Hammel, Eric. *Air War Pacific: Chronology, America's Air War Against Japan in East Asia and the Pacific, 1941–1945*. Pacifica, Calif.: Pacifica Press, 1998.

———. *Guadalcanal: Starvation Island*. New York: Crown, 1987.

———. *Munda Trail: The New Georgia Campaign*. New York: Orion Books, 1989.

Hammel, Eric, and John E. Lane. *Bloody Tarawa*. Pacifica, Calif.: Pacifica Press, 1998.

Hough, Frank O., Verle E. Ludwig, and Henry I. Shaw Jr. *Pearl Harbor to Guadalcanal*. Vol. I, *History of U.S. Marine Corps Operations in World War II*. Washington, D.C.: United States Marine Corps, 1958.

Lodge, O. R. *The Recapture of Guam*. Washington, D.C.: Marine Corps Historical Branch, 1954.

Lord, Walter. *Day of Infamy*. New York: Holt, Rinehart, & Winston, 1957.

Miller, Edward S. *War Plan Orange: The U.S. Strategy to Defeat Japan, 1897–1945*. Annapolis, Md.: Naval Institute Press, 1991.

Mondey, David. *Concise Guide to American Aircraft of World War II*. London: Temple Press, 1982.

———. *Concise Guide to Axis Aircraft of World War II*. London: Temple Press, 1984.

Nalty, Bernard C. *The Right to Fight: African-American Marines in World War II*. Washington, D.C.: Marine Corps Historical Center, 1995.

Olynyk, Frank J. *USMC Credits for the Destruction of Enemy Aircraft in Air-to-Air Combat, World War 2*. Aurora, Ohio: Frank J. Olynyk, 1981.

Shaw, Henry I. Jr., and Douglas T. Kane. *Isolation of Rabaul*. Vol. II, *History of U.S. Marine Corps Operations in World War II*. Washington, D.C.: United States Marine Corps, 1963.

Shaw, Henry I. Jr., Bernard C. Nalty, and Edwin T. Turnbladh. *Central Pacific Drive*. Vol. III, *History of U.S. Marine Corps Operations in World War II*. Washington, D.C.: United States Marine Corps, 1966.

Sherrod, Robert. *History of Marine Corps Aviation in World War II*. San Rafael, Calif.: Presidio Press, 1980.

Toland, John. *But Not in Shame*. New York: Random House, 1961.

———. *The Rising Sun: The Decline and Fall of the Japanese Empire, 1936–1945*. New York: Random House, 1970.

PERIODICALS

Hammel, Eric. "Assault on Bairoko." *Leatherneck*, July 1993.

———. "Guam." *Leatherneck*, July 1994.

———. "Jim Swett: World War II Flying Ace." *Leatherneck*, April 1993.

———. "Marine Air at Rabaul, Part I." *Leatherneck*, January 1994.

———. "Marine Air at Rabaul, Part II." *Leatherneck*, February 1994.

———. "Peleliu." *Leatherneck*, September 1994.

———. "The 4th Raiders and the New Georgia Invasion." *Leatherneck*, June 1993.

———. "The Invasion of Tarawa." *Leatherneck*, November 1984.

INDEX

Numerals in *italics* indicate an illustration of the subject mentioned.